Top 100 Attractions

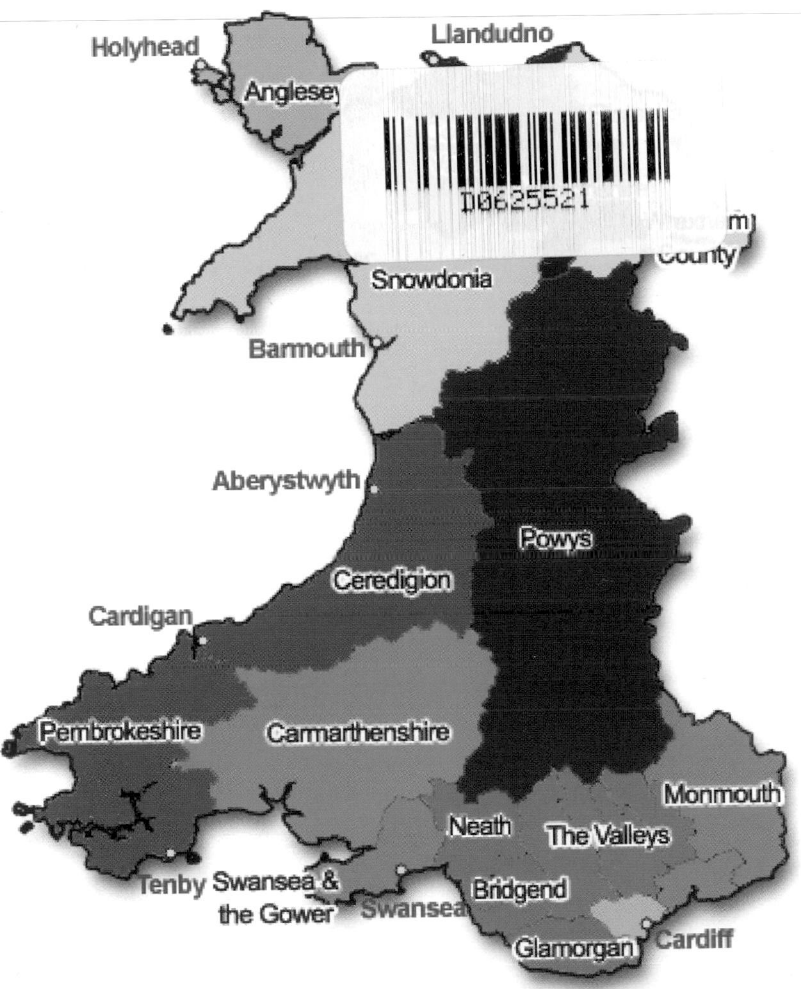

Published in 2013 by Plasma Media Ltd,

Plasma Media Ltd
Company Reg No. 07327527

Address for Plasma Media Ltd
Can be found by visiting,
Www.top100attractions.co.uk

A CIP catalogue record is available for this book,
and other In Plasma Media titles from the British Library.

Author: Joshua Stevenson
Designed by Gordon Milton
Edited by Joshua Stevenson
Design Manager: Gordon Milton
Photos: Joshua Stevenson, Neil lambert, Kevin Hughes, Tim Richmond, John Millar Arnhel de Serra, David Levenson, Paul Harris, Matthew Antrobus., Ben Hall, Chris Walling.

Every effort has been made to trace the copyright of various photographs used and we would like to apologize for any omissions. The author would be pleased to include appropriate acknowledgement in any subsequent book.

Because of the dynamic nature of the Internet, any web addresses or contact details in this book may have changed since publication and may not be valid. All telephone numbers, addresses, contact details and opening times were correct at the time of going to print.

ISBN: 978 0 9571957 1 4

Forward

We are grateful to you for picking this book from many of the fantastic books that are available on the great country of Wales. For many of you that have bought this book, I'm sure it was because you have been to Wales on many occasions, and like me, the country has left you with some very happy memories. For those of you that have bought this book because you haven't yet visited this magical land, then you are in for a special treat. Whatever your reasons for buying this book, we are sure that you will not be disappointed with its content. We at 'Plasma Media Ltd' have brought you the Top 100 of the very best Attractions within Wales and its borders, and with a sprinkle of some of the very best in places to sleep and eat, we are positive that you will want to visit many of the areas, and attractions that we have featured.

Another reason to be grateful to you is because we at Plasma Media Ltd are donating 49p from the profit of every book we sell, to local Welsh charities. Management from each of the 100 attractions within this book have chosen five worthy Welsh causes from a list of twenty charities that were provided to them. We will be publishing on our website, top100attractions.co.uk on the 15th December 2012, a full list of monies donated, and to which chosen charities that we're donated too, along with images of representatives from each chosen charity receiving cheques from us.

Finally, this book is just one in a range of seven of its kind. We will be bringing the Top 100 Attractions from the four corners of England, throughout the length and breadths of Scotland and finally attractions from all the 32 counties of Ireland. We have taken on the difficult task of looking at, visiting and determining which attractions are worthy of a Top 100 title. Also, If you have visited an attraction that left a long lasting imprint on your mind, why not visit top100attractions.co.uk and tell us about which attraction it was, where it is, and why you feel it should be investigated as being a Top 100 Attraction. If after investigating that attraction, we determine it too be worthy of a Top 100 title, we will with your permission, publish your name alongside that attractions page.

Visit the Top 100 Website for further information on all the Attractions, Accommodation, and Restaurants within this book.

www.top100attractions.co.uk

CONTENTS

ANGLESEY

Anglesey is one of those places that remain as magical and mysterious since it was invaded and made part of the Roman Empire 1,934 years ago. Ever since visiting here with the school many years ago, I have always had a soft spot for this geologically complex island. The island has several small towns dotted around it, Llangefni, Menai Bridge, Holyhead just to name but a few. But each one of the towns that you will come across on Anglesey each has something very unique to offer the thousands of visitors the island gets on a yearly basis. When you ask some people what springs to mind when they hear the name Anglesey, they would immediately associate it with getting the ferry from Holyhead to Ireland. But when you ask many others, they too have many fond childhood memories of the place.

Whilst writing and compiling this book I have got to meet so many interesting people, people from all walks of life, and a whole host of varied backgrounds. Whether it's a day on the beach you're after, or a trip to many of its great locations, Anglesey has it all! Anglesey also has a Coastal Path that spans some 200-kilometres (124) miles and boasts some absolutely spectacular views, no matter what kind of weather is thrown at you. All in all you will not be disappointed with your visit here, and once your holiday has come to an end, why not pop onto our website www.top100attractions.co.uk and tell me and our thousands of other readers what you thought.

Anglesey Circuit

t: 01407 811400 e: admin@angleseycircuit.com
www.angleseycircuit.com

Anglesey Circuit provides visitors with a challenging and exciting circuit in a breathtaking location.

Set on the west coast of Anglesey, overlooking the Irish Sea and the Snowdonia mountain range beyond, Anglesey Circuit provides visitors with a challenging and exciting circuit in a breathtaking location. Whether you are visiting the Circuit as a competitor, spectator, for driving instruction or as part of a corporate activity day, you are assured of a day to remember. It is one of the few circuits to be designed and constructed with an entirely new concept. Full advantage has been taken of the the undulating landscape and created a circuit with imaginative cambers, a blend of fast sections, technically challenging mid range corners complimented with two hairpin bends and a 10% banked corner. The alternative circuit configurations enable Anglesey Circuit to offer the ideal facility for a wide variety of events.

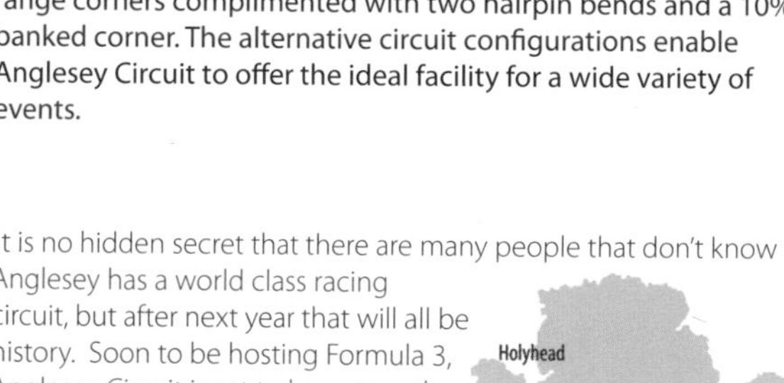

It is no hidden secret that there are many people that don't know Anglesey has a world class racing circuit, but after next year that will all be history. Soon to be hosting Formula 3, Anglesey Circuit is set to be put on the racing world map. I was very fortunate to be shown a few laps in a sports car, around this amazing track and that experience will be one I will never ever forget. Travelling at speeds in excess of 100mph I was taken into the world of Jenson Button and Lewis Hamilton. But these are not impossible dreams; these are dreams that can be made to come true at Anglesey circuit.

Anglesey Circuit, Ty Croes, Anglesey, LL63 5TF

Foel Farm

t: 01248 430646   e: info@foelfarm.co.uk
www.foelfarm.co.uk

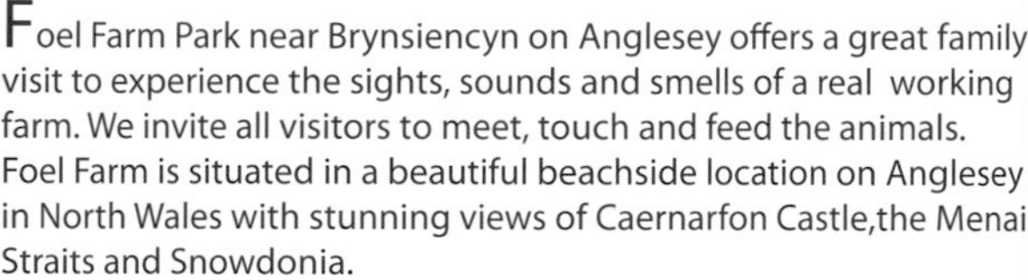

Attractions and Activities at Foel Farm Park on Anglesey!

Foel Farm Park near Brynsiencyn on Anglesey offers a great family visit to experience the sights, sounds and smells of a real working farm. We invite all visitors to meet, touch and feed the animals. Foel Farm is situated in a beautiful beachside location on Anglesey in North Wales with stunning views of Caernarfon Castle,the Menai Straits and Snowdonia.
There are tractor & trailer and quad bike & mini-trailer rides, ponyrides, chances to feed and meet the farm animals, and a lot more! There is also a Café & Bistro Bar, Gift Shop and even a Chocolate Workshop where you can see chocolates being made. Something for children and adults alike. The whole family can take a tractor & trailer tour of the farm to meet our shire horses and for the more adventurous we offer a thrilling mini trailer ride pulled behing the quad bike. Y Foel Bistro & Café Bar with its Mediterranean theme is a great venue for family meals. Relax and enjoy home cooking in our licensed restaurant and Café Bar.

I visited this attraction and was greeted by the owner "Bevis". It was very apparent during my time here, that this gentleman is very passionate not only about the attraction he has painstakingly built up over a long number of years but also about making sure every single visitor, young and old, enjoys their time at Foel Farm Park. Also for the chocolate connoisseurs, their homemade chocolatier shop onsite has to be the envy of North Wales. I cannot wait to return to Foel Farm Park!

Holyhead

Foel Farm Park, Brynsiencyn, Anglesey, LL61 6TQ

James Pringle Weavers

t: 01248 717171 e: simplythebest@ewm.co.uk
www.ewm.co.uk

The BIG name made the village famous, now the SHOPPING has made the village even BIGGER!

The big name made the village famous now the shopping is even bigger! This truly is a unique shopping experience with everything from luggage to lingerie, welsh whisky to wellingtons, you will surely find something for everyone in our large retail area, Welsh gifts, Hornby shop, clothing, souvenirs, Shoes shop, golf shop and so much more. There's a very large restaurant serving traditional Welsh Fayre, hot meals, snacks and refreshments served all day every day. The shortbread section at James Pringle Weavers, cannot be rivalled.

If anyone has ever wondered what Wales has in common with its Celtic neighbours of Ireland & Scotland, it has to be their love for high quality garments! James Pringle Weavers is one of The Edinburgh Woollen Mills flagship stores and has a vast array of quality clothing, including Cashmere, fashions, performance Outerwear, kids clothing, homewares, golf and shoe shop. There's also a great Welsh gifts shop and a Whisky & Real Ale shop (try before you buy!) The restaurant serves everything from Bara Brith to delicious Sunday lunches. I enjoyed my time at James Pringle Weavers that much, that I am going back very soon.

Holyhead

The Station, Llanfairpg, Anglesey, LL61 5UJ

Treftadaeth Menai Heritage

t: 01248715046 e: mbcht@btconnect.com
www.menaibridges.co.uk

A community project to celebrate our two world famous bridges!

Menai Heritage is an exhibition based around the history of the two famous bridges over the Menai Strait – Thomas Telford's Menai Suspension Bridge and Robert Stephenson's Britannia Bridge. We have artefacts dating from the construction of Telford's bridge (1819-1826) and its later alterations, and also from Britannia Bridge (1846 -1850) and its reconstruction after the 1970 fire. The history of the area is closely linked to the bridges and is included in the displays together with the Liverpool and north Wales pleasure steamers and HMS Conway. The geological and ecological significance of the Menai Strait is also covered. Visitors can watch DVDs about the bridges and take a guided walk along the waterfront. The children's corner (admitted free) will interest a range of ages. Open Sunday to Thursday at Easter, spring bank holiday and through summer, or arrange a group visit or workshop.

The Thomas Telford Centre is one of those attractions that are very different to many of the attractions we have in this book. This attraction has many themes, but is all based around both the Menai the Britannia Bridges, which are two of the most iconic bridges in Wales, let alone the UK. These two bridges will of course take you over to the idyllic island of Anglesey, where you can find a whole host of attractions and things to do. One of those things however that most certainly should be on your list is a visit to not only the bridges, but the Heritage Centre that houses all of the history and facts that tell the story about these amazing structures. Then once armed with the knowledge of Thomas Telford, Robert Stephenson and their bridges, I recommend taking one of the guided tours that can be arranged by the Heritage Centre.

Holyhead

Thomas Telford Centre, Mona Road, Menai Bridge, Anglesey, LL59 5EA

RibRide

t: 0333 1234 303 e: info@ribride.co.uk
www.ribride.co.uk

Boat Trips & Adventure BoatTrips!

Whether it's the adrenalin rush of high speed turns or the encounters with wildlife, you are sure to leave the boats with a smile on your face. We cater for individuals or groups of any age from 4 years old and up wanting a one-hour ribride. For those more adventurous types we offer the option of chartering a rib for the day to go around Anglesey or to chill out on a secluded beach. RibRides require no prior knowledge of boats, just the ability to make one largish step down into the boat. Our friendly and capable drivers will take care of the rest. Outside of extreme weather, rainy spells and the odd splash you will not get wet.... unless you want to! For those who aren't too fond of getting wet we do have waterproofs but please dress for the changeable conditions our country can offer. We provide lifejackets, all you need are soft soled shoes or boots and clothing suitable for a 5-8 degree drop in temperature.

RibRide is a new addition to our Top 100 Attractions books, and after winning their much earned 'Anglesey Tourism Award' for 2012, they have earned with pride their place in our new Wales edition. In my honest opinion, although Anglesey in itself, is a huge attraction and brings hundreds of thousands of visitors every year to this ancient celtic Island. Anglesey is still very lucky to of been chosen by RibRide as its base for all of its activities. This is not just a thrill seekers type of attraction, and even if your not confident on the water, their trained and informative set of staff will very quickly put your mind at ease. This attraction really does allow you to see this part of the North Wales coast in a totally different light, and for that very reason, RibRide offers total value for money.

Holyhead

Victoria Dock, Caernarfon LL55 1SR, Moel Y Don, Anglesey LL61 6EZ

Pili Palas Nature World

t: 01248 712474 e: info@pilipalas.co.uk
www.pilipalas.co.uk

Anglesey's Top Family attraction!

A day out at Pili Palas can be a magical experience for all the family, whatever the weather! So come along, enter a steamy environment full of lush vegetation and waterfalls with LIVE butterflies flying all around you. This is the magical world of Pili Palas. But there's a lot more than just butterflies to see. You'll meet Charlie, Elvis, Jake and a host of other feathered friends in our birdhouse. We have plenty of snakes and lizards of all kinds, and you're sure to be able to get up close to some of them in our popular animal handling sessions. If someone in your family likes bugs then they'll have the time of their life in our bug-zone, home to our hissing cockroaches, millipedes, locusts, giant snails and much more. Then we dare you to visit the tropical lair of tarantulas, scorpions and fire-bellied toads. Don't forget pets' corner where you can meet the rabbits and guinea pigs. Take a walk through our farmyard where our pygmy goats Milly and Molly live happily with Bert and Ernie.

We were just as selective in our selection process of the attractions here on Anglesey, as we were in any of our other areas, but one attraction we just had to have in, was Pili Palas. With new additions being added every year, it's not hard to see why this attraction gets thousands of visitors every season. With 2012's addition of the ever popular Meerkats, it just goes to show, the management here at this attraction, really have their fingers on the pulse when it comes to knowing what additions to make year in year out. I know it sounds a bit of a cliché, but this really is a place for all ages young or old. I will be visiting here again soon, and maybe this time, I just may get to see the Meerkats a bit closer than those on TV!

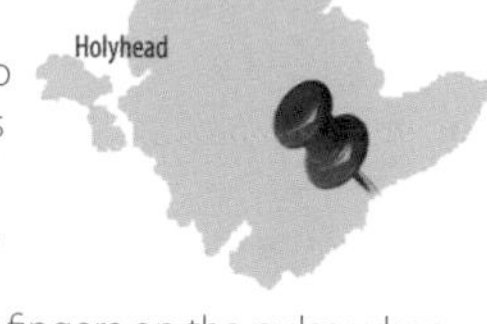

Penmynydd Road, Menai Bridge, Anglesey, LL59 5RP

Beaumaris Castle

t: 01248 810361 e: cadw@wales.gsi.gov.uk
www.cadw.wales.gov.uk

The most technically perfect castle in Britain has few equals.

Dare we say it, an absolute cracker of a castle with classic proportions and perfect symmetry. The last hurrah of Edward I's massive building programme in north Wales… just a shame he never got round to finishing it! With finances stretched to the limit and the Scots now increasingly effective in their resistance to the English monarch, his vice-like grip on Wales was beginning to slip. Edward or 'Longshanks', on account of his extraordinary height, was forced to focus his attention elsewhere and the rest is, quite literally, history…Technically perfect and constructed according to an ingenious 'walls within walls' plan, Beaumaris Castle was the 13th-century hi-tech equivalent of a spaceship landing unceremoniously on Anglesey today. You can usually complain if a neighbour's extension plans are a bit on the large side. Seven centuries ago the problem was resolved rather differently. The population of Llanfaes was forcibly moved 12 miles (19km) away to Newborough to make way for Edward's new castle. Want to create a fuss? You'd probably be better off keeping your head down…or risk losing it!

The jewel in Anglesey's crown has to be Beaumaris Castle. I visited here a couple of times with the school, but never imagined myself fortunate enough to be able to write a review on such a site. Cadw really has thought long and hard about the experience a visitor to this site would have. One thing that is a huge shame is that James of St. George never got to finish this architectural marvel.

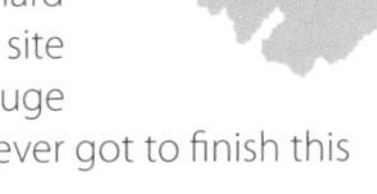

Castle Street, Beaumaris, Ynys Môn, LL58 8AP

Arlanfor B&B and Self Catering Accommodation

Moelfre, Anglesey, LL72 8HL

T: 01248 410555 www.arlanfor.co.uk E: enq@arlanfor.co.uk

Enjoy a fabulous nights sleep in our luxurious beds followed by a delicious home cooked Welsh breakfast served in the dinning room or on the deck, overlooking the sea.
The light and airy bedrooms are spacious, ensuite and have panoramic sea and mountain views. Located right on the coast in Moelfre we are ideal for walkers, bird watchers, fishermen, families or people who just want to watch the world go by. The sea is literally on our doorstep. Also available 2 luxurious self catering apartments.

Penyrorsedd Farm

Llanfachraeth, Isle of Anglesey, LL65 4YB

T: 01407 730630 www.penyrorseddfarm.com E: penyrorseddfarm@yahoo.co.uk

Relax and unwind... as a warm welcome awaits you at Penyrorsedd. Escape the stress of modern-day life and discover peace and tranquility in our charming 18th Century farmhouse. We aim to make your stay relaxing, comfortable, enjoyable and memorable...Penyrorsedd is a 360 acre working farm situated 3 miles from our beautiful coastline where there are many lovely beaches and coves which can be found just minutes away. Ideal location for coastal walks, bird watching at South Stack, golf, horse-riding. Both lake/sea fishing and exploring the islands many attractions.

Gazelle Hotel

Glyn Garth, Menai Bridge, Isle of Anglesey LL59 5PD

T: 01248 713364 www.thegazellehotel.com E: info@thegazellehotel.com

The Gazelle Hotel sits on the shores of the Menai Strait with panoramic views of the mountains of Snowdonia and is an ideal base for touring the Island and North Wales. We have a fine tradition of providing hotel accommodation and dining of the highest quality, choose from our a la carte menu in our thirty seater restaurant or from our grill menu in our cosy bar that overlooks the Menai Strait, we also have a slipway and a mooring just outside our front door so if you are sailing by feel free to sail in and come alongside for a pint and a meal. All of our rooms are en-suite with tea & coffee making facilities, colour TV and WiFi and offer breathtaking views of the Menai Strait or the Gazelle gardens.

Anglesey Arms Hotel

Mona Road, Menai Bridge, Anglesey, LL59 5EA

T: 01248 712305 www.anglesey-arms.co.uk E: anglesey@jwlees.co.uk

The Anglesey Arms Hotel, which is over 200 years old and recently received a huge makeover in August 2011. We offer a warm welcoming atmosphere with home cooked food and real ales. Supremely situated in the most prime of locations in Menai Bridge. Our pub restaurant has a relaxed, comfortable feel to it. Our menu is all about good, honest, home-cooked pub food. There's freshly prepared daily specials on offer too. There's also a bar area, to relax in after a long day. Our bar serves a fine range of JW Lees cask ale, along with our hand-picked wine list, as well as the usual spirits and soft drinks you'd expect.

Jasmine Cottage Bed & Breakfast

88 Breeze Hill, Benlech, Anglesey, LL74-8UA

T: 01248 851161 www.stayinanglesey.co.uk E: Mmaggiemccoy@aol.com

Jasmine Cottage is a modern, comfortable Bed and Breakfast, within walking distance of the beach and close to bars, shops, restaurants and access to the Anglesey coastal footpath.
With off road parking and Internet access, Jasmine Cottage is a great base for a holiday if you are taking it easy or visiting any of our places of interest.

Drws-y-Coed Farm B&B

Llannerch-y-medd, Isle of Anglesey, LL71 8AD

T: 01248 470473 www.drwsycoedguesthouse.co.uk E: drwsycoed2@hotmail.com

Situated on a large working beef, sheep and arable farm lies Drws y Coed farmhouse. It's a Visit Wales 5 Star B & B establishment to which guests return year after year. Centrally located Drws y Coed offers wonderful panoramic views of the rolling countryside and Snowdonia Mountain Range,a real place to enjoy peace and tranquility.The comfortable en-suite bedrooms are beautifully furnished and decorated with attention to detail.Varied selection of starters at breakfast and the traditional Welsh breakfast is freshly cooked to order.A spacious inviting lounge to relax infront of a log fire on chilly evenings.Interesting walks and Grade II*Listed farm buildings.

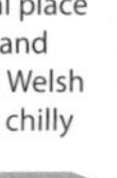

Cleifiog Bed & Breakfast

Townsend,Beaumaris, Ynys Mon, LL588BH

T: 01248 811507 www.cleifiogbandb.co.uk E: enquiries@cleifiog.co.uk

Cleifiog boasts magnificent panoramic views of the Menai Strait and Snowdonia it's charms include spacious panelled bedrooms, ensuite bathrooms and a magnificent panelled guest sitting room overlooking the Menai Strait. On a more contemporary note each room features a colour TV and DVD player and internet access. During your stay every effort will be made to help you to enjoy a tranquil and pampered 5 Star bed and breakfast interlude in this interesting and comfortable house.

Lastra Farm Hotel

Penrhyd, Amlwch, Anglesey, LL68 9TF

T: 01407 830906 www.lastra-hotel.com E: enquiries@cleifiog.co.uk

Lastra Farm - a lovingly restored 17th century farmhouse - is an excellent base for the discerning business traveller, with its fast Wireless and Ethernet broadband access, and its convenient location less than a mile from the main A5025 coast road. It's also a superb choice for a well-earned holiday or short break, just minutes from this stunning island's historic coastline, walks and beaches. All of the rooms are furnished and equipped to provide luxury, comfort and warmth for our guests and many of our customers return again and again just to experience the sheer pleasure of immersing themselves in this microcosm of rural Welsh life.

The Old Boathouse Café & Restaurant

Red Wharf Bay, Anglesey, LL75 8RJ

T: 01248 852731 www.boathouserestaurantanglesey.co.uk E: info@boathouserestaurantanglesey.co.uk

This super family friendly café/restaurant, with alfresco dining is overlooking the beautiful bay of Red Wharf. We serve breakfast, lunches, afternoon teas, evening meals. If you have any special dietary needs we will do our utmost to accomodate you. We are fully licensed with a good selection of wines to compliment your meal. we also have a good selection of beers. We have an extensive specials board, which changes daily and we are well known for our local fish dishes, such as Moules Mariniere, Smoked haddock gratin and grilled seabass.

Anglesey Arms Hotel

Mona Road, Menai Bridge, Anglesey, LL59 5EA

T: 01248 712305 www.anglesey-arms.co.uk E: anglesey@jwlees.co.uk

The Anglesey Arms Hotel, which is over 200 years old and recently received a huge makeover in August 2011. We offer a warm welcoming atmosphere with home cooked food and real ales. Supremely situated in the most prime of locations in Menai Bridge. Our pub restaurant has a relaxed, comfortable feel to it. Our menu is all about good, honest, home-cooked pub food. There's freshly prepared daily specials on offer too. There's also a bar area, to relax in after a long day. Our bar serves a fine range of JW Lees cask ale, along with our hand-picked wine list, as well as the usual spirits and soft drinks you'd expect.

Harry's Bistro

Henllys Hall, Henllys, Beaumaris, Gwynedd, LL58 8HU

T: 01248 812976 www.harrysbistro.com E: enquiries@harrysbistro.com

Chef Simon Doyle and front of house partner Nia Roberts are a well-known Anglesey combination. Their unique styles of bistro style food and service have built the reputation of Harry's being amongst the best restaurants on the Island.

"We offer traditional food with a contemporary style and our menu reflects the easy and relaxed restaurant that is Harry's. A unique and unhurried place to enjoy excellent food and wine at Henllys with its stunning views and heritage. There is always something new to enjoy and we are thrilled to see diners revisiting us on a regular basis, we work hard at our special offers with seasonal dishes prepared from fresh local ingredients."

Dylan's Restaurant

St George's Road, Menai Bridge, Anglesey, LL59 5EY

T: 01248 716714 www.dylansrestaurant.co.uk E: info@dylansrestaurant.co.uk

Dylan's restaurant sits at the water's edge, alongside the Thomas Telford bridge in the small town of Menai Bridge, Anglesey. The restaurant serves locally sourced, seasonal produce, specialising in freshly baked pizza and seafood. A passion for baking has driven us to create a range of specialist breads and pizza, made on the premises using traditional baking techniques and the finest flours.

Dylan's menu also includes some of the very best seafood sourced directly from the Strait such as our world famous Menai mussels, lobster and Anglesey sea bass. Our menu is a celebration of the abundant seafood and farm produce available to us on and around Anglesey - The Mother of Wales.

The Granary Restaurant

The Lastra Farm Hotel, Amlwch, Anglesey, LL68-9TF

T: 01407-830906 www.lastra-hotel.com E: booking@lastra-hotel.com

The Award winning Lastra Farm Restaurant & Bistro is an experience as unique as the island's history. We welcome you to come and experience it for yourself .
Drawing on a wealth of local farms and suppliers, our Restaurant is among the finest on the island. With a well deserved reputation for using the freshest of locally sourced ingredients, our very talented Chef and his team create truly unforgettable meals that lure visitors back time and time again.

Pier House Bistro

Seafront, Beaumaris, Anglesey, LL58-8BS

T: 01248-811055 E: robertcharlton1983@gmail.com

Pier House Bistro is situated on the seafront, Beaumaris set in idyllic North Wales. From our bistro and terrace, enjoy stunning views of the Menai Straits and the breathtaking Snowdonia mountain range. Our culinary influences are eclectic, inspired by flavours from around the world with our own unique twist. We source fresh local ingredients that are expertly infused with flavours known, loved and trusted. Our dishes are homemade with much care and attention. We offer a tasty selection of sweet bites and deserts for your fancy. To compliment our food we have a wide range of high quality teas and coffees, or, if you prefer, choose from our selection of wines and beers.

Gazelle Hotel

Glyn Garth, Menai Bridge, Isle of Anglesey LL59 5PD

T: 01248 713364 www.thegazellehotel.com E: info@thegazellehotel.com

We are proud of The Gazelle menus which offer a wide rangeof mouth watering meals from bar snacks to a la carte, our head chef, is frequently complimented and is always creating new dishes to tempt you even further. Don't forget! The Gazelle caters for Wedding receptions, Christenings, Birthday Parties, Anniversary Parties and Life Celebrations, call for details 01248 713364. For more information on our menus please contact us or any of The Gazelle staff and we'll be happy to help.

Tafarn Ty Gwyn

8 Holyhead Road, Llanfairpwllgwyngyll, LL61 5UJ

T: 01248-715599 www.tafarntygwyn.co.uk E: info@tafarntygwyn.co.uk

Situated next to James Pringle's Weavers and the famous Railway Station
Your hosts Brian & Veronica look forward to welcoming you. We offer excellent traditional home cooked meals, using the finest local ingredients and at a competitive price and pride ourselves on the quality and service we extend to all our customers. We boast an extensive daily menu that comprises of all your favourite dishes. Meals are served 12.00 – 2.30pm and 5.30pm -9.00pm Mon – Fri , 12.00 – 9.00pm Saturday and 12.00 – 8.00pm Sunday
"Anglesey's best Carvery, served every Sunday 12.00 – 6.00pm"

Tree Top Adventure

t: 01690 710914 e: info@ttadventure.co.uk
www.ttadventure.co.uk

ADVENTURE & ACTIVITY DAYS OUT!

Tarzan was King of the Jungle -- but we reckon he'd rather have been a jungle VIP at Tree Top Adventure. Tree Top Adventure gives a big Welsh welcome to family adventure, individuals, youth groups, birthday parties, stag and hen parties and corporate. Whatever the occasion we have the adventure. Our experienced instructors will tailor sessions to suit your specific needs in all our activities from Climbing and Abseiling to Gorge Walking and Hill Walking, not forgetting our premier high ropes course. Situated In North Wales, with di-vine views of Snowdonia National Park, this high-ropes course could test your Simian senses with balancing beams, zip wires, and rope bridges, before you scale Tree Top Tower to go bananas on the Powerfan Plummet -- one of the highest parachute simulators in the world at more than 100ft. Plus no need for the little monkeys to miss out with our unique Tree Tot Trail specially designed for 4 - 8 years old. Also whether it be a drink to calm your nerves or a snack while you spectate, our fully licensed Cafficoed serves good quality local produce throughout the day. Don't hang around -- Dare to be different and crown your self King of the Trees with Tree Top Adventure!

Nestled between the trees in the Conwy Valley lies Tree Tops Adventure. With everything you'd expect for a fun day out! A licensed Bar & Cafe, Toilets & Shower Facilities, Touch Screen Tourist Information Point not to mention professional and knowledgeable staff on hand to make sure your overall experience at Tree Tops is one you won't forget. Sean the proprietor of Tree Tops has put together a ropes course that is undeniably the best In its field. Whilst being there I saw and heard the comments from people who had just been around the course and everyone was truly positive. All in all whether it's the ropes course, team building activities or just a fun day out, your sure to find it at Tree Tops.

Llandudno

Llanrwst Road, Betws y Coed, Conwy County, LL24 0HA

CONWY VALLEY & DENBIGHSHIRE

Most of the areas that we have featured within this publication stand alone, but then there's some of the thirteen areas that are featured within this book, we have merged together, as they are so great, they all simply need showing off. This particular section in our book is one of those I am talking about. The huge area that makes up the Conwy Valley & Denbighshire section, spans from Prestatyn to Penmaenmawr and features some great little towns along the way. Take Llandudno for instance, once crowned the Queen of all Welsh holiday resorts this once great Victorian destination did, and still does, manage to pull in the crowds from far and wide. Speaking of pulling in the crowds from far and wide, leads me very nicely onto Conwy. This walled Bastion of a town complete with its quaint fishing quay, always seems to have visitors come rain or shine. Then there is Rhyl, this end of the pier style holiday destination with its sandy beaches and amusement arcades, has them flocking from all over the Midlands and the Northwest primarily. Not forgetting of course the unsung hero that is Llangollen. This small town, as far as I am concerned is the jewel in Denbighshire's crown, a town that can still manage to pull in the crowds most weekends in the winter, has to be applauded. So you see, you cannot fail to be hugely spoilt for choice in this area. Not only has it got some great attractions to visit, but the locations themselves truly are attractions in their own right!

Bodelwyddan Castle and Park

Museum, Gallery, Gardens, and much more....

t: 01745 584060 e: enquiries @bodelwyddan-castle.co.uk
www.bodelwyddan-castle.co.uk

Help us celebrate our museum's 25th Anniversary this year, come and visit our Victorian Castle with 260 acres of parkland, gardens, historic rooms and family-friendly galleries. Bodelwyddan Castle is a partner of the National Portrait Gallery with over 100 Victorian paintings displayed in magnificent period rooms. This beautifully restored Gothic-style house has open displays, which let you get up close to our fine collections. We have hands-on galleries, including Victorian inventions and amusements, dressing up and making portraits.
During school holidays we run family events. We also have a changing exhibitions programme throughout the year. The grounds are well worth a visit. There are rare World War 1 practice trenches within the deer park. The old walled garden is a quiet spot for enjoying the sun, maze and aviary. There is a new adventure playground and picnic area. And within the woodland you will find a bird hide, butterfly glade and orchard.
Bring this book or quote T100/13 and get cheapest entrant free.

Bodelwyddan Castle & Gardens has far more to offer than the name suggests. Set in its own 260 acre parkland the Castle has got a wide variety of attributes that is appealing to all age groups. With a multi dimensional approach the independent charitable trust set up to manage the property with the help of Denbighshire County Council has allowed a visit to the castle to be both educational and enjoyable, as I found to my delight on the day I visited. With a great little café serving a mouth-watering selection of savoury delights, cakes and pastries all at affordable prices, plenty of surprisingly free car parking and the audio tour being totally free, it all goes to make this attraction a great value day out for all the family.

Welsh Mountain Zoo

t: 01492 532 938 e: info@welshmountainzoo.org
www.welshmountainzoo.org

Get Up Close and Personal with some of our Amazing Animals!

The Welsh Mountain Zoo is set in North Wales, high above Colwyn Bay with panoramic views and breathtaking scenery. Its beautiful gardens are home to this caring conservation zoo. Roam the wooded pathways, relax on the grassy slopes and spend a lovely day learning about many rare and endangered species from Britain and around the world including Snow Leopards, Chimpanzees, Red Pandas and Sumatran Tigers! Enjoy our Penguin Parade, Chimp Encounter, Bear Falls, Lemur Lookout, Condor Haven and the Children's Farm plus much more. Visit 'Sea Lions Rock' and watch our Californian Sea Lions being trained. Enjoy the exciting and extensive Jungle Adventureland and Tarzan Trail Adventure Playground. For the more technically inclined, visit our Media Centre, where you can do a virtual tour of the Zoo and play some great educational games. OPENING HOURS: April to October: Gates open at 9.30am, last admission just before 5.00pm, Zoo closes at 6.00pm.November to March: Gates open at 9.30am, last admission just before 4.00pm, Zoo closes at 5.00pm. Closed Christmas Day.

Visiting all the attractions that makes Wales such a special place is truly an honour. Not only is it an honour for the attractions to make their way into these books, but the memories they have given me will stay with me for the rest of my life. I say this now because I have some very fond memories of my visit to the Welsh Mountain Zoo. There is no zoo on this earth that offers the same views as can be found here, and the magnificent range of animals they have, really did put a smile on my face. Open all year round, this attraction offers amazing value for money by way of its annual pass, and the idea of being able to be a 'keeper for the day ' truly excited me! This attraction owes itself to its founder, the late Robert Jackson who opened the zoo back in 1963. It is also my opinion that Colwyn Bay owes a debt of gratitude to Robert Jacksons vision, and to his family for continuing to keep that vision alive.

Llandudno

Colwyn Bay, Conwy, North Wales, LL28 5UY

Cae Dai 50s Museum

t: 01745 817004 e: caedaitrust@btconnect.com

A private collection will appeal to all with an interest in the 50's

The Cae Dai Trust is based in the countryside just 1 mile outside the market town of Denbigh. After the closure of North West Wales largest psychiatric hospital in 1994, the Cae Dai Trust was established to provide support for vulnerable adults. Cae Dai is able to give limited temporary accommodation; which provides the"umbrella" of support required to enable the beneficiary's time to gain confidence, self esteem and life skills essential to moving on and living independently in the community. The main source for this support is in the 1950's museum, a fantastic resource and attraction for the local and wider community. The museum has a collection of classic cars, sport, music, film and crime memorabilia. Our beneficiaries also enjoy looking after the animals on our farm and a spot of gardening in the woodland and community orchard. Please visit Cae Dai and help us to continue.

The 50's museum here in Denbigh is one of those little hidden gems you will hear talked about a fair bit in this book! Having seen fire's destroy one of the main buildings last year due to an arson attack, like a Phoenix from the Ashes Cae Dai 50's museum is hoped to be back to its full glory again from April 2012. Then you will be able to enjoy looking around such vehicles as the original lorry that was used in the real 'Great Train Robbery' also featured at the museum is the car that belonged to 'Christine Keeler' the 50's & 60's model that sparked the whole 'Profumo' scandal that rocked the then conservative government. Plus many more treasures from the 50's era. So whether you're a 50's enthusiast or just somebody who appreciates the past, do not overlook this amazing little museum.

Cae Dai Trust, Cae Dai, Denbigh, LL16 4SU

Bodafon Farm Park

CARTWHEEL CAFE, BAR & BBQ.

t: 01492 549060 e: info@bodafonfarmpark.com
www.bodafonfarmpark.com

A Genuine working Welsh Farm attraction!

Bodafon Farm Park is only a stone's throw from the sea front in beautiful Llandudno, and is very easy to find – it's just off the Promenade towards the Little Orme by the fields.
Come and experience life on a genuine working farm. There's lots to do at Bodafon farm or just come and relax in our cartwheel cafe and courtyard where our unique BBQ is situated.
For the children we have ride on tractors and an adventure playground where adults can sit on our sunset terrace and watch the kids play. We have a wide variety of animals which you can feed or take a tractor trailer ride around the fields. We also offer pony rides and we are home to the north Wales bird trust with a large collection of owls and unusual birds to walk around. We also have stunning views over Llandudno bay, so come and enjoy a day out with great food and a relaxed atmosphere.

Combining both coast and countryside, Bodafon Farm Park really does have a lot to offer. They have one of the biggest birds of prey areas that I have seen at a farm park, which was a sheer delight to see, Owls, Hawks just to name but a few and all very friendly I found. As I walked around the farm park all the animals seemed to make their way to where I was standing, I was beginning to think I must be a kind of Dr Doolittle figure, when I suddenly remembered that people can feed these animals by buying feed in the cafe, so it clearly wasn't me they were interested in, but merely what I may of had in my hand! Story of my life! Ha! Another thing that really impressed me was that for 2013, it is totally free to visit Bodafon, so what are you waiting for?

Llandudno

Bodafon Road, Llandudno, Gwynedd, LL30 3BB

Conwy Water Gardens

t: 01492 650063 e: info@conwywatergardens.co.uk
www.conwywatergardens.co.uk

Come and visit and share this beautiful part of Wales with us!

Conwy Water Gardens is set within the Snowdonia National Park in the picturesque Conwy Valley, North Wales. Besides our fully licensed Dutch Pancake House & Restaurant we have lots to offer – 3 fully stocked coarse fishing lakes,Otters, Capybaras and lots of ducks and wildlife.
A newly constructed nature walk which includes numerous ponds, woods and waterfalls. Also available is an outside eating area, children's play area, an aquarium with over 100 species of fish, a reptile House with all sorts of creepy crawlies and an aquatic centre for all your fish and pond supplies.
Whether you want to just look round and feed the ducks or spend a day here, come and visit and share this beautiful part of Wales with us!
Open every day except Mondays (but open on Bank Holiday Mondays) from 9.30am to 5.30pm.

This attraction has to be one of the Conwy Valleys hidden gems. The owners despite opening their attraction free to the general public have maintained this site to a very high standard, and are continuing to expand the gardens to ensure the walks are user friendly to all. Then there is the "Dutch Pancake" house on site with pancakes of all types that were just to die for!
After I visited Conwy Water Gardens I was left gobsmacked that all this was for free! Now that's what I call value for money! Miss this at your peril!

Llandudno

Bodnant Welsh Food

t: 01492 870447 e: info@gomines.co.uk
www.greatormemines.info

A visit to Great Orme Mines is both an enjoyable and educational experience!

Bodnant Welsh Food serves up a tasteful food experience. In an age of mass produced and chemically balanced sameness, Bodnant offers food as it used to be. Dairy items, such as freshly made ice-cream using milk gathered from cows across the river, hand packed butter, unhomogonised milk and creamy hard cheese are produced in the Bodnant dairy, whilst a selection of artisan breads and traditional cakes are freshly baked daily. Butcher Miles sources many of the best local cattle, sheep and pigs to be enjoyed in N Wales. No traceability issues here! Sausages are made onsite and include pork, apricot and cheese, whilst the beer or whisky flavoured bacon adds a new dimension to breakfast! Allied to the above, more than 70% of shop food items are made in Wales, mostly in North Wales, and the unique Bodnant range of artisan foods are featured on innovative menus served in the Furnace Tearoom and Hayloft Restaurant.

Want to learn more? See website for details on fun and interactive cookery experiences for all ages coming up in the cookery school.

Relatively speaking the Bodnant Welsh Food Centre is a new attraction to the Conwy Valley, but once visited, you would never of known. The Food Centre itself is a foodie heaven, and this slick operation has people flocking from not only the county of Conwy, but from further afield also. Not only can you sample Welsh delicacies in their amazing farm shop, but the dishes in the Restaurant are second to none. The Tea Room has also some great lunch alternatives, or if your just looking for a snack they have it all. But what really does set this attraction apart from others of its kind, is the fact they also have some amazing accommodation that you can stay in. With the close proximity to the National Trusts Bodnant Garden, Collectively, this attraction has so much going for it, and is most definitely worth a visit.

Llandudno

Furnace Farm, Tal-ycafn, Conwy, LL28 5RP

Venue Cymru

t: 01492 872000 e: info@venuecymru.co.uk
www.venuecymru.co.uk

Llandudno's Premier Theatre

Set beneath the glorious foothills of Snowdonia and occupying spectacular views out to sea, Venue Cymru is one of the finest locations for professionally managed conferences. Located in Llandudno, in the centre of the North Wales coast, Venue Cymru is well served by all transportation methods. The A55 dual carriageway connects the town to both the M56 and M53; in travel terms both Manchester and Liverpool are just one hour's drive away, as are their respective airports. Venue Cymru has been recently expanded to include modern, purpose built conference facilities for anything from 5 to 5000 delegates. It hosts a full range of rooms and services available for events and conferences of all sizes. Whatever your specifications, our dedicated events team will be able to meet your needs.

Venue Cymru has to be the brightest jewel in the Queen of british holiday resorts crown. Llandudno isn't only a seaside from Victorian times gone by, but the town is also home to one of the most modern and vibrant theatres Wales has to offer. Venue Cymru isn't just a theatre but a very busy conference centre and Live music arena to boot. Playing host to a wide variety of artistes such as Stereophonics, Manic Street Preachers, Mike Peters, Status Quo, Ian Brown, Duffy, The Kooks, Feeder, Pendulum and many more....

Llandudno

As I was being shown round Venue Cymru I was gobsmacked to realise just how diverse the venue is and how important the theatre was to not only North Wales but also to the hundreds of thousands of visitors to North Wales on a yearly basis.

The Promenade,Llandudno, LL30 1BB

Rhyl Sun Centre

t: 01745 344433 e: admin@clwydleisure.co.uk
www.rhylsuncentre.co.uk

SO MUCH TO DO AT RHYL SUN CENTRE!

There's no better way to enjoy a cracking day out than at Rhyl's own tropical paradise, The Rhyl Suncentre.
Whatever the weather, temperature at the Suncentre averages 80 degrees and in this tropical atmosphere there is something for everyone - waves and tropical storms, a superb surfing pool (surf boards supplied), and lots of slides to suit all. There are no extra costs for our rides, all charges are included in the admission price, if you dare, try the BLACK Thunder, pick up an inflatable and go for the Buzz,(300ft Slide) and there's more, in fact, something for everyone. Even thrill seekers need a break and food is available all around the pool hall with freshly made take-away menus and Lite Bite selections too. Should the real sun appear then catch some rays on our open air sun decks which overlook the promenade and the wide expanses of Rhyl's fine golden beaches.

Please check opening times!

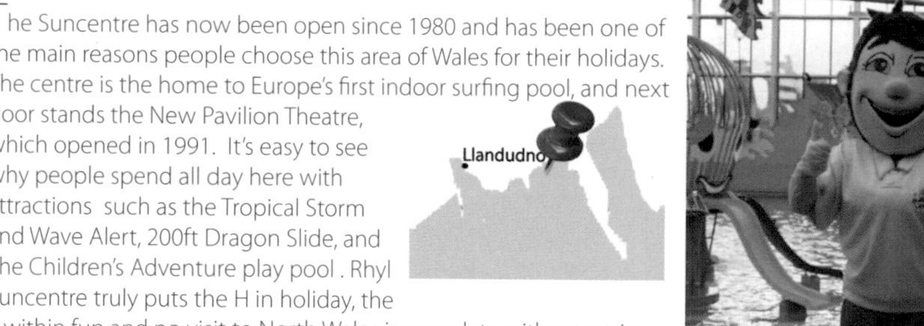

The Suncentre has now been open since 1980 and has been one of the main reasons people choose this area of Wales for their holidays. The centre is the home to Europe's first indoor surfing pool, and next door stands the New Pavilion Theatre, which opened in 1991. It's easy to see why people spend all day here with attractions such as the Tropical Storm and Wave Alert, 200ft Dragon Slide, and The Children's Adventure play pool . Rhyl Suncentre truly puts the H in holiday, the F within fun and no visit to North Wales is complete without a trip here.

Rhyl Sun Centre, East Parade, Rhyl, LL18 2QD

Hot Tub Safari

t: 01824 790732 e: info@pentremawrcountryhouse.co.uk
www.hottubsafari.co.uk

THIS ISN'T JUST GLAMPING!!

Want a safari style holiday but don't want the airport queues, the long haul flights and the jet lag! When you get there it's all worthwhile but getting there and the threat of cancelled flights! Pack up your troubles, "c'mon get happy", sounds good but singing a song, dancing around the bedroom and throwing a few items in to an open suitcase isn't quite so easy as getting away from those demons of responsibility is usually far,far away. So we thought go right back to one of the holiday wonderments from childhood. Camping. This isn't just any camping. This is camping with whistles and bells on, king size large beds, bath robes, huge bathrooms with free standing baths and a private terrace hot tub. (actually we made up the whistles and bells bit). The Canvas lodges, as inspired by our african trips, are a camping model firmly focused on luxury.

I had heard whispers of a new craze that was sweeping not only the UK, but the wider world. But when it's a new craze that is tourism related, I know I have to go and check it out! Some would say that it's strange that such an idea would end up being one of the Top 100 Attractions in Wales, but once you've experienced not only Glamping, but Glamping done well, you'll know there's nothing strange about it at all. After a fantastic meal in Pentre Mawr's cosy restaurant, I sat outside in the hot tub. Even though it's was 11.30pm, it wasn't hard to imagine a Giraffe poking its long stiff neck over my secluded garden, I then retired to have one the best sleeps I've had in ages! Hot Tub Safari are set to become one of the leading Glamping sites in the UK, and we wanted to be first to tell you all about it.

Pentre Mawr Country House, Llandyrnog, Denbighshire, LL16 4LA

Plas Mawr

t: 01492 580167 e: cadw@wales.gsi.gov.uk
www.cadw.wales.gov.uk

Plas Mawr stands as a symbol of a prosperous, buoyant age.

The Elizabethan era. A golden age? Think Renaissance and Shakespeare. Think Plas Mawr. An Elizabethan gem worth its weight in gold. The finest town house of its period in Britain. Its owner Robert Wynn, an influential merchant of great repute, was particularly fond of grandeur and colour. He also liked entertaining. Lavishly. Behold his finest hour, a grand house built between 1576 and 1585 in the heart of medieval Conwy's narrow cobbled streets. A house which more than matched his grandiose ambitions. Particularly exquisite is the ornamental plasterwork in the hall, now repainted in vivid original colours. There's not an inch that doesn't impress, from plasterwork ceilings to friezes and skilful carpentry. Look out for the initials 'RW' on various crests and coats of arms, lest you forget the master of the mansion and payer of all bills. If wealth was measured in style, then this well-travelled Welsh gentleman was absolutely fabulously wealthy. While not available in Wynn's day, you can now take advantage of multi-sensory displays to delve deeper into Plas Mawr's history. We positively encourage you to be hands-on with our touch-screen technology!

Plas Mawr is reputed to be the best kept Elizabethan property in the UK, but let me put you straight on that, Plas Mawr truly is the best preserved Elizabethan property in the UK! Withstanding all that has been thrown at it, together with the test of time, this house is more than just a tourist attraction. I went round the house twice, as I wanted to make sure I had not missed anything. The children will thoroughly enjoy themselves here, as the staff at Plas Mawr make learning just that little bit more fun.

Conwy

Rathlin Country House

48 Kings Road, Colwyn Bay, LL29 7YH

T: 01492 532173 www.rathlincountryhouse.co.uk E: enquiries@rathlincountryhouse.co.uk

Rathlin Country House is situated in a beautiful conservation area just minutes from Colwyn Bay town centre. This imposing residence, within its own grounds of almost an acre, offers 5 Star Visit Wales Luxury Bed and Breakfast accommodation for the more discerning traveller. All rooms are en-suite and appointed to a very high standard. There is an outdoor swimming pool and sauna which is available for guests during the summer months.

Abbey House B & B

52 Abbey Road, Llandudno, LL30 2EH

T: 01492 873328 www.visitllandudno.org.uk/ E: marymccann@hotmail.co.uk

Parking guaranteed. Newly refurbished for 2012. Flat screen TV, king pillow top beds, new bathrooms, separate dining tables. Weekly discounts available. Between the two Shores at the foot of the Great Orme. Always a warm welcome in our lovely Victorian house. Excellent value with wonderful breakfasts and 5 Star services from experienced hosts Mary and Bernie McCann.

Sychnant Pass Country House

Sychnant Pass Road, Conwy, LL32 8BJ

T: 01492 596868 www.sychnant-pass-house.co.uk E: info@sychnantpasscountryhouse.co.uk

A welcoming country house set in three acres of landscaped gardens on the edge of Snowdonia National Park. With 12 bedrooms, an indoor swimming pool, sauna and hot tubs, it provides the perfect place to relax and unwind. We have 12 bedrooms, each one different. Some have 4-posters; some are twin bedded; some have jacuzzi baths; others have showers. Almost all have stunning views of the Snowdonia nationa park. Our restaurant is open to residents and non residents and our award winning chef prepares a 5-course meal - and there's a different menu each night.

The Groes Inn

Tyn Y Groes, Conwy, LL32-8TN

T: 01492-650545 www.groesinn.co.uk E: enquiries@groesinn.co.uk

The Groes Inn has fourteen beautifully presented rooms that perfectly blend the features of the 16th century inn with the requirements of a modern guest. Offering luxury and relaxation each room has its own style. All rooms have a magnificent view either of the foothills of Snowdonia or the Conwy Valley. Some also have their own private terraces or balconies from which to enjoy the afternoon and evening sun across open fields.

Escape B&B

48 Church Walks, Llandudno, Conwy, LL30-2HL

T: 01492-877776 www.escapebandb.co.uk E: info@escapebandb.co.uk

Welcome To Escape. Llandudno's Premier Boutique Bed & Breakfast, offering exclusive, stylish and luxurious accommodation in a unique Victorian Town Villa.
Contemporary in style & offering 9 individually designed rooms with luxurious features such as, Flat Screen TV's, Bose IPod docking stations, Blu-Ray DVD players and high speed wireless broadband access.

The Kinmel Arms

The Village,St George, Abergele, Conwy, LL22 9BP

T:01745-832207 www.kinmelarms.co.uk E: info@thekinmelarms.co.uk

The Kinmel Arms North Wales, offers luxury rooms and exquisite gourmet food set within the stunning scenery that is St.George, Abergele. Ideally situated along the main rambling routes of North Wales, The Kinmel Arms is located just off the A55, 15 mins from Llandudno and 25 mins from Chester. With gourmet food of the very highest quality and four luxurious bedrooms that really must be seen to be believed the Kinmel Arms is a real jewel in the North Wales coastline, perfect for romantic getaways, weekend breaks and businessmen working in the area.

Lympley Lodge Bed & Breakfast

Alastair Sawday's

Colwyn Road,Craigside, Llandudno LL30-3AL

T:01492-549304 www.lympleylodge.co.uk E: info@lympleylodge.co.uk

Lympley Lodge is a Victorian residence built in the castellated style of the 1870's and is situated beneath the Little Orme overlooking Llandudno Bay. The house is set within lovely walled gardens with splendid views.
Situated on the edge of the town, Lympley Lodge is a perfect base for visiting North Wales' many famous beauty spots, such as Snowdonia, Betws Y Coed, Conwy and Anglesey.

The Queens Head & Storehouse Cottage

Glanwydden, Conwy, LL31-9JP

T:01492-546570 www.queensheadglanwydden.co.uk E: enquiries@queensheadglanwydden.co.uk

Lovingly and sympathetically restored, The Old Storehouse standing opposite The Queen's Head in the village dates back to the early 18th century and was once the original storehouse of the Llangwstennin Parish. Every attention to detail has been taken to ensure a comfortable and decadent stay. Superb accommodation for self catering or bed and breakfast.

Osborne's Cafe & Grill

Promenade, 17 North Parade, Llandudno, LL30-2LP

T: 01492-860330 www.osbornehouse.com E: sales@osbornehouse.com

Osborne's Cafe and Grill is open every day from 10.30am to 10.00pm (Sunday 9.00pm) Lit by a multitude of candles, with opulent drapes and dazzling chandeliers, gilt edge mirrors and original art. This romantic bistro/cafe with brasserie style food has a diverse a la carte menu prepared and presented in a modern way with an air of informality.

Dawsons Restaurant

The Castle Hotel, High Street,Conwy. LL32 8D

T: 01492-582800 www.castlewales.co.uk E: mail@castlewales.co.uk

Our Head Chef, Andrew Nelson is ably supported by his team of young aspiring Welsh chefs being mentored in all that's good about Welsh food. Consultant Chef/Director Graham Tinsley is the Manager of the Welsh Culinary Team and as you can imagine, passionate about his food! Peter Lavin and Graham have worked together for over 25 years and have always shared the belief that a good hotel must have a good food. Dawson Bar's great new look is now complimented by the new look lounge and garden courtyard with an even better atmosphere and range of hand pulled beers & fabulous wine list.

Pentre Mawr Country House

Llandyrnog, Denbigh, Denbighshire, LL16-4LA

T: 01824-790732 www.pentremawrcountryhouse.co.uk E: info@pentremawrcountryhouse.co.uk

Both Bre and Graham cook and though neither consider themselves chefs, Graham trained (many years ago) at Gleneagles in Scotland. They have an AA dining award and both have a love of cooking and enjoy fusing together different flavours. They're reinstating the vegetable garden and hope soon to be providing all the vegetables for the restaurant at Pentre Mawr. Everything is homemade even the bread. The menu changes slightly, nightly. (Try saying that with a few glasses of wine!!!) They also have a dedicated vegetarian menu and are more than happy to make adjustments to the menu for dietary needs or just coz you prefer a different sauce with your main course!

L's Coffee & Bookshop

7 High Street, Conwy, LL32 8DB

T: 01492-596661 E: garethlavin@yahoo.co.uk

L's Coffee & Bookshop is a great little shop with lot's of character. With nearby parking in the castle hotel, together with great food and a warm welcome, you will not be disappointed. L's tries to accommodate all people with a diverse range of food, including home made gluten free cakes, with a plan to extend their range to include gluten free Pizzas. They also sell Coffees, Chocolate Fondues, preserves and curds.

The Kinmel Arms

The Village,St George, Abergele, Conwy, LL22 9BP

T:01745-832207 www.kinmelarms.co.uk E: info@thekinmelarms.co.uk

Good, fresh food is at the heart of the Kinmel Arms Restaurant. We try to source as much produce as possible from North Wales and North West England, however quality knows no boundary!
We delight in serving fantastic fish and meat. All our desserts are hand-made in our own kitchens using only the purest ingredients. Our menu at lunch is of a Brasserie style, evenings see a more 'a la carte' atmosphere. Whenever you dine with us you can be sure of only the very freshest ingredients we can find served in a simple but creative way.

The Queens Head & Storehouse Cottage

Glanwydden, Conwy, LL31 9JP

T:01492-546570 www.queensheadglanwydden.co.uk E: enquiries@queensheadglanwydden.co.uk

The Queen's Head is a most remarkable country pub in terms of good food, wine, beer, welcome and character.
Priceless chefs who have a passion for local produce, excellent staff, effortless charm and a warm welcome. The bar, with its relaxed atmosphere and roaring log fire, is a lovely pre-dinner drink venue. The Queen's Head offers a warm welcome to pre theatre dinner guests with Venue Cymru just a 5 minute drive away or a welcoming respite after a long day's shopping.

Split Willow Restaurant

Penmaenmawr Road, Llanfairfechan, Conwy, LL33 0PA

T: 01248-680647 www.splitwillow.co.uk E: splitwillow@hotmail.co.uk

Split Willow is in the small town of Llanfairfechan, off the A55 midway between Bangor and Conwy. Excellent location, good parking, landscaped garden and menus to suit all budgets, the perfect venue of family gatherings or a quiet meal. A reasonably priced lunch menu is available Tuesday to Saturday. A popular Traditional Sunday Lunch is on offer 12 – 2pm, £8.50 for main course (£11.95 for 3 courses) bookings advisable. Restaurant evening meals are only available by reservation.

The Seahorse Restaurant & Bistro

7 Church Walks , Llandudno, Conwy, LL30-2HD

T: 01492-875315/ 877924 www.www.the-seahorse.co.uk E: seahorsellandudno@gmail.com

Chef Proprietors Don & Gill Hadwin. We extend a very warm welcome to you. Our motto is, "Fresh, local produce prepared with love, thought and care." Why not celebrate your special occasion here at The Seahorse restaurant Llandudno? We have held several wedding breakfasts in our upstairs dining room, seating up to 38 people comfortably, and on one occasion 45 people! We can discuss your individual requirements for your menu choice.

SNOWDONIA MOUNTAINS & COAST

I have travelled to many places in the UK and abroad, and have seen some fantastic scenery along the way, but none more beautiful than that of Snowdonia. It's sometimes rugged but Spectacular Mountain ranges are simply breathtaking at times, and one can't fail to see why millions of people travel to the area every year, either on holiday, for the weekend, or as I do on many occasions simply just for the day. I have become to know the area just like the back of my hand and when that happens, then you can truly say how magnificent a place is. But enough about me! If after reading this book you're wondering where to start, then, make Snowdonia, Mountains & Coast the first stop on your adventures.

You are truly spoilt for choice when it comes to Activities, Attractions, Quaint Villages, and Blue Flag Beaches, Snowdonia, Mountains & Coast simply has the lot! But don't just take our word for it; the proof is merely in the pudding as they say. We have included a great line up of accommodation providers, & restaurants that are absolutely top notch, so there you have it, get reading, get booking and have a fantastic time whatever you decide to do first.

The Railway Station-Betwys

t: 01690 710747 e: info@alpinecoffeeshop.co.uk
www. alpinecoffeeshop.co.uk

A Fabulous Day Out!

Betws-y-Coed Railway Station is located in the heart of the beautiful Snowdonia National Park. The station was first opened to passenger trains in 1868, it was purchased by Robert Hughes (Bob 17) in the 1980s and remains in the family today where it is still a functioning station for trains travelling between Llandudno and Blaenau Ffestiniog. There are a number of shopping outlets and restaurants running along the station, at the centre of these is The Alpine Coffee Shop, which is a lively and welcoming coffee shop catering for all dietary requirements, including vegetarian, vegan and gluten free. The coffee shop prides itself on being entirely Palm Oil free, the reason for this being, to raise peoples awareness of the impact palm oil has on the environment and to help save the apes of the world. Watching over the Coffee Shop and the rest of the station is a Gorilla fountain, which helps to raise vital funds for saving the apes. Upcoming projects include self-catering holiday apartments and a gallery is opening in the basement of the railway station.

There are lots of tourist attractions along the North Wales coast that are known the countrywide, many of them are in this Top 100 Attractions book. But as you may of gathered reading through this book, that it is not just about the big attractions that we write about, but a number of what we like to call hidden gems. Set back slightly, away from the coast, is the Railway Station and Retail Village , hidden away in the sleepy yet vibrant village of Betws-y-Coed. This attraction is one of those hidden gems that just I had to let my readers know about. You won't hear about this attraction, because its one of those attractions that doesn't need a flyer, brochure or travel agent to promote it, but more word of mouth by the people that have visited, or travel writers like myself.

Caernarfon

Station Road, Betws y Coed, LL54 5TP

The Retail Village-Betwys

The place is busy all year round with people, and even on a wet day, I'm surprised how many people still visit this place. That's where the Alpine Coffee shop comes into it. There are a few eateries situated here and all are big names, such as Cadwaladers Ice Cream & Spinnakers Fish & Chip Shop, all serving the best food within their field and famous in their own rights, but then there's another place that caught my eye called the Alpine Coffee Shop. Along my travels I have eaten and drank in a number of great places, but this place was totally different to anywhere else I have been in. Firstly, they have to be the only coffee outlet that is 100 percent palm-oil free, not just on all of their hot drinks, but also on all of their foods as well, and despite a little extra cost, the owner assures me that every food outlet could become palm-oil free with out any major headaches. The Cafe Is also dog friendly (ask about their sausages for dogs loyalty card), which did make me chuckle!

Due to open in the Summer of 2013 is an 'Art Gallery' underneath the Staion, which is to house a number of amazing artworks etc that were before, dotted around the coffee shop itself. But now with the collaboration of other artists, they have now added yet another reason to visit this already amazing place.

Although there are many varied accommodation providers in and around the village, self catering accommodation is quite scarce in the area, and for this very reason. The owner of the Railway Station & Retail Village has invested a huge amount of time and money into renovating some of the station buildings into state of the art self catering apartments. I very cheekily asked to be shown one or two of these apartments and I have to say I was completely bold over with what I saw as I was being given my tour. Each apartment has been individually designed by the owner himself, Jacha Potgieter. They have been fitted with bespoke kitchens and furniture that were also designed by himself, and built by a local Blacksmith. I will go as far as to say that no matter where you go in our very huge planet, you will never see a bed, kitchen or bathroom quite like the ones that are furnished here within these apartments.

Station Road, Betws y Coed, LL54 5TP

Electric Mountain

t: 01286 870636 e: info@electricmountain.co.uk
www. electricmountain.co.uk

ELECTRIC MOUNTAIN & DINORWIG POWER STATION.

Have you ever wondered how electrical appliances we rely on most in our day to day lives are powered? Or how does the National Grid cope during periods of exceptionally high demand? These questions plus much more are answered as you witness the creation of electricity at Electric Mountain.Visitors can take a guided tour around Dinorwig Power Station starting with a sound and vision spectacular at Electric Mountain, illustrating the role that pumped storage plays in ensuring the country's electricity demands are always met, before descending deep inside the ancient Elidir Mountain's labyrinth of dark and imposing tunnels. Electric Mountain's friendly and knowledgeable guides show you the main features of the complex, from the massive main inlet valve chamber to closeup views of the world's fastest response turbine-generators. These units have a dynamic response capacity from zero output to full power within seconds, and are housed in Europe's largest man-made cavern.

I took a tour inside the Electric Mountain, knowing what to expect as I have taken a tour inside this world famous power station on many occasions, and what you will find for those who also have been before, is that every time you take a trip inside the mountain, you notice or learn something new every time. You cannot fail to be amazed by the ingenuity of this power station and the importance it places in our everyday lives from making a cup of tea in the adverts of 'Corrie' to turning the hoover on, the electricity we are using has a good chance of coming from the Electric Mountain in the beautiful and picturesque village that is Llanberis.

Caenarfon

Electric Mountain, Llanberis, Gwynedd, LL55 4UR

Childrens Farm Park

t: 01766 780247 e: hello@childrensfarmpark.co.uk
www.childrensfarmpark.co.uk

Come and see all your favourite animals on the farm!

Floss the donkey and her friends, various pigs, rabbits, calves, ducks, hens, small pigmy goats and many other birds and animals too.

All the animals are housed in farm buildings, so you'll have a great time no matter what the weather is like, we also have an indoor play barn, which is a must on wet days. In spring and early summer you can have a go at bottle-feeding the lambs and calves. Animal feed is available from the reception through out the season for you to hand feed the goats, lambs, calves, ducks and chickens.

Situated at the Children's farm park we have a small family campsite for tents, motor vans and caravans. Facilities include toilets, mains water and hot showers.

The farm park here in Llanfair has grown from strength to strength over the years. There is always something to capture the imaginations and hearts of all ages of children and if their totally honest the adults also. What I liked about this attraction was the great family atmosphere that surrounds the place and the views across the Cardigan bay, Shell Island etc. are absolutely breath taking. With the proximity of the Slate Caverns being so close it would be a shame not to do both, or if you have small children and teenagers you could send dad off with the teenagers down to the slate caverns leaving mum and the little ones to enjoy feeding the animals. What I liked so much about this site is there something for everybody and you can use your ticket for a free return visit should you not have the time to see everything.

Caernarfon

Cae Gethin, Llanfair, Harlech, Gwynedd, LL46 2SA

Galeri Caernarfon

t: 01286 685 250 e: post@galericaernarfon.com
www. galericaernarfon.com

GALERI CREATIVE ENTERPRISE CENTRE, LOCATED ON THE VICTORIA DOCK IN CAERNARFON IS AN INDEPENDENTLY OWNED ENTERTAINMENT COMPLEX..

The award winning £7.5m building includes:

- 394 seat theatre and cinema
- Workspace units
- Art Space (exhibiting a mixture of work by local, national and international artists)
- Rehearsal studios and soundproof rooms
- Meeting rooms
- DOC Café Bar (serving a fresh, local home-cooked menu)

Galeri has over 400 events on an annual basis, ranging from workshops, music concerts, theatre / drama, film screenings, dance and comedy.
International stars often perform at Galeri, from Llŷr Williams to Bryn Terfel and Lee Evans, Rob Brydon and Alan Carr.

The building of this state of the art theatre and conference centre couldn't have come at a better time. Caernarfon itself has always been famous for its castle and if you were to ask anyone else that would be it. The company (Galeri Caernarfon Cyf) that owns the centre have been responsible in my opinion for giving Caernarfon a lease of new life, and a visit to this theatre only goes to strengthen that. Since 2005, the award winning centre has been pulling in the masses with such names as top UK comedian 'Lee Evans' and the Welsh opera singer 'Bryn Terfel' Check out their website above and book your tickets, sit back in luxury and enjoy the show!

Caenarfon

Doc Victoria, Caernarfon, Gwynedd, LL55 1SQ

Ffestiniog & Welsh
Highland Railways

t: 01766 516000 e: enquiries@festrail.co.uk
www.festrail.co.uk

Steam, Scenery, Snowdonia!

The Ffestinog and Welsh Highland Railways are two of the Great Little Trains of Wales, together offering a wide variety of travel options through northern Snowdonia. The Ffestiniog Railway runs between Blaenau Ffestiniog and Porthmadog. Built to carry slate from the quarries, the little steam trains now haul carriages of passengers through the beautiful Vale of Ffestiniog. The newly reopened Welsh Highland runs through from Caernarfon to Porthmadog sharing a station with the Ffestiniog. The impressive Beyer Garratt locomotives haul modern comfortable carriages on this coast to coast journey through the Snowdonia National Park. The scenery is breathtaking as the train crosses the lower slopes of Snowdon before plunging through the forest and alongside the river in the Aberglaslyn Pass on its way to Porthmadog. Refreshments are available with hot snacks on many Welsh Highland services. Trains run daily from late March until the end of October plus selected dates in winter.

There are 5 railways featured within this book and each one deservedly so. The task we undertook choosing which 5 railways we would feature wasn't an easy one. The Ffestiniog & Welsh Highland Railway is a slick operation with some of the best scenery routes Wales has to offer. With three main stations in Snowdonia you'll never be far away from catching one of these great little trains, and with the schedules being the way they are, it's quite easy to do both the Ffestiniog Railway & Welsh Highland Railway in one day. The reason I say this is because both routes here in Snowdonia like our other trains featured in this book have something completely different to offer. So whether you're a train enthusiast or not, you will not be disappointed here. What we also liked about this attraction was its restaurant Spooners' serving anything from a fresh sandwich to a full Sunday dinner all at prices that are totally affordable.

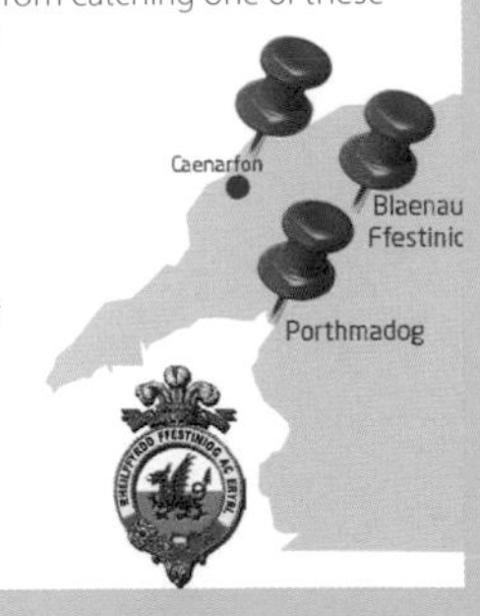

SNOWDONIA Mountains & Coast

Caernarfon, LL55 2YD-Blaenau Ffestiniog, LL41 3HE-Porthmadog, LL49 9NF

Go Ape - Coed-y-Brenin

t: 0845 643 92 15 e: info@goape.co.uk
www. goape.co.uk

LIVE LIFE ADVENTUROUSLY!

Go Ape is the UK's number one tree-top adventure. Head to Go Ape! Coed-y-Brenin, nr Dolgellau for two to three hours in the trees, taking on zip wires, Tarzan swings, rope ladders and a variety of high-wire crossings, all set in the UK's most beautiful forests.

There are now 27 Go Ape courses dotted around the UK, which means there's one near you. No two courses are the same so if you've been before, check out another site for a whole new adventure. And bring your Tribe!

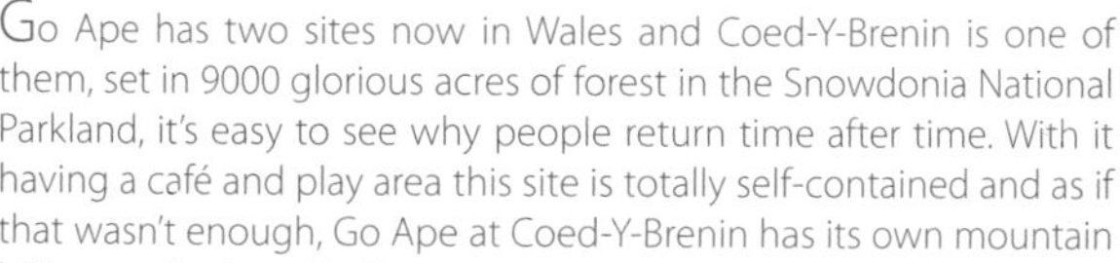

Go Ape has two sites now in Wales and Coed-Y-Brenin is one of them, set in 9000 glorious acres of forest in the Snowdonia National Parkland, it's easy to see why people return time after time. With it having a café and play area this site is totally self-contained and as if that wasn't enough, Go Ape at Coed-Y-Brenin has its own mountain biking trails also. Challenging enough as they are the tree-top crossings & wind-in-your-face zip wires all go to make this attraction a firm favourite for all prospective tree dwellers! All in all Coed-Y-Brenin has something to offer the whole family and I guarantee you'll be booking your next trip back within days if not hours!

Dolgefeiliau, Dolgellau, LL40 2HZ

Glasfryn Parc

t: 01766 810202 e: info@glasfryn.co.uk
www.glasfryn.co.uk

Wales' Premier Activity and Adventure Centre!

Whatever the weather, there's loads of fun to be had at Glasfryn Activity Parc near Pwllheli. Whether you take the challenge of the go kart circuit or quad bike safari or try your hand at wakeboarding, ten pin bowling or archery or just let the children enjoy the magic of the Soft Play Centre, Glasfryn Parc offers the ideal day out for everyone. Full instruction and protective equipment is included where appropriate and homemade meals and snacks are served until late. Visit the award-winning Farm Shop at Glasfryn Parc which sells farm-raised meat, traditionally cured bacon, homemade ready meals, sausages (including gluten free), burgers, and locally sourced cheeses, pate, preserves, biscuits and other gourmet treats and everyday essentials. Open everyday from 9am until late, Glasfryn Parc's entrance is located on the A499,15 miles south of Caernarfon and 4 miles north of Pwllheli. For older Sat Navs please use (LL53 6RN). Admission to the Parc is free and there's plenty of free parking.

There are attractions within this book that are fabulous indoor and excellent outdoor. Glasfryn Activity & Adventure Centre has it all, and too much to name all in this short review. As I walked around the site I was flabbergasted at just how much is here. Jonathan Williams-Ellis the proprietor of Glasfryn claims to have the biggest Activity and Adventure centre in North Wales, I disagree! I think Glasfryn is one of the biggest of its type in the whole of Wales. The centre is only closed on Christmas Day so the fun truly doesn't stop! The site also has holiday cottages and lots of space for camping so you can make a weekend of it. In short, Glasfryn has to be up there with some of the top attractions in Wales.

Caenarfon

Glasfryn Parc, Y Ffôr, Pwllheli, Gwynedd, LL53 6PG

Llanfair Slate Caverns

t: 01766 78024 e: caverns@llanfairslatecaverns.co.uk
www.llanfairslatecaverns.co.uk

CHWAREL HEN, LLANFAIR SLATE CAVERNS

The entry to this old but important slate mine is through the main tunnel, under the twin arches of the crypt, and into the lofty cathedral cavern. Remember that the tunnels and caverns you are about to see are all man made over a 100 years ago with only a candle for lighting. The slate in this mine, which is found in veins between layers of ancient Pre-Cambrian rocks, is among the oldest in the world. Many industrial towns in Britain and Ireland have the original roofs made of Llanfair slate. Descend Jacobs ladder and wonder through the tunnels and chambers, and look for the old drilling holes, and the likeness of a human face in the mighty no 6 cavern. As you emerge from the caverns, you face the breathtaking view of Cardigan Bay, from the Preseli mountains in the south to the Lleyn peninsular. Look down at Shell Island and the Artro estuary, and at low tide trace the fourteen mile long natural causeway of St Patrick.

In this book, are silver/lead mines, copper mines and even slate and coal mines, but the slate caverns here near Harlech, are something equally as special. These caverns were man made over a hundred years ago and would even give Dan Yr Ogof Show Caves a run for their money. Like many slate quarries in this area, thousands of homes throughout Britain and Ireland have been roofed by Llanfair slate. But as if that wasn't enough prestige for the owners to be proud of, the caverns have been featured in great feature films such as First Knight starring Sean Connery & Framed, with Trevor Eve, just to name a few. Llanfair Slate Caverns has got a great tearoom which serves all types of snacks, so an ideal location for lunch. Although there is a separate charge, the caverns are also part of the Llanfair children's farm park so there is more than enough on this site to satisfy all ages.

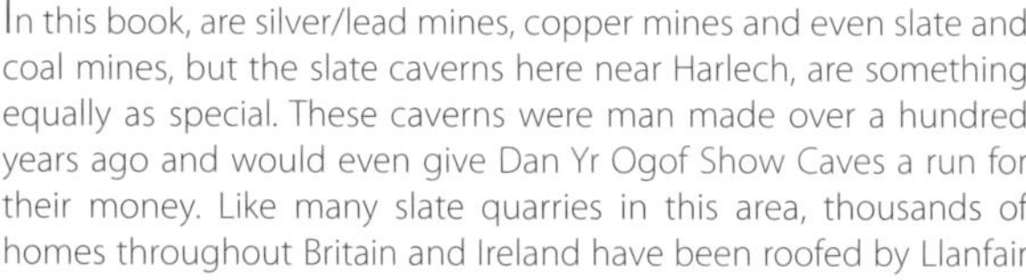

Cae Gethin, Llanfair, Harlech, Gwynedd, LL46 2SA

Go Below

t: 01690 710108 e: ask@go-below.co.uk
www.go-below.co.uk

An Underground Adventure!

Go Below is a totally unique all weather adrenalin activity near Betws-y-coed. Participants experience a thrilling guided underground adventure through the abandoned mines of Snowdonia!

The way through this fascinating subterranean environment is via a series of exciting roped challenges, such as an abseil, a zip line, boating across an underground lake, scrambling, climbing a waterfall and a scaling a shaft etc. On your journey under the mountain you will encounter forgotten deep blue lakes, lofty caverns and ancient mining machinery lying forgotten in the darkness. Experienced trip leaders are also willing and able to inform on the Welsh mining industry and its history.

No experience necessary, no potholing or squeezing through small gaps, and activities can be bypassed if preferred. All equipment and footwear provided. Open all year.... So come on down...adventure starts where daylight ends...

Go Below is so unique we just had to have them in our book! Where else in the UK can you experience being deep underground in a disused mine and journey through it in such an exciting way? On that basis alone, this attraction is total value for money! Just when you thought Frodo in the Lord of the Rings trilogy had a tough journey, your adventure has only just begun! The mines explored are in the local area and you can be transported there in one of their classic Landrovers. One popular trip involves taking a boat across a flooded underground cavern and then travelling across a zip line to your next destination. Then, with the company of your colleagues, you abseil down an underground cliff face to reach a further awe inspiring chamber.

Then it's time for a well earned lunch break, where you'll be able to talk amongst yourselves about the brave quest you have taken so far! After lunch, your group leader will take you on a waterfall climb and your ascent back to Terra Firma is via a steep climb up the mine shaft! And if that isn't enough to get your pulse racing, their newest underground adventure lays on even more challenging roped activities and is not for the faint hearted! Any spaces on tomorrow's trips you'll hear yourself ask!

Caenarfon

Penmachno, Betws-y-coed, Conwy, LL24 0PN

Zip World

t: 01690 710 914 e: info@zipworld.co.uk
www. zipworld.co.uk

the Largest zip Wire Experience in the Northern Hemisphere!

Zip World is the largest zip wire experience in the Northern Hemisphere and will see visitors fly through the skies for over a mile at speeds of up to 75mph.

Located in the world's largest old slate quarry, Zip World is a first for the UK and will take visitors over 700ft through the air above a mountain lake with panoramic views out over Snowdonia, to the Isle of Anglesey and even the Isle of Man on a clear day.

The journey starts at ground level with guests being collected in ex-military vehicles and taken high up into the Welsh mountains on a three hour fully guided interactive exploration of the area with commentary. Adventurous visitors will then get the chance to ride the mile long zip wire and fly through the air back to ground level. Guests will get chance to find their feet first with a short taster on the Little Zipper, before stepping up to the big wire. Participants will be supplied with a flying suit to wear that is wind and shower proof. Helmets and goggles will also be supplied. Prices start from £45 for adults and £36 for children.

Snowdonia has been waiting for this attraction for so long now, partly because of the magnitude of this attraction's size, and mainly because, Zip World is the second largest Zip Wire in the world, the largest one being in South Africa, which then, makes this the largest Zip Wire in the Northern Hemisphere. Because of my great fear of heights, I have not sampled this particular attraction, but I have visited the site, and it is absolutely breath taking to see. In my opinion the Ogwen Bank side of Snowdonia is the rugged brother of the area which means the terrain lends itself very well to this attractions charm. Taking a trip in the military vehicle up to the summit will make the hairs on the back of your neck stand on end, and this once in a lifetime opportunity will then become very real!

Caenarfon

Penrhyn Quarry, Bethesda, Bangor,Gwynedd, LL57 4YG

King Arthur's Labyrinth

t: 01654 761584 e: info@kingarthurslabyrinth.co.uk
www.kingarthurslabyrinth.co.uk

An Underground Adventure...

Grab a hard hat and set sail, with a mysterious Dark Age boatman, on this underground storytelling adventure. Sail underground, through a waterfall and back across a thousand years into the darkest of the Dark Ages. You have travelled back to the time of King Arthur and to a time of myth and magic. Guided by your boatman, explore vast underground caverns and winding tunnels whilst tales of King Arthur and other ancient Welsh legends are told with dramatic scenes, light and sound. A real adventure for all ages in all weathers.
Open daily 10am to 5pm from 31st March to 4th November 2012. Find us deep in the mountains of Southern Snowdonia, an area steeped in myths and legends. King Arthur's Labyrinth starts from the Corris Craft Centre which is also home to 9 craft studios.

This attraction is both unique and diverse as it isn't just the one attraction here it's several. Let me start with King Arthur's Labyrinth. Steeped in legend and mystery, this attraction has it both in abundance. As you take a journey back in time you can't help but get caught up in it all! The Labyrinth's main aim is achieved within a very short time. It's both exciting and mysterious and I promise that once you come back above ground you will want to go back down. Then of course as if that wasn't enough, there are more stories to be told in the Bard's Quest, a self-guided tour that allows you to take as long as you like to enjoy stories of olde. But if you want to hear them again, no problem! Even though the Bard's Quest suggests 45 minutes you can quite clearly go at your own pace making a visit to King Arthur's Labyrinth and surrounding attractions a value for money day. Now that can't be bad can it!

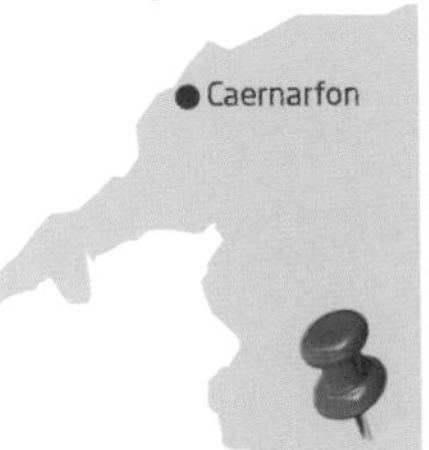

Corris Craft Centre,Corris, Machynlleth, Powys, SY20 9RF

Portmeirion Village

t: 01766 772311 e: info@portmeirion-village.com
www.portmeirion-village.com

Enjoy a Magical Day at Portmeirion!

This unique village is set on its own private peninsula on the southern shores of Snowdonia. It was created by Welsh architect Clough Williams-Ellis (1883-1978) to demonstrate how a naturally beautiful place could be developed without spoiling it. Portmeirion is made up of about 50 buildings most of which are used as hotel or self-catering accommodation and surrounded by 70 acres of sub-tropical woodland gardens. On the main driveway is Castell Deudraeth, a Victorian mansion recently restored as a brasserie style restaurant and hotel. Portmeirion is one of Wales' premier visitor attractions, welcoming 250,000 visitors every year. With free parking, complimentary guided tours and audio visual show, six cafes and restaurants, half a dozen shops, gardens and beaches it is the perfect day out for all the family.Surrounding the village are 70 acres of exotic woodlands with easy to follow woodland trails and coastal walks. Portmeirion is open every day of the year from 9.30am to 7.30pm. We look forward to welcoming you.

Portmeirion has been a tourist attraction for a number of years now and many generations of families have enjoyed walking through the streets of this famous Italianate village. I myself have visited here on many occasions and everytime feels like the first! The village has a strange pull on its visitors and its not hard to see why they return time upon time to these famous cobbled streets! People always associate Portmeirion with the Cult Tv series 'The Prisoner' but the site was a popular tourist destination long before the show started filming there and it's all down to the forward thinking of Sir Clough Williams-Ellis who started building and creating Portmeirion from 1925 to 1975 a strong testament to a strong minded man. I would highly recommend a visit to Portmeirion, and see for yourself what makes this place so special and why it leaves such a strong mark on all those who visit!

Caenarfon

PORTMEIRION, Minffordd near Porthmadog, LL48 6ER

Llechwedd Slate Caverns

t: 01766 830306 e: bookings@llechwedd.co.uk
www.llechwedd-slate-caverns.co.uk

WE ARE OPEN FROM 10.00am to 6pm (5.00pm OCTOBER - MARCH)

Explore the underground world of the Victorian Slate Miner!

These wonderful Slate Caverns at Blaenau Ffestiniog are part of a living, working slate mine that has been active since 1836. With spectacular underground tours - we take you deep inside the Welsh mountains. Come rain or shine outside, the temperature in the mine remains at around 54° F - the ideal family day out whatever the weather. Descend nearly 500 feet... go underground in Europe's steepest mining cable railway and discover the world of the Welsh Slate Miner during the late 19th Century.

Meet 'Sion Dolgarregddu' the ghost of the mine who guides you through the Deep Mine. Sion was born in 1841 and was only 12 years of age when he first came to work in the vast chambers of the mine, alongside his father and uncle. Enjoy a ride of nearly half a mile along the Miners' Tramway and a personally guided tour to discover the world of Welsh Slate Mining 170 years ago.

Llechwedd Slate Caverns really is an attraction within an attraction! What I really like about Llechwedd is it's ability to be as much of an interesting indoor attraction as well as an outdoor one. The charming Victorian Village complete with it's shops/ pubs and houses, really have had a lot of thought put into them. With the restaurant offering great food at even greater prices it makes sense to have lunch here to. I would most definitely allow a good few hours to be able to see and experience everything at Llechwedd. There is something for every member of the family here and in saying that Llechwedd really is a value for money attraction.

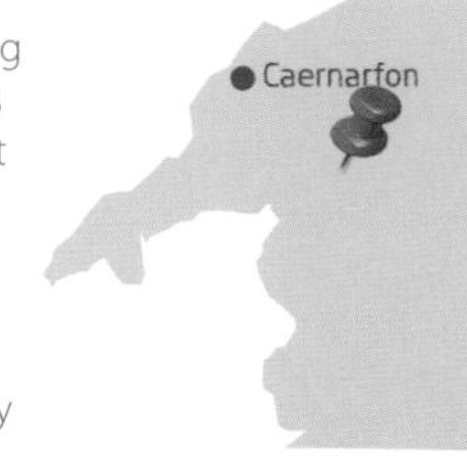

Blaenau Festiniog, Gwynedd, LL41 3NB

GreenWood Forest Park

t: 01248 670076 e: info@greenwoodforestpark.co.uk
www. greenwoodforestpark.co.uk

Award Winning Adventure Park!

Voted Best Family Attraction in North Wales for 2011 and 2012, days out don't get much better than this! GreenWood Forest Park is set in 17 magical acres, where you will discover bags of woodland adventure, awesome attractions and Forest Family Fun.

Jump aboard the world's only people powered roller coaster, zoom down Wales' longest sledge run or embark on the Jungle Boat Adventure. Head inside the Enchanted WoodBarn, full of the latest indoor play. Young explorers will love it! Plus, find extraordinary entertainment in the Forest Theatre or get creative in the craft area and make something unique to take home with you!

With so much to do on a day out, you'll need a break! In the GreenOak Café, choose from delicious hot and cold meals, as well as a great selection of Fairtrade and locally sourced products. Or during school holidays, grab a bite from one of the onsite snack bars.

Snowdonia is the ultimate outdoor destination, and with many of the tourist attractions within this area having an outdoor theme, there is no way you can ever get bored visiting here. GreenWood Forest Park is a great example of that outdoor fun I speak about, fun that can be enjoyed by all ages of the family. Nestled in a prime location between Bangor & Caernarfon, GreenWood really was an attraction that took me by surprise. I visited here late in the summer of 2012, and was very impressed with what I saw. The staff were friendly, helpful, and there was hardly any litter on the floor whatsoever, which tells me an awful lot about an attraction! I know I talked a lot at the beginning of this review about outdoor fun, but I was so surprised at the amount of indoor fun here as well! Definitely worth a visit!

Caenarfon

Bush Road, Y Felinheli, LL56 4QN, Sat Nav,LL55 3AD

Snowdon Mountain Railway

t: 0844 493 8120 e: info@snowdonrailway.co.uk
www.snowdonrailway.co.uk

A MAJESTIC MOUNTAIN TOP ADVENTURE!

Let Snowdon Mountain Railway take you on a journey of a lifetime to the rooftop of Wales. Snowdon, at 3,560ft dominates the landscape of Snowdonia National Park in North Wales. Claim this mountain peak, the highest in Wales, as a lifetime's achievement. With stunning scenery and awe-inspiring views it's all part of a great day out for you and your family in North Wales. The new visitor centre is a uniquely designed structure built of granite with large views from the "window on the world" wall of glass which makes up the front of the centre. It acts as a terminus for the Snowdon Mountain Railway providing refreshment facilities, toilets and interpretation of the mountain, its history and ways to enjoy it. Much of the interpretation is built into the structure.

This railway needs no introduction, for those of you that have walked Snowdon, or even taken the train, you will be familiar with this unique railway service. The railway has been servicing Snowdon since 1896 and hasn't stopped since! Every year the railway sees more and more visitors and once you've taken a trip on this famous little narrow gauge railway it's easy to see why. I personally like to walk up Snowdon and get the train down, but no matter what your preference, upon your visit to Snowdon, no trip is complete until you've closed that carriage door and smelt the steam coming through your windows. No matter how many times you've ridden the train the views just get better and better, so what are you waiting for?

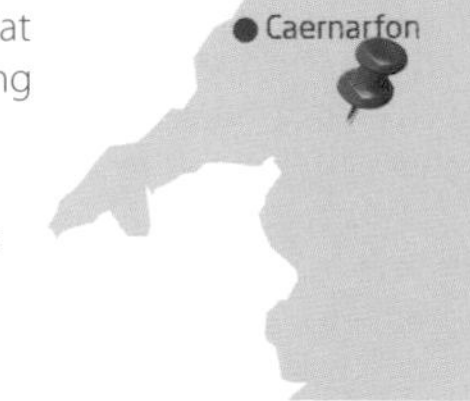

Snowdon Mountain Railway, Llanberis, Gwynedd, LL55 4TY

National White Water Centre

t: 01678-521083 e: info@ukrafting.co.uk
www.ukrafting.co.uk

Come and raft the stunning natural rapids of the River Tryweryn!

The National White Water Centre is set on the banks of the River Tryweryn, near Bala. The Tryweryn is dam controlled ensuring great water conditions all year round and the centre prides itself on providing the best white water rafting experiences in the UK. The NWWC pioneered commercial rafting in the UK in 1986 and remains the country's most popular white water rafting destination. Experience the thrill of the Tryweryn for yourselves, with rafting sessions ideal for groups, individuals and families, as well as the brand-new tandem kayak and canyoning sessions. For a more relaxed view of the river, take a walk along the delightful Tryweryn Trail as you explore mossy oaks and delicate willows in this magnificent setting. Or simply enjoy a warming cup of tea in the new riverside cafe; Caffi Celyn as you watch your friends and family whizz past you! Call the centre on 01678 521083 for more details or to book.

The National Whitewater Centre in Bala is undoubtedly one heck of a slick operation. It is true to say, there are plenty of whitenuckle rides to be enjoyed in various theme parks dotted across the UK, but what this attraction has to offer, far surpasses anything man made that is on offer at any of them! When I visited this attraction only recently, I was given a guided tour by the manager Bleddyn, who is clearly very proud of what they have achieved with this attraction, and so he and his team should be! Whether you are a hardened rafter or a novice, the team will look after you all just the same, and if the rapids don't take your breath away the scenery in its surrounding location will do!

Canolfan Tryweryn, Frongoch, Bala, Gwynedd, LL23 7NU

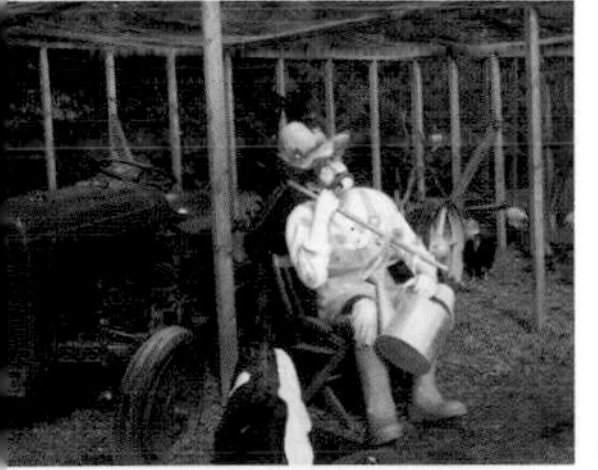

Gypsy Wood

t: 01286 673133 e: info@gypsywood.co.uk
www. gypsywood.co.uk

Come and experience the Gypsy Wood Magic at our Fun Filled Activity Park... we are unique in North Wales!

We're a must North Wales attraction for all animal, train, nature and fairy lovers - There's lots to do and see for the whole family. Gypsy Wood is an enchanting outdoor attraction for the whole family and is situated in the foothills of Snowdonia, North Wales. Set in 20 acres of natural beauty, visit us and discover one of Wales's best kept outdoor secrets. Enjoy the park's magical fantasy land – explore the wood and find the fairies and make a wish. If you feel adventurous, bring your wellies to explore the wetland walk. Bring a picnic – Gypsy Wood offers light refreshments and afternoon teas. Finish off your visit by taking home a little keepsake from our gift shop. Gypsy Wood is filled with friendly animals of many different types – our animals will be pleased to make friends with you – come and see where we live and you can watch us play in our beautiful Gypsy Wood home!

It's not often, that you get to visit a Top Attraction and, use an award winning loo all in the same day! But with a visit to Gypsy Wood that is exactly what you will be doing! I knew this site was going to be great before I got here, but just how great, I did not know. It's no big secret that this attraction is predominately for twelve's and under, but I have to say that adults find it hard not to share in the magic that this enchanting attraction has to offer. I dare say the owners Chris and John wouldn't of known how popular this attraction would be to all of its visitors, but in my professional opinion, not only should this attraction be winning this award, as one of Wales's Top 100 Attractions but so should its owners, for their creativity, and ingenuity, in their sheer brilliance that is, Gypsy Wood.

Caernarfon

Bontnewydd,Caernarfon, Gwynedd LL55 2YA

Caernarfon Castle

t: 01286 677617 e: cadw@wales.gsi.gov.uk
www.cadw.wales.gov.uk

After all these years Caernarfon's immense strength remains undimmed.

A brute of a fortress. Caernarfon Castle's pumped-up appearance is unashamedly muscle-bound and intimidating. Picking a fight with this massive structure would have been a daunting prospect. By throwing his weight around in stone, King Edward I created what is surely one of the most impressive of Wales's castles. Worthy of World Heritage status no less. Most castles are happy with round towers, not Caernarfon! Polygonal towers were the order of the day, with the Eagle Tower being the most impressive of these. You will also note the colour-coded stones carefully arranged in bands. The site of this great castle wasn't chosen by accident. It had previously been the location of a Norman motte and bailey castle and before that a Roman fort stood nearby. The lure of water and easy access to the sea made the banks of the River Seiont an ideal spot for Edward's monster in masonry. Edward wasn't one to miss an opportunity to tighten his grip even further on the native population. The birth of his son, the first English Prince of Wales, in the castle in 1284, was a perfect device to stamp his supremacy. In 1969, the investiture of the current Prince of Wales, HRH Prince Charles took place here. Caernarfon is one of eight sites chosen by Cadw as a hub for community projects in support of the Cultural Olympiad celebrations in Wales.

I always leave Caernarfon Castle filled with more wonder than the moment I arrived. This hugely famous bastion has got more going for it than just history, it is steeped in Welsh myth and legend and no matter how many times you visit, you will always spot something that wasn't spotted before. It is not hard to see why we voted this site as one of the Top 100 Attractions in Wales, now all that's left to do is go and see for yourselves.

Caenarfon

Castle Ditch, Gwynedd LL55 2AY

The Waterloo Hotel (Best Western)

Holyhead Road, Betws y Coed, Snowdonia, LL24 0AR

T: 01690 710411 www.waterloo-hotel.info E: reservations@waterloo-hotel.info

Offering a modern and contemporary venue Bar 1815 is the ideal place to drink and relax after a busy day out and about in North Wales....

As well as an endless array of hot, cold, alcoholic and non alcoholic beverages our wine list features old and new world wines especially chosen to accompany the flavours that our menus offer. Ask your server about our Fairtrade wine selection and our wine of the week!

After your meal at the Bridge Restaurant unwind on our sofas in front of the fire with a nightcap...but beware..........many have been known to fall asleep at this point!

Plas Bodegroes

Pwllheli, Gwynedd, LL53-5TH

T: 01758-612363 www.bodegroes.co.uk E: gunna@plasbodegroes.co.uk

Plas Bodegroes stands in its own secluded grounds (just a mile from the beach!) on the wild Llŷn Peninsula, on the far north west of Wales. The Llŷn Peninsula is one of Britain's first designated Areas of Outstanding Natural Beauty. With mile upon mile of open sandy beach, glorious gulf stream light, tranquil seclusion and a coastal path edging the whole peninsula, this is a wonderful, unspoilt region well worth a visit. Our bedrooms are all individually designed, and overlook the gardens. All are non-smoking with ensuite, Flatscreen digital TV with 40 Freeview channels, phone and CD Player. All mattresses are pocket sprung, bedlinen is Egyptian cotton and duvets are goose-down.

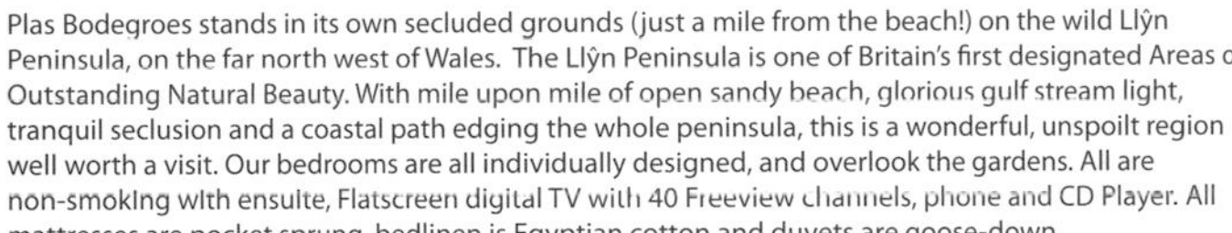

Caerwylan Hotel

Beach Bank, Criccieth, Gwynedd, LL52-0HW

T: 01766-522547 www.caerwylan.co.uk E: info@caerwylan.co.uk

The Caerwylan is a friendly, privately owned 3 star hotel, with wonderful sea views. We are the ideal base to explore Criccieth, Llyn Peninsula and Snowdonia. We have renovated the hotel to a high standard and now have 24 individually designed en suite bedrooms, a tranquil sea facing lounge and a contemporary bar. Our elegant Tonnau Restaurant is open to residents and non residents for dinner 7 nights a week and at Sunday lunch time, when we serve traditional Sunday roasts. Visit www.caerwylan.com for more information.

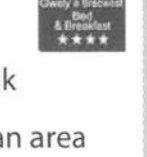

Llwyn Onn Guest House

Pentrefoelas, Betws Y Coed, Conwy, LL24 0TW

T: 01690 770124 www.llwynonnguesthouse.co.uk E: bookings@llwynonnguesthouse.co.uk

Situated at the gateway of Snowdonia's National Park, this small, family-run B&B is set within an area of natural beauty, amidst the rolling heather moors of Hiraethog. Our beautiful Guest House has five rooms; three double en-suite rooms, one twin room and one triple/family en-suite room. All our guest rooms are tastefully decorated with simplicity, quality and charm in mind ensuring you have the most relaxing stay.

Glyn Peris Guest House

Glyn Peris, Llanberis, Caernarfon, Gwynedd, LL55 4EL

T: 01286-872711 www.glynperisguesthouse.com E: : stay@glynperisguesthouse.com

Glyn Peris is ideally located for Snowdon, the coast, castles and steam trains. Our philosophy is of 'cleanliness' and 'comfort' and for you to always feel at home during your stay. Hearty breakfasts, pack lunches and free flask filling service set you up for exploring Snowdonia. Then with contemporary décor, modern bathrooms, and a cosy guest lounge, along with a drying room, private parking and bike/kayak storage you have everything you need to relax afterwards. Complete your Snowdonia experience with a guided walk up Snowdon with one of our guides.

The Joys Of Life Country Park B & B

Coed -y-Park, Bethesda, Gwynedd, LL57 4YW

T: 01248-602122 www.thejoysoflife.co.uk E: enquiries@thejoysoflife.co.uk

The Joys of Life Country Park is a popular, pleasantly secluded centre for holidays, B & B, family gatherings, reunions and courses. This stunning holiday and meetings centre combines formal gardens with natural woodland paths and a small lake. The indoor accommodation and the nearby small secluded caravan park have all been totally refurbished over the last 5 years. All bedrooms are now ensuite and there is a range of accommodation styles to choose from, ranging from family rooms to twin or single-occupancy, and independently rated from 4-stars to 5-stars by the North Wales Tourist Board.

Groeslon Ty Mawr - Tearooms & B&B

Groeslon Ty Mawr, Llanddeiniolen, Gwynedd, LL55 3AW

T: 01248 352791 www.tymawr-bandb.co.uk E: ruth@tymawrbb.wanadoo.co.uk

Ty Mawr is a family run guest house (B&B) with a licensed restuarant.We are ideally situated in the heart of Snowdonia.

The picturesque views from all our bedrooms and restaurant are quite breathtaking, Ty Mawr is conveniently situated being only 10 minutes from Llanberis, Snowdon railway, Caernarfon castle, and Bangor university & city centre. Groeslon Ty mawr is also a stones throw from the isle of Anglesey.

Glanarvon House

Penmaenmawr Road, Llanfaifechan, Conwy, LL33 OPA

T: 01248 681105 www.glanarvonhouse.com E: glanarvonhouse@hotmail.co.uk

Glanarvon House is a new guest house in the picturesque village of Llanfairfechan in Conwy. We have three individually designed rooms with en-suite facilities. Glanarvon House is smoke free throughout. Unfortunately we are unable to accommodate pets and children under the age of 18. Our rooms are individually designed for your comfort and enjoyment. All rooms have a shower en-suite with complementary toiletries . Hair dryers are also a standard feature. All bedding is Egyptian cotton in our sumptuous beds for a great night's sleep. All rooms have a flat screen TV and DVD players & complementary tea & coffee and mineral water. Free Wi Fi.

WAL Restaurant

Palace Street, Caernarfon, LL55 1RR

T: 01286 674383 www.walrestaurant.co.uk E: reservations@walrestaurant.co.uk

WAL 's eclectic menu serves up everything from satisfying lunchtime burgers to top end fillet steaks. Owner, John Tyrrell , has sourced all his meat from Llanfair Hall, just four miles up the road. The meat of the herd of Welsh black cows grazing there yields a wonderful flavour, thanks to the lush grass and meadow flowers of their pasture, and a stress-free lifestyle spent alongside the Menai Strait. In addition to delicious steaks, Wal is serving up perfect pasta dishes, risottos and pizzas. A traditionally mouth-watering day menu of soup, sandwiches, all-day breakfasts, burgers, fish and chips and the like, promises to keep hunger pangs at bay without draining your wallet.

Sopna Tandoori Restaurant

Rhosbodrual, Caernarfon, Gwynedd LL55 2BB

T: 01286-675222 www.sopna.co.uk

Our fully licensed 65 seat restaurant offers the very best in Bangladeshi cuisine. But don't just take our word for it, we where voted 2007 Welsh Curry House of the Year, and North Wales Winners in 2010.Each dish is freshly created for your order, using the highest quality ingredients.
We at Sopna present to you the most pleasant flavoured Balti dishes and hope that your evening spent with us will be, both a culinary and a social event, to be savoured. All our dishes are cooked fresh to order. If however you require a different dish or have a specific requirement, please ask, we will do our utmost to help.

Castell Deudraeth Brasserie

Minffordd, Penrhyndeudraeth, Gwynedd, LL48 6ER

T: 01766 770000 www.portmeirion-village.com E: info@portmeirion-village.com

Castell Deudraeth's brasserie menu is based on the best fresh local produce from land and sea. You are welcome to call in at Castell Deudraeth for a morning coffee, a sandwich, or a brasserie style lunch or dinner using the best seasonal ingredients from the surrounding countryside. Peter Hedd Williams, Head Chef and Mark Muscroft, Sous Chef oversee the kitchens at Castell Deudraeth, ably assisted by Pastry Chef Yahia Mohand. Restaurant Manager Laura Holden ensures a prompt, friendly service.

The Black Boy Inn

Northgate Street,Caernarfon, Gwynedd, LL55 1RW

T: 01286 673604 www.black-boy-inn.com E: info@black-boy-inn.com

At the Black Boy Inn, the locals' favourite, diners are offered a wealth of choice and flavours. Depending on your mood, taste or occasion you can choose between our hearty à la carte restaurant menu and our chalkboard of seasonal specials.
Head chef, Marius Cepoiu, and his team pride themselves on their unfussy but skilful preparation of quality ingredients, with a passion for fresh seafood and a commitment towards using the best locally sourced organic Welsh produce.

Plas Bodegroes

Pwllheli, Gwynedd, LL53-5TH

T: 01758-612363 www.bodegroes.co.uk E: gunna@plasbodegroes.co.uk

In the 25 years since we first opened Plas Bodegroes, our restaurant has gained top awards from all of the leading guides, including (for 14 years) Michelin star, Egon Ronay star, and UK Restaurant of the Year in the Good Food Guide. Our reputation is based upon the modern interpretation of traditional dishes, concentrating upon the superb local ingredients. In addition, we try to source our fish as sustainably as possible, and do not use endangered wild species. As a result some of our fish is now farmed from sustainable sources. These include Icelandic cod, Norwegian halibut and Shetland organic salmon and sea trout.

Tonnau Restaurant

Caerwylan Hotel, Beach Bank, Criccieth, Gwynedd, LL52 0HW

T: 01766-522547 www.caerwylan.co.uk E: info@caerwylan.co.uk

Experience our new fine dining Tonnau Restaurant, overlooking Cardigan Bay and Criccieth castle. Our contemporary restaurant has an unpretentious approach to quality cuisine with the varied menu changing everyday. Our experienced chefs source as much as possible from local suppliers. We also have an extensive wine list which perfectly compliments the flavours our menu offers. After dinner relax over coffee in one of our deep settees in the sea facing lounge.

Jenny's Cafe & Restaurant

High Street, Porthmadog, Gwynedd, LL49 9LP

T: 01766-513760

The restaurant offers a wide variety of dining options from early morning breakfast for a hearty start to the day, through lunchtime with daily specials available and Sunday Roast to late afternoon dinning, we also offer a Junior Menu for our younger customers. Jenny's cafe offers the option of a lighter meal or snack, with the deli section within the cafe having a vast array of takeaway available and picnic hampers. Favourites from the deli section include the home roasted meats, pies, salads, with special requests catered for. For those summer days we have outdoor seating available. Special occasions are catered for in the function room and outdoor catering is also provided.

The Groes Inn

Tyn Y Groes, Conwy, LL32-8TN

T: 01492-650545 www.groesinn.co.uk E: enquiries@groesinn.co.uk

Diners at The Groes Inn have a wealth of choice: they can choose between our dining room, our bar menu, and our famous chalkboard of specials depending on their mood and requirements. All offer top quality food with a bias towards locally sourced, seasonal ingredients in an atmosphere that brings the best of the old together with the best of the new.

WELSH BORDERS

Throughout our Top 100 Attractions book, we have we have put a lot of thought into the attractions that have been featured. The reason for that simply lies with the huge expectations we come to expect when we go on holiday. If you were travelling abroad, there would be a good chance you are going for the sun and on that basis, wouldn't be as focused on attractions as a main reason for picking your holiday destination. Holidaying in the UK however, because we don't normally see the types of temperatures commonly associated with those abroad we base our UK holidays a lot of the times on what to see and do!

The reason I bring this up in this particular section of the book is because in the Welsh borders area, we don't have a wide array of beaches as it is a land locked area. Therefore tourist attractions are a very important part of a visit to this locality. We have chosen a great selection of attractions for you to visit, I'm sure you will not be disappointed with them one bit. Whether it's a trip on a train, Zorbing down a mountainside or just a relaxing visit to one of the many National Trust properties in the area. There is something to wet all your tourist tastebuds.

The magic of the Welsh borders section is that even if you are staying in great places such as Chester or Shrewsbury, a trip across the border is one that you could and must make. It will certainly be a trip that will help you plan your next holiday, a holiday in Wales for sure.

Llangollen Motor Museum

t: 01978 860324 e: owenann@tiscali.co.uk
www.llangollenmotormuseum.co.uk

"Funny and informative" - "A trip down memory lane"
"Wonderful "as is" museum. - "Excellent but very strange"

We try to be interesting and informative but most of all to demonstrate the charm and character of our motoring past. The museum is not just two rows of old cars quietly rusting away. Most of our vehicles are on the road. The collection includes a model"T"Ford, a 30/98 Vauxhall, several Austins and Citroens. Among the motor bikes are most of the names that bring back memories of "British Bikes". The Norton, the Triumph, the Ariel, the Sunbeam and the B.S.A.. An experience not to be missed. More than 60 vehicles from cars to invalid carriages and pedal cars, a 50's village garage scene complete with owners quarters, the cars that grandad used to drive .

Llangollen Motor Museum is probably Llangollen's best kept secrets. Hidden just a mile out of the town, going out towards the Abbey and the Horseshoe Pass, blink and you could miss the entrance, but miss this attraction and you could be missing out big time! Apart from being a big fan of Top Gear I wouldn't say I was a huge Car or Bike enthusiast, but this attraction has the power to be able to stir up that interest very quickly! Every vehicle on display here has been tender lovingly restored and are a credit to the family that have owned this attraction for many years.

Pentre Felin, Llangollen, LL20 8EE

Llangollen Railway

t: 01978 860979 e: info@llangollen-railway.co.uk
www.llangollen-railway.co.uk

Travel through the beautiful north wales countryside!

Llangollen Railway is a Heritage Railway line starting at Llangollen Station, located beside the Dee River Bridge in Llangollen Town and continuing 7 ½ miles upstream to the village of Carrog. The railway was started in 1975 by a group of enthusiasts who saw the potential for a scenic heritage line through the Dee Valley.
The line passes through one of the most beautiful and historically interesting valleys in Britain. with the Berwyn Mountains towering above on either side as it follows the course of the River Dee. The Dee is classed as a Site of Special Scientific Interest (SSSI) Historical sites abound, some like Castell Dinas Bran having Arthurian legends associated with them; during medieval times the valley was heavily involved in border warfare and the rebellion of Owain Glyndwr. As Britain moved into the industrial revolution the work of great engineers especially Thomas Telford, had a major impact on the valley. Telford was to build both the London to Holyhead road and the beautiful Llangollen Canal which flows close to the line. The line is currently being extended another 2 ½ miles to the town of Corwen, which is hoped to be completed by the end of 2012.

As I stood on the platform awaiting the arrival of my train, I could quite easily have been waiting for the Hogwarts Express to be taking me back to Hogwarts to start another school term. I was instantly transported back in time to when these steam trains were the backbone of our Industrial era. The puff of smoke as the train pulled into the station was truly magical, and made the hairs on the back of my neck stand on end. I travelled 7 ½ miles up the track to the village of Carrog where the train pulled into the station, I had lunch at the station café and was transported back to Llangollen again. I can now truly see why a huge portion of the staff here donate their time to this railway and why passengers return time and time again to ride on this amazing piece of history that time just refuses to forget.

The Station, Abbey Rd, Llangollen,Denbighshire, LL20 8SN

Llangollen Wharf

t: 01978 860702 e: bill@horsedrawnboats.co.uk
www.horsedrawnboats.co.uk

Take in the magical sights and sounds of the beautiful Llangollen Canal.

Llangollen Wharf is one of the major attractions in the North Wales market town of Llangollen. From the Wharf you can embark on either a horse drawn boat trip along the feeder for the main canal, or a motorised aqueduct cruise which takes you across the famous Pontcysyllte Aqueduct built by Thomas Telford. Both these trips take in the magical sights and sounds of the beautiful Llangollen Canal. Longer horse drawn trips can be arranged for large groups. Lunches and cream teas can be pre-ordered for the aqueduct trips. The whole canal in this area is now a World Heritage Site.

We also have a self steer day hire boat for groups of up to 10 people, on our purpose built 32' narrow boat the "Dydd Un". This is an ideal way to take a leisurely cruise along the Llangollen Canal and across the unforgettable Pontcysyllte Aqueduct. This is a perfect way for a family, group of friends or a corporate team to have their own private boat for the day.The Tea Room and Gift shop at Llangollen Wharf is located in the old canal warehouse. All our food is prepared and cooked on the premises so that you know it will always be fresh.

The Llangollen Horse Drawn Boats has something to offer everybody, whether you want a relaxing stroll along the canal side in Llangollen or a leisurely cruise across the famous Aqueduct built by the industrial genius himself "Thomas Telford" I actually took a trip across the aquaduct and enjoyed a scrumptious Welsh Cream Tea. I have to be totally honest with you I was a bit concerned about how high the aqueduct might be as I don't really have a head for heights. But after being on the boat ten minutes and listening to the speech perfect vocal commentary by the boats very able captain I truly forget how high I was and just sat back at ease and enjoyed the rest of the cruise.

Wrexham

Wharf Hill, Llangollen, Denbighshire, LL20 8TA

Park Hall

t: 01691 671123 e: info@parkhallfarm.co.uk
www.parkhallfarm.co.uk

The Countryside Experience!

Discover the delights of Park Hall Countryside Experience, the national award winning farm attraction. There's a day packed with animal antics, action, fun and adventure waiting for all the family. Get up close to your farmyard favourites with a regular schedule of interactive events. Bottle feed lambs, pet micro-pigs, groom ponies, or lead the heavy horses. Try hand milking a real cow or cuddle gorgeous bunnies, and don't miss the spectacular pig racing event each day. This all weather attraction has two massive indoor play barns, while outside there are adventure courses, climbing areas, play houses and great walks for all the family. 2012 sees the introduction of a Science Illusion Zone with lots of hands on scientific fun. Best of all for the kids are the brilliant driving experiences for different ages. The junior driving school, the 4x4 land-rovers and quad bikes (6-14yrs) are amazing and the barrel train ride to the woodland is also a must!
At a more sedate pace visit the wonderful heritage exhibits, the Victorian School, depicting the life of the Victorian child, the Welsh Guards Museum, and the Iron Age Roundhouse.

After featuring a few Children's Farm parks in this book, I thought I knew what I would be expecting. I couldn't of been more wrong! This attraction has everything whether it is indoor or outdoor activities you seek, this attraction has it all!
Just when I thought I had seen it all, there was something else to see, from an indoor Victorian museum to educational farming and Welsh Guards Museum, this site certainly has everything. In the short words I am allocated in this book I simply cannot tell you everything that Park Hall has to offer you! But one thing I can say is that when it comes to simple value for money this site cannot be beaten.

Wrexham

Stiwt Theatre

t: 01978 841300 e: admin@stiwt.co.uk
www.stiwt.co.uk

A first class venue for the performing arts and cultural activities

With live theatre and entertainment seeing a huge resurgence in popularity, the Theatr Stiwt Wrexham has been transformed into a state-of-the-art venue for entertainment in the region. Our vision remains to nurture and develop the creative, cultural and recreational aspirations of all people in the immediate vicinity and wider community of Wales. The Theatr Stiwt continues to offer a first class venue for the performing arts and cultural activities while also providing training and education for young people in the arts and creative activities. We hope to recreate the community spirit which was the original intention of the hardworking mining community in the 1920s by uniting past present and future generations within this grand old building for many years to come.

Theatr Stiwt Wrexham is the perfect venue for you to entertain guests, celebrate a special occasion in a venue with a difference or as a unique conferencing venue to impress your clients. We guarantee that you won't find a comparable or more splendid venue anywhere else in the region.

Theatr Stiwt was formerly the villages miners institute, but even after all these years this great venue itself has turned more into an institution. It is now one of the area's biggest theatres and although it boasts some very modern facilities it still hasn't lost some of its old Welsh charm. When I visited this Theatre I could not get over how warm and friendly the place is. The venue itself plays host to many different performances not only from top comedians, singers and great bands but also hosts many well-known plays and theatre companies, not forgetting its traditional yearly Pantos. Theatr Stiwt is worth a visit at any time of the year no matter what your performance tastes are.

Broad St, Rhosllannerchrugog, Wrexham, LL14 1RB

Planet Zorb

t: 07522 107 811 e: info@planet-zorb.com
www.planet-zorb.com

The Latest & Greatest Adventure Activity to hit Wales

Planet Zorb is the place to come to experience an extensive range of adrenaline pumping adventure activities such as zorbing, gorge walking and white water rafting. Whether a day out with your family, friends or colleages, you will have the time of your life! Located in the picturesque Welsh countryside between Bala and Corwen on the A494, we are situated only 4.4 miles from the A5. Being so well located in northern Wales, why not make a weekend of it in this beautifully landscaped area by visting the nearby Snowdonia national park and staying in local hotels, you won't find yourself short of other exciting activites to see and do.

WELSH BORDERS

For many years now Bala has only ever been famous to tourists for its vast lake and its great outdoor pursuit's activities such as yachting, canoeing, and not forgetting its world famous 'White Water Rafting' But Bala needs to brace itself as theirs a new craze in town! 'Zorbing' whether your thing is Harness or Hydro Zorbing, Planet Zorb has it all to offer here at its secluded purpose built course. As if that wasn't enough, they also offer 'Gorge Walking' as well. Situated within the outstanding scenery of the Welsh countryside between Bala and Corwen, this attraction is all you need to finish your holiday off. But you have to definitely book in advance, due to its popularity and coupled with the fact there are but only a few sites in the UK offering this kind of experience, it's not the kind of attraction you can just turn up and have a go. But having said that the team at Planet Zorb are a great bunch, and I'm sure once you've given them a call they will do their best to accommodate you.

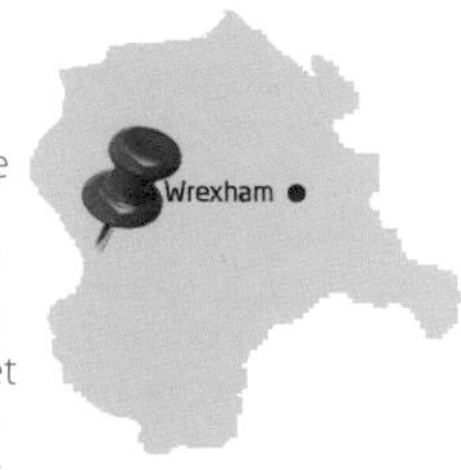

Ty-uchaf, Bethel, Bala, LL23 7LA

Plassey

t: 01978 780 277 e: enquiries@plassey.com
www.plassey.com

Bring the family for a fun and unique day out at The Plassey!

Multi-award winning Plassey is set in 247 acres of magnificent parkland in the beautiful Dee Valley, and is host a dazzling array of over 25 retail & craft outlets, fun activities, and food outlets, all wrapped up with the charming Edwardian buildings. We have everything in one location, from Delicatessen, ladies fashions, accessories, photography, bridal wear, handmade Jewellery, picture framing, Caravan & Camping accessories, unique gifts and much more…For the active there are 2 miles of nature trail walks, cycle paths, and an outdoor adventure playground. Those that play golf have an excellent full size 9 Hole Golf Course, or for those new to the game can hire golf clubs and go onto our own mini Pitch & Putt Golf Course too! After all this activity, why not sit and relax and have tea & home-made scones in the Coffee Shop tea garden that has stunning panoramic views over the valleys, or indulge yourself with a fantastic meal in our restaurant that using quality local produce.

Plassey has always been a favourite place of mine going back to the days when I myself lived in the Wrexham area. Now I have moved away, it's always still very much a pleasure to return, when I do, there is always something different to see. Being a family run business, the family have played a huge part in this attractions success and are constantly reinvesting to make the site better. Plassey has a multitude of different hats, one part of the site plays home to a holiday park, where you can bring your caravan,tent or the likes. The other part hosts a vast array of diverse retail businesses that will make you feel you are in shopping heaven, with more arriving all the time.

Wrexham

Plassey Village accommodates both a restaurant and a tearoom catering for all your culinary needs. A really enjoyable morning or afternoon awaits you here, what are you waiting for!

Plassey, Eyton, Wrexham, LL13 0SP

Glanllyn Lakeside Caravan & Camping Park

Bala, Gwynedd, LL23 7SS

T: 01678 540227/540441 www.glanllyn.com E: info@glanllyn.com

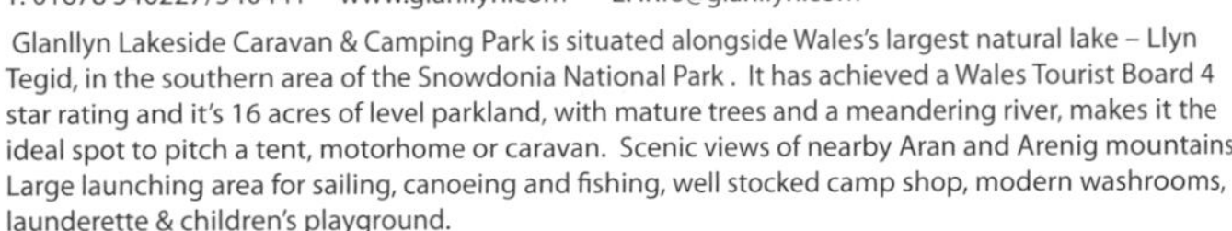

Glanllyn Lakeside Caravan & Camping Park is situated alongside Wales's largest natural lake – Llyn Tegid, in the southern area of the Snowdonia National Park . It has achieved a Wales Tourist Board 4 star rating and it's 16 acres of level parkland, with mature trees and a meandering river, makes it the ideal spot to pitch a tent, motorhome or caravan. Scenic views of nearby Aran and Arenig mountains. Large launching area for sailing, canoeing and fishing, well stocked camp shop, modern washrooms, launderette & children's playground.

The Bunkroom

106 Brook Street, Chester, Cheshire, CH1 3DU

T: 01244-324524 www.thebunkroom.co.uk E: admin@thebunkroom.co.uk

The Bunkroom in Chester is a small independent hostel located only 2 minutes walk from the train station and 4 minutes walk from Chester city centre.Beautifully presented in a 120 year old Georgian town house with a mix of old world charm and very modern facilities, The Bunkroom hostel sleeps a total of 26 in large spacious rooms of 2, 3, 4 and one room of 6 .Facilities include en-suite bathrooms, quality linen and duvets, free tea and coffee, free WI-FI, excellent self catering facilities, residents bar and lounge and an outdoor garden with BBQ facilities. Our hostel is surrounded by cafes, pubs and shops, making this the perfect location for all visitors, backpackers, groups and families

The Royal Oak Hotel

The Cross, Welshpool, Powys, SY21 7DG

T: 01938 552217 www.royaloakhotel.info E: relax@royaloakhotel.info

Formerly the manor house of the Earl of Powis and a coaching stop, The Royal Oak Hotel continues to provide the best of local fare, ales, comfort and good cheer to both local and travelling folk, as it has for 350 years. There are 25 comfortable bedrooms with options of Contemporary & Classic styled bedrooms if you prefer. A choice of well-equipped function and conference rooms are available, accommodating up to 180 guests.

Glencoed Bed & Breakfast

Cross St, Pentre, Chirk, Wrexham, LL14 5AN

T: 01691 778148 www.glencoed.co.uk E: glencoed@croeso.net

Glencoed is a stone built traditional Welsh Cottage dating from the early 18th century with alterations carried out in the early 1950's and the late 1980's. The cottage is located in one acre of its own grounds adjacent to the Llangollen Branch of the Shropshire Union Canal, and approximately ten minutes walk from the world famous Pontcysyllte Aqueduct built by Thomas Telford. We have ample car parking and are happy for our visitors to leave their cars while they explore the surrounding area by train, boat, or on foot.

The Squirrels Guest House

Abbey Road, Llangollen, LL20 8SP

T: 01978 869041 www.squirrelsllangollen.co.uk E: lilian@squirrelsllangollen.co.uk

First class hospitality offered in this well-loved Victorian house. Bedroom One, Bedroom Three, Bedroom Four and Squirrel's Gallery are double en-suite rooms. Bedroom Four and Squirrel's Gallery can accommodate an extra single bed. Bedroom Five is a twin en-suite room and Bedroom Six is a twin room with a private shower adjacent (robes provided). All your creature comforts are provided. TV/DVD players in all rooms. We have a drying room for outdoor activity people's clothing. Your car will be safe in our car park. We are a three minute leafy walk from the town centre.

Glasgwm Bed & Breakfast

Abbey Road, Llangollen, LL20 8SN

T: 01978 861975 www.glasgwm-llangollen.co.uk E: glasgwm@llangollen.co.uk

Glasgwm is a Victorian townhouse run by John Spicer and Heather Petrie, located close to the centre of the historic town of Llangollen. Just a short walk from all of the town's many attractions, Glasgwm offers plenty of off-road parking at the front of the property. The four en-suite bedrooms have views, either across the beautiful valley at the front of the property, or into a quiet, terraced garden at the back. Glasgwm is ideal for those wishing to explore the wider attractions of North Wales, and also the border counties of Cheshire and Shropshire (Chester is only 30 minutes drive and Shrewsbury 40 minutes drive away).

The Hand Hotel

Church Street, Chirk, Wrexham, LL14 5EY

T: 01691 773472 www.thehandhotelchirk.co.uk E: info@thehandhotelchirk.co.uk

The Hand Hotel is located in Chirk making it one of the best hotels to stay at while in the local area. We are local to Chirk Catle, Offa's Dyke, Llangollen and Chirk Marina. All the hotel's guestrooms have all the conveniences to suit guests' utmost comforts.The guestrooms are all non smoking.Guests can experience the high standards of comfort while staying with us and everything you need is right on site such as bar/pub, restaurant, business center. For a more enjoyable stay, guests can take advantage of a variety of our recreational facilities, including garden.

Bryn Tegid Country House

Llanycil, Bala, Gwynedd, LL23 7YG

T: 0167 8521645 www.balawales.com/bryntegid E: info@bryntegid.co.uk

Bryn Tegid Guest House is a fine Victorian Country House which has been restored & lovingly maintained by the recent owners keeping many of the original features. The house enjoys an elevated position within its 9 acres of private woodland and beautiful lawned gardens which guests are free to enjoy. The guest rooms overlook Llyn Tegid, (Bala Lake), and its splendid surrounding scenery. Birdwatchers will appreciate the variety of species to be observed and fishermen will find the area to be a paradise with its mix of fly & coarse fishing in the lakes & rivers. There is secure storage for canoes, cycles etc and a useful drying area. Child friendly with a family room.

The Boathouse Cafe, Bar & Restaurant

Chirk Marina, Chirk, LL14 5AD

T: 01691 772493 www.theboathouseatchirk.co.uk info@theboathouseatchirk.co.uk

The Boathouse is a charming canal side cafe-bar and restaurant. Located at Chirk Marina on the Llangollen Canal, all are welcome to enjoy a drink from our selection of fine wines or real ales, and choose from a menu of traditional home cooked food, all locally sourced and lovingly prepared for your enjoyment. Open all day, The Boathouse is a great place to relax and meet up with friends old and new. Savour a quiet pint in front of the open fire, or take in the stunning views of the Llangollen Canal from our outdoor terrace and extensive grounds. We look forward to welcoming you into The Boathouse very soon!

Gallery Restaurant

15 Chapel Street,Llangollen, Denbighshire, LL20 8NN

T: 01978 860076 www.thegalleryrestaurantllangollen.co.uk

E: info@ thegalleryrestaurantllangollen.co.uk

Food we know you love is what we offer at the welcoming Gallery Restaurant in Llangollen, Wales. No nonsense, no pretence, just generous portions of hearty, flavourful food created from the best locally sourced ingredients. Sumptuous steaks cooked just the way you like them, pizzas topped with your favourite toppings and pasta in a variety of tasty options are just some of the dishes on our menu. Join us when you want to savour a meal that is both flavourful and reasonably priced, we can even cater for small private functions.

The Walls

Welsh Walls, Oswestry, Shropshire, SY11 1AW

T: 01691-670970 www. the-walls.co.uk E: Info@the-walls.co.uk

Almost twenty years have flown past since we began the creation and operation of The Walls, at the time a very lovely but unloved, boarded-up schoolhouse. The Walls has a truly great reputation for providing really good food for large numbers of people with more choice than anywhere else and a minimum of fuss. Our food is what it says it is: we call a pie a pie, the bread is fantastic and we make all the soups, sauces and puddings. Our wine list is spectacular, full of real gems and even the house wines pass muster. We're great at hosting weddings, birthday parties, fashion shows, dinner dances, musical and theatrical events, casino nights, talents shows and even find time to be a restaurant!

The Hand Hotel

Church Street, Chirk, Wrexham, LL14 5EY

T: 01691 773472 www.thehandhotelchirk.co.uk E: info@thehandhotelchirk.co.uk

The Hand Hotel is located in Chirk making it one of the best hotels to stay at while in and around Wrexham. All the hotel's guestrooms have all the conveniences to suit guests' utmost comforts. Our menu is constantly changing with the seasons. With our fantastic recently appointed Head Chef you can be assured a quality dining experience. Our restaurant and bar is available for guests and visitors alike. We have promotional evenings running throughout the week. Bookings are taken and are strongly advised.

The Bison Grill & Bistro

Rhug Estate, Corwen, Denbighshire, LL21 0EH

T: 01490 413000 www.rhug.co.uk E: contact@rhug.co.uk

The Rhug Estate Farm shop incorporates a delicatessen, butchers, traditional farm shop, award winning bistro and take away burger bar. The Bison Grill Bistro produces all its meals from scratch using Rhug Organic's own award winning meat and was recently named the "Best on Farm Restaurant" in the UK by the FARMA organisation. The restaurant is headed up by talented head Chef Daniel Hughes who insists on using only the best ingredients to produce truly memorable food. Around the farm shop there is a play area for Children and walks around the farm and bison enclosure.

The Dragons Rest Cafe

St Asaph Rd, Lloc, Nr Holywell, Flintshire, CH8 8RF

T: 07860 643214 Opening times: 8.30am - 4.30pm - 6 days a week. (Closed Tues)

Here at The Dragon's Rest Café, a family run business, we offer the best in home cooked food. Being conveniently located just off junction 31 of the A55, The Dragon's Rest Café truly is the gateway to Wale's culinary delights. We offer all types of home cooked food, from snacks, all day breakfasts, daily specials to roast dinners, made from locally sourced produce. Our homemade cakes and Welsh ice creams are to die for as well. You will receive a very warm welcome from our staff, then place your order and relax! Also we can cater for busy people on the move with food to go. We also have for sale Welsh Jams, preserves, chutneys and fudges as well as lots of collectables and gifts for sale.

The Eagles Inn (Tafarn Yr Eryod)

Llanuwchlyn, Bala, Gwynedd, LL23 7UB

T: 01678 540278 www.yr-eagles.co.uk E: eagles-inn@btconnect.com

The Eagles Inn (Tafarn Yr Eryod) is a wonderful stone built building, even older than the village church! With a well stocked bar including real ales, inglenook fireplace, beer garden, fine wines and a dining room boasting a menu which would be the envy of many a restaurant, the family run Eagles Inn is in Llanuwchllyn the headquarters village of the Lake Bala narrow gauge railway. And here, you are definitely on the right tracks! The excellent menu of home cooked dishes is complemented by a small but impressive wine list. Such is the popularity of the food served at the Eagles Inn that advance booking, particularly at weekends, is strongly advised.

Plas-yn-Dre Restaurant

23 High St., Bala, LL23 7LU, Gwynedd

T: 01678-521 256 Open: 12-2pm, 6-9pm

Whether it's a light lunch ranging from local granary bread sandwiches to battered fish, homemade chips and mushy peas or a full on a la carte meal-ie pan-fried scallops, local lamb shank then finishing with creamy homemade banoffee pie you're after, then Plas-yn-Dre is the place for you. Specialising in local produce and award-winning local ales served in a relaxed, friendly atmosphere, Plas-yn-Dre caters for couples and families alike. Children are welcome and have their own menu.

MID WALES / BRECON

As one of the three Welsh National Parks, the Brecon section of this book needs no introduction. With not as many attractions featured here as some of the many other areas in the book, the reason being quite simply, is the Brecon National Park is an massive attraction in itself. That being said, we have assembled an excellent cast that guarantees to be a big crowd pleaser. Whether your a keen walker, nature enthusiast, avid historian or just simply someone who visited the Brecon area as a child, there will not be enough hours in the week to take it all in! Maybe you should book two? Because in this book we have specifically focused on the tourist attractions of the thirteen main great areas of Wales, we haven't been able to focus on some of the great walking routes the Brecon Beacons and other areas play home to.

But don't be too disappointed, if you visit our website, www.top100attraction.co.uk you will find a great, selection of walking routes, walking clubs and some amazing tips for everything outdoorsy in the Brecon Beacons, and surrounding areas.

Also whilst visiting our website, why not leave a comment or even a request on things we've featured or things you would like to see featured within the site. We will jump to it to make sure we respond to every comment and suggestion you feel you would like to make.

Talyllyn Railway

t: 01654 710472 e: Enquiries@talyllyn.co.uk
www.talyllyn.co.uk

Why not come and visit us for a great family day out?

The Talyllyn Railway is a historic narrow-gauge steam railway, set in the beautiful Mid-Wales countryside. Running from Tywyn to Abergynolwyn and Nant Gwernol, the line passes the delightful Dolgoch Falls and there are excellent forest walks at Nant Gwernol. Experience the nostalgia of historic steam trains in some of Wales' finest countryside. The railway starts on the coast at Tywyn, snakes through the foothills of Cader Idris to Dolgoch Falls, Abergynolwyn and Nant Gwernol. The train clings to the hillside as it passes through woodland and over ravines. The trip takes about an hour each way. Your ticket allows you to break your journey and extend your day. You could take a country walk, explore wooded paths, discover waterfalls or visit the beach. Tywyn Wharf station is home to the Narrow Gauge Railway Museum, which tells the story of little railways across Britain, and King's Cafe which has hot and cold menus, lunch time specials and a licensed bar. Quarryman's Tea Room at Abergynolwyn serves a range of refreshments and light bites.

Being hidden on the west coast of Wales, you could be forgiven for missing The Talyllyn Railway. But now I've told you about Talyllyn there can be no forgiveness for not visiting it. This railway has everything the bigger named railways have, and if truth be known just as bigger history to boot. Taking you from the coast to the countryside, you get to see a short glimpse of what Wales is all about. When doing my research on this attraction I visited every station along its route, and I found every member of staff to not only be totally professional, but the stations were totally immaculate right down to the public toilets. In today's day and age these things matter and the management and staff realise this and its clear to see that they care about every single one of their passengers. A true breath of fresh air!

Newtown

Wharf Station, Tywyn, Gwynedd, LL36 9EY

Dragonfly Cruises

t: 07831 685 222 e: info@dragonfly-cruises.co.uk
www.dragonfly-cruises.co.uk

Enjoy cruising the beautiful Monmouthshire & Brecon Canal!

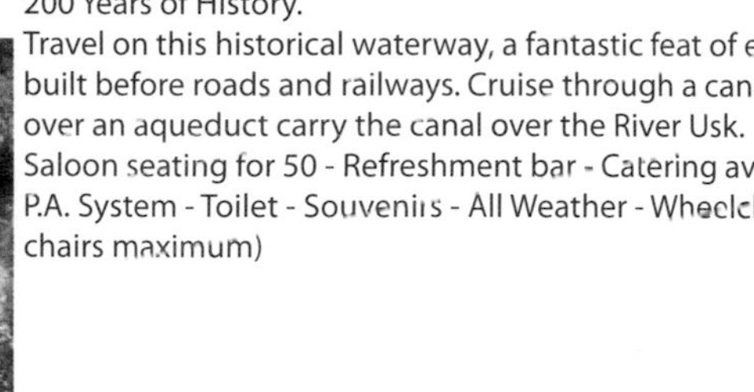

Spend a delightful few hours cruising through some of the most beautiful scenery in Britain, lying within the Brecon Beacons National Park.
The Monmouthshire and Brecon canal hugs the mountainside above the valley of the River Usk. Through the four seasons there a fine views and an abundance of wildlife to be seen.
200 Years of History.
Travel on this historical waterway, a fantastic feat of engineering, built before roads and railways. Cruise through a canal lock and over an aqueduct carry the canal over the River Usk.
Saloon seating for 50 - Refreshment bar - Catering available
P.A. System - Toilet - Souvenirs - All Weather - Wheelchair Lift (2 chairs maximum)

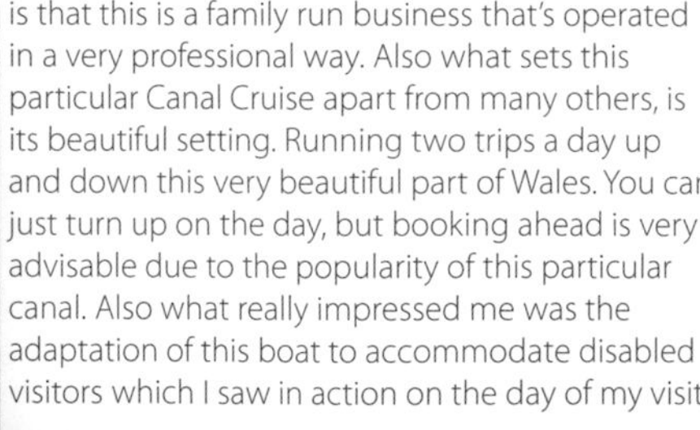

Dragonfly Cruises is one of only two canal cruises featured within this book of Wales's Top 100 Attractions, I have to say that a trip on this fine vessel is worth every penny. There are many of these canal style boat trips throughout the UK, all offer a good trip. But what I liked about this particular cruise, is that this is a family run business that's operated in a very professional way. Also what sets this particular Canal Cruise apart from many others, is its beautiful setting. Running two trips a day up and down this very beautiful part of Wales. You can just turn up on the day, but booking ahead is very advisable due to the popularity of this particular canal. Also what really impressed me was the adaptation of this boat to accommodate disabled visitors which I saw in action on the day of my visit.

Canal Wharf, Brecon, Powys, Mid Wales, LD3 7EW

MID WALES / BRECON

Gigrin Farm

Red Kite Feeding Station & Rehabilitation Centre

t: 01597 810 243 e: chris@gigrin.co.uk
www.gigrin.co.uk

Spend a fantastic day out watching Red Kites!

The Red Kite feeding station at Gigrin Farm attracts as many as 600 of these beautiful birds of prey, together with buzzards, ravens and other species. Five permanent hides, three of which are wheelchair friendly, allow the visitor to see their stunning aerial displays as they dive out of the sky to pick up the food. Specialist hides for photographing, and filming, are also available. Gigrin Farm attracts a variety of rare and interesting birds, as well as otters, polecats, badgers and hares, and the spring and summer flowers are breath taking. The farm has an interpretive centre where visitors can use interactive computer displays, see into a red kite nest and watch video recordings of the farm's badgers. Feeding takes place at 2pm in winter and 3pm in summer (kites don't know that we change the clocks!) But for Christmas day, the farm is open from 1pm every day.

The Powell family that own Gigrin Farm would never have known just what they were starting back in the early 90's when the late Mr Powell had the foresight in accepting the RSPB's request to make the kite feeding at Gigrin Farm a permanent fixture. A visit to see the Kite feeding at Gigrin will make the hairs on the back of your neck stand on end and confirm to you a sight that you've never seen before. If you are a bird enthusiast or not you can't help fall in love with these birds of prey and see just how easy a decision it was all them many years ago for the late Mr Powell to set up this now very important feeding station and rehabilitation centre. Thats right, the centre allows kites, that have fallen ill or been injured, to recuperate after having any required veterinary care elsewhere. Forget your binoculars at your peril!

Newtown

Gigrin Farm, South Street, Rhayader, Powys, LD6 5BL

The Spaceguard Centre

t: 01547 520247 e: mail@spaceguarduk.com
www.spaceguarduk.com

The Largest Telescope in Wales Coming to Spaceguard!

The Spaceguard Centre is the only organisation in the UK addressing the hazard of Near Earth Objects. NEOs are asteroids and comets that come close to, and sometimes collide with the Earth. Such impacts can have devastating effects – they have in the past and will in the future unless we use available technologies to prevent them. The aim of Spaceguard UK is to develop and maintain a world class facility for astronomical research and science education,with a specific emphasis on the Spaceguard project. We want to bring the wonders of the universe to everyone in a fun and understandable way.
Spaceguard UK operates the Spaceguard Centre located in Knighton, Powys, UK from where we provide timely information to the public, press, media and education about the threat of asteroid and comet impacts, and the ways in which we can predict and deal with them.

Forget Hollywood films such as Armageddon, Deep Impact, Deadly Skies and the like. The Spaceguard Centre is doing it all for real. During my visit to the Spaceguard Centre I was absolutely blown away to learn members of Spaceguard UK have already been active in promoting the assessment of the United Kingdom's contribution to the international NEO detection effort. The founders of this amazing space observatory high in the Welsh Powys hills have been scanning our skies for many years now and are very keen to pass on their knowledge to all visitors to the centre. Whether you are a keen enthusiast or not, you will leave the Spaceguard Centre feeling very glad you came and I'm sure planning your next visit back to this truly remarkable attraction.

Llanshay Lane, Knighton, Powys, LD7 1LW

Penderyn Distillery

t: 01685 810651 e: keitht@welsh-whisky.co.uk
www. penderyn-distillery.co.uk

Nestled in the foothills of the Brecon Beacons, and there we have created the best little distillery in Wales.

Due to the success & demand of visitors to the Distillery, we are now offering evening & corporate tours, to parties of 10-25. Penderyn is the only distillery in Wales & home of the award winning Single Malt Welsh Whisky & other award winning spirits. The distillery includes an exhibition about key elements of wysgi making & Welsh culture. There is an opportunity to see our distillery at work, learn about the process & the unique product range. At the dawn of the new millennium, a group of friends from the beautiful country of Wales set out with a simple vision. As the first Welsh distillers in more than a century, we were determined to break with convention & pledged to realise our dream. We're located in the old village of Penderyn, nestled in the foothills of the Brecon Beacons less than 40 minutes from Cardiff. The standard Madeira finish is available nationally in Tesco, Sainsbury's, Asda & Morrisons. We have been distilling since 2000 & bottling since 2004. In addition we are currently exporting to France, Spain, Germany, Canada, USA etc.

Not widely known but Whisky has now been distilled and enjoyed in Wales since the Middle Ages, but production died out in the late 19th century. In the 1990s attempts were made to revive the practice, resulting in the establishment of Wales's first distillery in over one hundred years, Penderyn. At Penderyn, whisky and their vast spirits range isn't the only thing they do well! Their tour is great to, with a tour around the distillery, and a tasting session thrown in for good measure, it's no wonder the tourists flock to Penderyn every year. Whether you're a whisky or spirit drinker you will find a visit here to the distillery and fascinating one. I don't drink myself but I was taken a back at the long history that whisky has here in Wales and the long journey it has been on, only to now, be up there with some of the best whiskies in the world!

Newtown

The Welsh Whisky Company, Penderyn Distillery, Penderyn, CF44 9JW

The Hall at Abbey-Cwm-Hir

t: 01597 851 727 e: info@abbeycwmhir.com
www.abbeycwmhir.com

WHERE STYLE MEETS BEAUTY IN A TIME FROM THE WORLD!

Mid Wales most unique, remarkable and beautiful stately home/ historic house. A 52 room, Grade 11* Gothic Revival mansion in 12 acre gardens overlooking the ruins of the 12th c cistercian abbey. Daily guided tours available to the public. Visitors enjoy the combination of outstanding architecture, stunning interiors, fascinating collections and magnificent gardens.
15 mins from Llandrindod Wells/Rhayader/The Elan and Wye Valleys. 30 mins from Presteigne/ Builth Wells/Knighton/Kington. 1hr from Ludlow/Hay/Hereford/Shrewsbury/Aberystwyth.

Original features include:

23 marble and wrought iron fireplaces; gothic widows and shutters; Maw and Co tiled floors; slate slab surfaces and Rococco and stained glass ceilings etc. The house bursts with interior design ideas: images handpainted on to wallpapers; rooms themed to trains/castles/the 1930`s; a billiards room celebrating The Arthurian Legend and the Garden Room with its 136 enamel signs.

The Hall at Abbey-Cwm-Hir is not only in Wales - but also in a different world! My visit to The Hall left me spelbound - 52 rooms stylishly furnished with the greatest possible attention to detail. The house and gardens are open throughout the year, with Paul and Victoria decorating each of the 52 rooms to individual themes for Christmas (Nov.1st-6th Jan) and Easter (the month of April) annually. Something unique in the UK.The tour left me with warm feelings for days, and I really cannot wait to go back. But d`ont just take my word for it! The Hall at Abbey-Cwm-Hir is set for great things, so take a tour yourself, and be amazed and astonished.

Newtown

MID WALES / BRECON

Abbey Cwm Hir, nr. Llandrindod Wells, Powys, LD1 6PH

Centre for Alternative Technology

t: 01654 705950 e: visit@cat.org.uk
www.cat.org.uk

Europe's leading eco centre.

CAT educates for a sustainable society. We run Masters courses in renewable energy and sustainable architecture; have short courses on all aspects of sustainable living; hold regular events and are open to visitors. We have created some of the most innovative low impact buildings in the UK, including the multi-award-winning Wales Institute for Sustainable Education (WISE). Our Graduate School of the Environment offers Masters programmes in renewable energy and sustainable architecture taught by leading professionals in the industry.

There is something for everyone who wants to learn more about creating a sustainable society at CAT. Through short courses, publications, research, engaged members and a Visitor Centre, we are inspiring and enabling people to take action for a sustainable world. Our Visitor Centre is open seven days a week. Interactive displays show global issues such as energy generation and transport, and practical, everyday solutions for everyone.

From the minute you arrive in the car park of this attraction, it hits you that you've arrived somewhere completely different. The excitement starts to build as you journey up to the centre on a water-pumped cliff railway - one of only a handful in the world. As I walked around CAT, it hit me just how much we take for granted and many questions were answered along the way. Questions like, 'how would we cope without electricity, gas' just a few of the many daily elements we take very much for granted. There is so much to see, too much to tell you about in just a short amount of words, but what I can say is, you will definitely not be disappointed with your visit here. But you don't need to just come for the day, the attractions website will guide you to all the many courses they have available here.

Machynlleth

Llwyngwern Quarry Pantperthog, Machynlleth, Powys, SY20 9AZ

Gliffaes Country House Hotel

Gliffaes Hotel, Crickhowell, Powys, NP8 1RH

T: 01874 730 371 www.gliffaeshotel.com E: calls@gliffaeshotel.com

The only Four Star Hotel in the Brecon Beacons National Park .If you are looking for a small luxury Country House hotel in a stunning location, which offers good food and service with neither exorbitant prices nor a lot of pretension; you may well have found what you are looking for. Just 3 miles from Crickhowell and about 10 miles from Brecon, you will be right in the heart of the Brecon Beacons and the glorious Black Mountains.

Highbury Farm Bed & Breakfast

Llanyre, Llandrindod Wells, Powys, LD1 6EA

T: 01597 822716 www.highburybandb.co.uk E: highbury.farm@btinternet.com

A warm welcome awaits you at our delightful home one mile northwest of the Spa town of Llandrindod Wells The accommodation offers two tastefully furnished ground floor bedrooms ensuite. One with bath/shower and one with walk in shower Colour TV's, clock/radio and hospitality tray. A separate T.V. Lounge is also available downstairs where breakfast can also be served upon request. The Dining room is situated upstairs with views of the surrounding hills. Centrally situated offering a beautiful location for a relaxing holiday touring the sites and reservoirs of the Elan Valley with its magnificant walks where Red Kites are frequently seen gliding across the skies.

Tynllwyn Farm B&B

Groes Plaun, Welshpool, Powys, SY21 9BW

T: 01938-553175 www.tynllwynfarm.co.uk E: info@tynllwynfarm.co.uk

Tynllwyn is a large farmhouse dated 1861 on a working beef and sheep farm and guests are welcome on the farm all year round. The farm is approached up a long private drive a mile out of Welshpool with beautiful views of the Severn Valley and Long Mountain. All rooms are ensuite with central heating, colour TV and tea making facilities. The large Guest Lounge has colour TV and open log fires in the winter. You are assured of a warm welcome and country hospitality. In the Dining Room we serve plentiful farmhouse meals and an English Breakfast. Home produced honey, eggs and vegetables are used in season.

Peterstone Court,Country House, Restaurant and Spa

Llanhamlach, Brecon, Powys, LD3 7YB

T: 01874 665387 www.peterstone-court.com E: enquiries@peterstone-court.com

Hidden inside a beautiful Georgian House, the essence of Peterstone Court is informal, chic and relaxing. A sense of history remains, but it's complemented with modern, stylish touches and a friendly ambience. The twelve en-suite rooms are large and light spaces with contemporary touches which guarantee total comfort and affordable luxury. The Spa and pool add another special dimension to ensure the perfect escape from everyday life. Food is the real focus at Peterstone, offering award winning simplicity with modern British food, using the best seasonal, locally sourced ingredients to create fresh, timeless dishes, inspired by the exceptional 360* Brecon landscape.

The Old Ford Inn

Llanhamlach, LD3 7YB,

T: 01874 665391 www.theoldfordinn.surf3.net E: enquiries@theoldfordinn.co.uk

The Old Ford Inn is a centuries old Coaching Inn, offering affordable, comfortable B&B accommodation, licensed Bar and Restaurant facilities in the heart of the Brecon Beacons National Park. Cosy, beamed bars and restaurant offer excellent value and choice, with a menu resourced large-ly from fresh local produce. Food is served lunchtime and evenings with real ale and good wine to accompany. Upstairs there are five comfortable en-suite bedrooms with colour television and beverage trays. Brecon itself offers a whole range of activities for both the outdoor lovers and townies alike.

Bryndu Farm B&B

Llandefalle, Brecon, Powys, LD3 0NF

T: 01874 754227 www.byndu.co.uk E: mary@byndu.co.uk

Bryndu is a traditional working Welsh 17th Century farmhouse in the Brecon Beacons and Black Mountains area, offering superb bed and breakfast accommodation, 4 poster beds, large en suite bathrooms with bath and shower, LCD TV'S with DVD'S, holistic and beauty treatments, available. The B&B is attentively run by its owners Mary & Wayne. The farmhouse has been lovingly refurbished to a high standard has a wealth of charm and character with exposed beams and stonework, and offers double and single room accommodation complete with en-suite facilities. Children are welcome but sorry no pets are allowed. Internet service is available to visitors.

Lasswade Country House & Restaurant

Station Road, Llanwrtyd Wells Powys, LD5 4RW

T: 01591 610515 www.lasswadehotel.co.uk E: info@lasswadehotel.co.uk

With a fine reputation for Good Food and Service, it is no wonder that guests return. Lasswade is a period Country House with a 2 A.A. Food Restaurant (special diets can be arranged with pre-booking and our Restaurant is open to the Public), with adorable views, 8 en-suite spacious bedrooms and all modern amenities, WIFI and most rooms with views of the Mid Wales Countryside. This is the perfect location for tranquillity and peace of mind. Groups, Families and re-unions welcome.

Our Conservatory and its panoramic views will ensure you have a good start to your day with a well presented Breakfast. Located between the Natural Cambrian Mountains and the Brecon Beacons in the town of Llanwrtyd Wells, Powys. Ideal central position for visiting attractions, castles, mines,

The Bear Hotel

High Street, Crickhowell, Powys NP8 1BW

T: 01873 810408 www.bearhotel.co.uk E: bearhotel@aol.com

Cymru Wales Gwesty Hotel ★★★

The Bear, a hotel famous far and wide for its welcoming atmosphere, historic character, convivial surroundings and good food. A cobbled forecourt, archway into the inner courtyard and 19th-century stagecoach timetable in the bar are all reminders of the Bear's former role. All bedrooms feature remote controlled colour television, direct dial telephone with modem access, hairdryer, tea / coffee making facilities, etc.. Family Rooms. We have a number of rooms throughout the hotel that can accommodate extra beds, please call with your requirements to discuss. The regularly changing restaurant menu surpasses the high standard set by the bar bistro. uk & recognition worldwide.

The Usk Inn

Talybont-on-usk, Brecon, Powys, LD3 7JE

T: 01874 676251 www.uskinn.co.uk E: uskinn@intamail.com

The Usk Inn has been transformed from an ordinary village pub into a country inn and restaurant with rooms of excellence. The Usk has been completely refurbished in sympathetic style, returning to it the atmosphere and ambience of a traditional village inn. The spotless bedrooms are bright and cheerful, finished in a refreshing choice of colours. The Usk's location is as good as it gets - attracting a healthy local trade as well as visitors to the Brecon Beacons National Park. It's close to the heart of the Beacons, and also handy for South and Mid Wales. Guests can go walking, fishing or cruising the Monmouthshire and Brecon Canal, which flows through Talybont.

The Griffin Inn

The Griffin Inn, Llyswen, Brecon LD3 0UR

T: 01874 754241 www.griffininnllyswen.co.uk E:contactus@griffininnllyswen.co.uk

Its position in the pretty village of Llyswen, makes the Griffin Inn an ideal visiting point for locals and visitors to Mid Wales. With its ivy clad exterior, old beams and welcoming log fires this traditional Inn offers a friendly service and homely hospitality in which to enjoy the selection of real ales, excellent food and fine wines. A menu of carefully selected, locally sourced produce, is on offer in both the bar and restaurant. The cosy bar and lounge area both have original real fireplaces and beams. Guests can enjoy a drink and food surrounded by fishing and hunting memorabilia. The Griffin Inn is open from 11am to 11pm during the Summer, and serves bar meals at lunchtime with the restaurant open in the evening.

The Hours Cafe & Book Shop

15 Ship Street, Brecon, Powys, LD3 9AD

T:01874 622 800 www.the-hours.co.uk E: thehours@btinternet.com

'The Hours' is a place, to relax with good food and a good read; to meet friends and family, or to peruse an eclectic selection of books. We wanted to create the kind of place we'd like to stumble across if we were meandering around a Welsh Market town ourselves. In this beautiful listed building you'll find flagstone floors, wooden beams, and rustic furniture that provide the perfect spot to spend an hour or two. Each and every thing you find on the menu in our tranquil and welcoming cafe promises to delight both your tastebuds and your pocket and we are proud to say we make the best coffee around using only freshly ground fair trade beans... and a little bit of love.

Tipple N Tiffin

Theatre Brycheiniog, Canal Wharf, Brecon, Powys, LD3 7EW

T: 01874 611866 www. tipplentiffin.co.uk E: Info@tipplentiffin.co.uk

Tipple'n'Tiffin is an individual restaurant set in the glorious Brecon Beacons. With the canal on it's doorstep Tipple'n'Tiffin offers a friendly and relaxed atmosphere where you can enjoy the globally influenced eclectic menu. Offering a tapas style menu whereby sharing and grazing is largely encouraged this restaurant is ideal for a light bite or a heartier meal. Also open in the mornings for coffee's Tipple'n'Tiffin is perfect in adapting to your needs.

The Bear Hotel

High Street, Crickhowell, Powys NP8 1BW

T: 01873 810408 www.bearhotel.co.uk E: bearhotel@aol.com

We have two Dining Rooms: One small & rather intimate, the other, which is also used for breakfast, is longer and slightly more involved with the activity of service to the bar. The latter has recently undergone a refurbishment. Yet still inkeeping with its 14th century origins. The small candlelit restaurant is next on the list for a face lift, but we still want to follow the romantic theme currently evident. The regularly changing restaurant menu surpasses the high standard set by the bar bistro. Making the most of wonderful locally sourced produce, the kitchen brigade cook dishes to a high standard that has won many awards in the uk & recognition worldwide.

The White Swan

Llanfrynach, Brecon, Powys, LD3 7BZ

T: 01874 643234 www.white-swan-brecon.co.uk E:info@white-swan-brecon.co.uk

The White Swan Inn stands in an area of natural outstanding beauty in the foothills of the mountains or the Brecon Beacons. Producing fine food from Bistro-style gastropub food - perfect if you are walking through the beacons and fancy a wonderful but not too heavy lunch, through to Bespoke Wedding Packages and Fine Dining menus. If you've been exploring the local countryside, and are in need of a well earned rest, then The White Swan is the ideal place to unwind. With a relaxing bar area serving a range of real ales, beers and soft drinks, this is a perfect place to sit back and watch the world go by.

Bistro 7

7 Hall Street , Welshpool, Powys, SY21 7RY

T: 01938-552879 www.thethreehorseshoesllandovery.co.uk E: djwmorgan@hotmail.co.uk

A Bar where you can eat, a restaurant where you can drink. Bistro Seven is a newly established family run bistro providing home cooked simple meals using inspiration from Great Britain and the Mediterranean. At Bistro Seven we wanted to offer something different to Welshpool, sourcing our raw ingredients from local producers wherever possible. Aiming to promote a relaxed atmosphere, our meals are cooked to order which means you can request changes to your favourite dish if required, while being look after by our friendly staff. Our Meze menu offers a buffet style service of a sample selection of popular dishes to larger groups. This has proved popular with customers who try something different and return to have the full size meal!

Iechyd Da Health Foods & Produce

11 Broad St, Llandovery, SA20 0AR

T: 01550 720703

Iechyd Da, is housed in what could be one of the oldest houses in Llandovery! Reputed locally as possibly being the first ever Lloyds TSB bank, this building that is now the towns most popular store for organic, fairtrade and just generally healthy food. With many locally sourced products in stock and available to order, it is not surprising Iechyd Da is such a hit with the locals. Also last but not least Jake the owners 'Artisan Bread' selection is to die for.

CEREDIGION / CARDIGAN

t's very hard to know which county you are in whilst venturing round Wales, as one is just as stunning as the other, until of course you come to Cardigan or Ceredigion as the locals would now ike it to be known! With it's gigantic sweeping sea cliffs, rolling hills, quaint villages and its vibrant nightlife, Cardigan/ Ceredigion, is very unique indeed. I spent a few very pleasant days here, met some wonderful people, tasted some outstanding food and it didn't rain once either! Don't get me wrong though, I'm not saying it never rains here in Cardigan, but what I am saying is that no matter what the weather, Cardigan has something to offer come rain or shine.

f your considering driving from North Wales to South Wales, one would be forgiven for being tempted into driving via England, down the M6 to Birmingham, M5, M42, M40 corridor and then take The M4 direct to South Wales! However, we all have to be strong and not give in to our temptations. Let me take you a more refreshing way! Depending where in North Wales you are leaving from, let's say Llandudno ok! Here goes, A470, A487, A40! Thats it! 3 roads! Ok it may add about half an hour onto your journey? But boy it's worth it!

Animalarium

t: 01970 871224 e: animalarium@btconnect.com
www. animalarium.co.uk

Welcome To The Animalarium - Borth Zoo

The Animalarium is set in the pretty seaside town of Borth, near Aberystwyth. It is a small Zoo with a difference. Most of our animals are unwanted exotic pets or unwanted from other Zoos or private collections. Many people like to keep exotic pets, however they require a long term commitment, and some of them grow very large and are very long lived. Some are dangerous, even our Leopard was a pet until he tried to kill his owner! Our collection includes several species of monkey and lemur, wallabies, birds, large snakes and caiman. We offer pony rides in the summer, free hands on reptile encounter, and cat feeding times. You may buy feed pots and feed the animals yourself all day. We also have play areas, free car park, gift shop and café. We have a good local bus service and train station.
Open daily all year.

Borth has always been a favorite spot of mine, with it's three miles of sand this beach is backed for the most part by a pebble storm beach,and to the north by dunes. But nestled within the centre of Borth is it's Animalarium ran by Jean Mumbray. Jean's love for all animals cannot be denied. I have never met a more passionate animal lover as this lady. During my time at the animalarium it became completely clear to me that this attraction isn't just an attraction that has a high number of visitors every year but one that is the source of many jobs locally, a place that allows animal lovers from all over the local area to come and work, care and protect even the most smallest of their inhabitants.

Aberystwyth

Ynisfergi,Borth, Ceredigion, SY24 5NA

Devil's Bridge Falls

t: 01970 890233 e: visit@devilsbridgefalls.co.uk
www.devilsbridgefalls.co.uk .co.uk

A PLACE OF OUTSTANDING NATURAL BEAUTY!

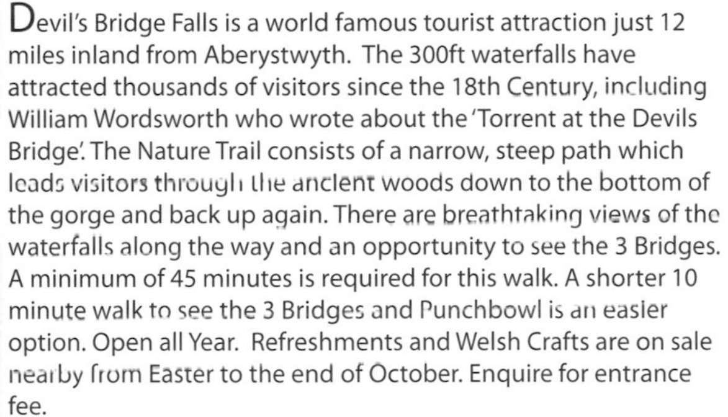

Devil's Bridge Falls is a world famous tourist attraction just 12 miles inland from Aberystwyth. The 300ft waterfalls have attracted thousands of visitors since the 18th Century, including William Wordsworth who wrote about the 'Torrent at the Devils Bridge'. The Nature Trail consists of a narrow, steep path which leads visitors through the ancient woods down to the bottom of the gorge and back up again. There are breathtaking views of the waterfalls along the way and an opportunity to see the 3 Bridges. A minimum of 45 minutes is required for this walk. A shorter 10 minute walk to see the 3 Bridges and Punchbowl is an easier option. Open all Year. Refreshments and Welsh Crafts are on sale nearby from Easter to the end of October. Enquire for entrance fee.

There are devils bridges all over the world from Europe to South America, built mainly in medieval times. But what makes this Devils Bridge so different from the rest is that three bridges coexist here, each one built above the next. This attraction has been enticing tourists for hundreds of years and once you've visited too, you will see exactly why! As if the bridges weren't enough of an attraction there are the waterfalls to see as well. Devils Bridge is served by Devil's Bridge railway station on the historic narrow-gauge Vale of Rheidol Railway, which opened between Aberystwyth and Devil's Bridge in 1902. The railway is also featured in this book and both attractions compliment each other nicely. When doing our research on the bridge and falls we wondered why the entrance fee for such an attraction was so low. After my visit, it became very apparent that the now owners of the site don't just see the bridge and falls as a money making scheme and want as many people as possible to enjoy them like thousands of people have before them.

Aberystwyth

Woodlands, Devil's Bridge, Aberystwyth, Ceredigion, SY23 3JW

The Silver Mountain Experience

t: 01970 890620 e: info@silvermountainexperience.co.uk
www.silvermountainexperience.co.uk

ADVENTURE & ACTIVITY DAYS OUT!

Silver Mountain will provide a first rate themed attraction utilising the old mine workings and former mine buildings as a stage on which actors will interact and entertain visitors in one of Wales' scariest underground experiences. The stories and special effects will make a dramatic and memorable visit to this special part of Wales. Above ground a fantasy realm caters for younger children making the whole site a 7 acre fantasy world with characters too. The existing water wheels, leets and stream will become an interactive water based play area to augment the facilities for children. The old mine site, high in the ancient Cambrian Mountains, has tumbling streams, mysterious forests and a continuous storyline going back through centuries of time. In these remote lands the links with the past are tangible and the re-launched attraction will grow out of the myths and legends of the locality.

The Silver Mountain Experience is only several miles away from a couple of our other Top 100 Attractions, Devils Bridge & Falls and The Vale of Rheidol Railway, which in my opinion could all be done on the same day. This award winning attraction really does have it all, as well as being 'Value for Money'', a trip underground was both informative and educational, and the tour guide really did know his stuff which always makes a difference. It's now after my visit, very apparent why people are itching to film at Llywernog as did the BBC's ' Countryfile' team a couple of years ago. With loads to see and explore there's a lot to occupy yourselves with, and what makes it extra special is that apart from the underground tour you are pretty much left to your own devices. Which as you will see the kids love? As if that wasn't enough the surrounding area at Llywernog is breathtakingly beautiful so once your done at the mine go and explore the surrounding area.

Aberystwyth

Ponterwyd, Aberystwyth, Ceredigion, SY23 3AB

New Quay Honey Farm

t: 01545 560822 e: info@thehoneyfarm.co.uk
www.thehoneyfarm.co.uk

A real working honey farm producing truly natural products!

There are lots of reasons to visit New Quay Honey Farm - a fantastic location in its own valley near New Quay, an Exhibition that shows you the life of the honeybee, with live exhibits behind glass; a shop selling honey from the Farm's 600 odd hives, mead made in its own meadery, and a tea room which serves locally sourced food of the highest quality; as well as the wildlife walk and picnic area. The honey Farm was started in 1995 to bring the beautiful honey of the area to a wider public and to share with visitors our fascination with the incredible life of the honeybee, the world's most studied insect. THE EXHIBITION spreads over the whole of the top floor of the converted chapel and shows the life of the honeybee and its importance in a combination of video displays, interpretation boards, and five live exhibits of actual full sized colonies of honeybees. THE SHOP sells a wide range of honey and honey products as well as books about bees, wildlife and nature, candles and other beeswax products. THE MEADERY also has a small exhibition and you can sample the meads in the shop. THE TEA ROOM serves many items made with our own honey, alongside the best the area has to offer, together with a great cup of tea or coffee.

Never before have I met two people so dedicated to what they do as Gerald & Mariana Cooper. It is clear to see that this is just, so much more than a tourist attraction to them. It is their life, their passion, and they want to share that passion with as many people as possible. We have Farm Parks in this book and they are the 'Crème De La Crème' of farm parks! But what makes the Honey Farm so unique is, it's all about one insect, an insect that we often don't think too much about, but we should, for honey is used in far more than we imagined and it's all to be learned about here at New Quay Honey Farm. Then there's the tearoom, which is a treasure trove of some of those products that are made from the very bee's here at the farm. So for a completely unique and fascinating experience, plan a visit here, you will not be disappointed, and you won't be able to help yourself when it comes to taking a souvenir away with you!

Cross Inn, New Quay, Ceredigion, SA44 6NN

Magic of Life Butterfly House

t: 01970 880928 e: info@magicoflife.org
www.magicoflife.org

Free-flying butterflies in a luxuriant tropical display!

The Trust was established in 2000 with the aim of encouraging an appreciation and understanding of nature. The idea was to set up a centre where people could learn first-hand about plants and animals.

What you'll see ...

* Hundreds of colourful butterflies
* Giant caterpillars and bizarre insects
* Collections of rare and endangered plants
* Woodlands, walks and waterfalls nearby in the stunning Rheidol Valley
* An environmental Trust run by biologists

Open March 27th - November 3rd, 2013
Open daily from 10.00 am till 5.00 pm
Coach groups welcome
10% Discount for groups of six and above!

There are many magical attractions throughout Wales, and within this book you will find one hundred of the very best of them. The Magic of Life is most definitely one of those attractions that deserves its place within this book. One of the many things that I liked about this attraction is the fact that it is not just a money making machine, it is a charitable trust that has been set up to ensure that all of its visitors understand everything that they are trying to achieve there. With colourful butterflies, Giant caterpillars and bizarre insects being just some of the many things that can be seen here, together with woodlands galore, walks and waterfalls nearby, I would say there is at least 3 to 4 hours worth of fun. Giving you great value for your admission fees, which is another thing we love here at Top 100 Attractions.

Aberystwyth

CwmRheidol, Aberystwyth, Ceredigion, SY23 3NB

SeaMor Dolphin Watching Boat Trips

t: 07795 242 445 e: info@seamor.org
www.seamor.org

The finest way to see the stunning Rheidol Valley!

SeaMôr is a small company running dolphin watching boat trips and private boat charter in the picturesque fishing village of New Quay and the Victorian town of Aberaeron in West Wales. Look for the dolphins onboard our wildlife watching and research boat Islander and learn about the dolphins and porpoises of Cardigan Bay and how you can help with their research and conservation! We carry a hydrophone (underwater microphone) and will show you how to listen to dolphins and porpoises every time we see them.
Join us for a coastal excursion or have a private picnic lunch by a remote beach! Our commercially coded and fully insured boat is also available for private hire, research, and media charter.
Sunset Trips are our ever popular evening tours of the Bay with feeding dolphins in the glow of the setting sun!

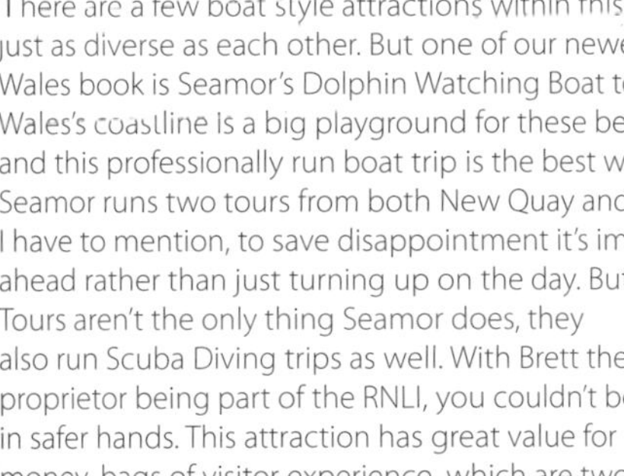

There are a few boat style attractions within this book and all are just as diverse as each other. But one of our newest additions to the Wales book is Seamor's Dolphin Watching Boat tours. This part of Wales's coastline is a big playground for these beautiful creatures and this professionally run boat trip is the best way to see them. Seamor runs two tours from both New Quay and Aberaeron but I have to mention, to save disappointment it's important to book ahead rather than just turning up on the day. But Tours aren't the only thing Seamor does, they also run Scuba Diving trips as well. With Brett the proprietor being part of the RNLI, you couldn't be in safer hands. This attraction has great value for money, bags of visitor experience, which are two of the main factors looked for when choosing our Top 100 attractions.

Aberystwyth

Quayside Gifts, New Quay, SA45 9NP

Summat Else - Bed & Breakfast

New Road New Quay, Dyfed SA45 9SE

T: 01545 561418   www.bedandbreakfast-directory.co.uk   E: blakemore12@btinternet.com

Located on the picturesque hertitage coastline Summat Else is situated 1 mile from the centre of New Quay and the picture book harbour, of Dylan Thomas fame, within easy reach of local pubs and restaurants and blue flag beaches. Excellent for Walkers, cyclists, bikers and watersports.Your hosts Kit & Angela provide all the care and pesonal attention that goes with a small guest house. Comfortable ensuite bedrooms and breakfast menu that includes Full English, fish, vegetarian and Welsh dishes. Private parking available.

Maesglas Uchaf - Bed & Breakfast

Ysbyty Ystwyth, Ystrad Meurig, Ceredigion SY25 6DD

T: 01974 282571   www.maesglasbandb.co.uk   E: info@maesglasbandb.co.uk

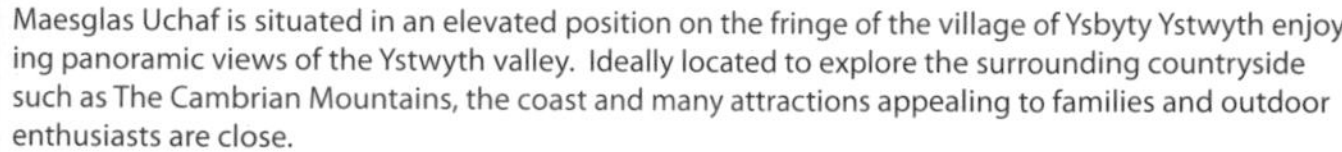

Maesglas Uchaf is situated in an elevated position on the fringe of the village of Ysbyty Ystwyth enjoying panoramic views of the Ystwyth valley. Ideally located to explore the surrounding countryside such as The Cambrian Mountains, the coast and many attractions appealing to families and outdoor enthusiasts are close.

Our two guestrooms on the first floor are spacious and comfortably furnished, and our home cooked breakfast will set you up for the days activities.

Gwesty'r Marine Hotel

Marine Terrace, Aberystwyth, Ceredigion SY23 2BX

T: 01970 612444   www.gwestymarinehotel.co.uk/   E: info@gwestymarinehotel.co.uk

Located on the picturesque promenade of Aberystwyth, the Marine is a relaxed, friendly hotel close enough to the town centre but away from the hustle and bustle of town life. The Marine is an ideal place to stay while exploring this beautiful part of Mid-Wales and what better way to enjoy the amazing sunsets over Cardigan Bay than in one of our many refurbished, comfortable en-suite bedrooms. We aim to provide all of our guests with excellent facilities, home-cooked traditional food and warm friendly service. We aspire to cater for your every requirement - whether it's a special champagne weekend break in one of our deluxe suites, a rest on your business travels, a conference or a wedding celebration - we would like to extend to you all a very warm Welsh welcome.

Llety Ceiro Country Guest House

lon ceiro, Bow street, Aberystwyth, Ceredigion, SY24 5AB

T: 01970 821900   www.lletyceiro.com   E: lletyceiro@hotmail.co.uk

Set in the idyllic countryside setting of the Eleri Valley, a warm welcome awaits you at this fabulous country guest house. Just 4 miles from the University town of Aberystwyth and a mere 2 miles from the popular seaside resort of Borth, Llety Ceiro is the perfect base for walkers, bird watchers and cyclists alike. Equipped to the highest standards, Llety Ceiro offers 11 en-suite bedrooms with telesion, hairdryer, iron, a safe and tea/coffee making facilities as well as Wi-Fi. The Guest House also has a bedroom fully equipped with disabled facilities. Llety Ceiro has a licensed bar, private car parking facilities and restaurant.

Bryncarnedd Country Cottages

Clarach Road, Aberystwyth, Ceredigion. SY23 3DG

T: 01970 612444 www.aberholidaycottages.com E: info@aberholidaycottages.com

Located just outside of the seaside town of Aberystwyth this wonderful cottage complex offers the best of both worlds, set within walking distance of the town and shops, but also far enough away from the hustle and bustle of town life, providing a relaxing and peaceful setting for your holiday. Once an important dairy farm to the local area, the buildings have been sympathetically converted into self-catering accommodation. Ranging from 1 to 4 bedrooms, these cottages have all been uniquely designed to accommodate everyone's needs. Pets welcome. Nightly, weekly or long stays.

Llety Teifi Guesthouse

Pendre,Cardigan, Ceredigion, SA43 1JU

T: 01239 615566 www.llety.co.uk E: mail@llety.co.uk

Llety Teifi is a relaxed family run Guest House located in Cardigan on the West Wales coast. Situated just off the main high street, the guest house is close to town but away from the hustle and bustle of town life. The guest house is located in a converted Grade II, elegant Georgian town house and aims to provide Cardigan with premier boutique accommodation. Each of our 10 en-suite bedrooms have been designed to offer our guests a comfortable stay, making the Guest House a perfect location to explore this beautiful part of Mid Wales.

Harry's Hotel Bar & Bistro

40-46 North Parade, Aberystwyth, Ceredigion, Wales. SY23 2NF

T: 01970 612647 www.harrysaberystwyth.com E: enquiries@harrysaberystwyth.com

Harry's Hotel Aberystwyth offers excellent accommodation and is located in the heart of town. As well as Hotel rooms, Harry's offers undoubtedly Aberystwyth's most luxurious and stylish bar, making it the perfect place for socialising with friends. Harry's offers a comfortable and personal experience in a warm and friendly environment. A seductive Beer Garden, where you can enjoy the summer sun, which will give you a feel of absolute bliss not matter what the weather. Harry's Hotel in Aberystwyth was newly renovated in 2008, making all rooms en-suite. Harry's Hotel has a range of accommodation from single rooms to deluxe rooms, which will suit all types of travellers.

Woodlands Caravan Park

Devils Bridge ,Aberystwyth, Ceredigion, SY23 3JW

T: 01970 890233 www.woodlandsdevilsbridge.co.uk E: enquiries@woodlandsdevilsbridge.co.uk

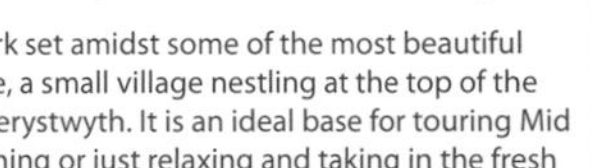

The Woodlands is a well established, family run caravan park set amidst some of the most beautiful scenery Mid Wales has to offer. It is situated in Devils Bridge, a small village nestling at the top of the Rheidol Valley, 12 miles inland from the coastal town of Aberystwyth. It is an ideal base for touring Mid Wales, walking, cycling, mountain biking, birdwatching, fishing or just relaxing and taking in the fresh air. The Touring Park is quiet and picturesque, and is away from the static caravans. It has both level hard ground and grassy pitches. Electric hook ups and TV aerial points are available if required.

The Hive

Cadwgan Pl Aberaeron, Dyfed, SA46 0BU

T: 01545 570445 www.thehiveaberaeron.com E: info@thehiveaberaeron.com

The Hive Grill offers an American style menu with a European influence, with a variety of dishes on offer from burgers, Steaks, fish and shellfish. The Hive kitchen is run by Jason Jones, our head chef who has a passion for using the freshest produce to prepare the style of food we all love to eat....
The Hive bar is open throughout the day from 10am in the morning, until late in the evening. Why not try one of our cocktails whilst relaxing in our conservatory and watch the world go by. The Hive is the home of the famous Honey Ice Cream. Made on the premises by our master Ice Cream makers Kevin and Mateusz.

Harry's Hotel Bar & Bistro

40-46 North Parade, Aberystwyth, Ceredigion, Wales. SY23 2NF

T: 01970 612647 www.harrysaberystwyth.com E: enquiries@harrysaberystwyth.com

Harry's Bistro is a hidden gem, with it's low lighting and relaxed atmosphere, beautifully decorated oasis. Refurbished to indulge that warm cosy feeling, Harry's set's the feeling of a relax, enjoyable evening while serving up sumptuous food. Whether it is a family occasion or a romantic evening meal, this Bistro is an ideal venue with a varied menu that will make everyone's mouth water. Harry's Bistro is the ideal location to hold your special occasion let it be a birthday celebration, anniversary or your little one's communion, confirmation or christenings. We can design a menu to suit your tastes, needs and budget nothing is too big or too small.

Llety Ceiro Restaurant

Lon Ceiro, Bow Street, Aberystwyth, SY24 5AB

T: 01970-821900 www.llety ceiro.co.uk E: info@lletyceiro.co.uk

We are open from early morning to late evening, seven days a week, making it an excellent choice for any occasion. We cater for breakfast, morning coffee, lunches, afternoon tea and dinner. In addition we also cater for private parties, wedding celebrations, business meetings and funeral gatherings. We also offer a traditional sunday carvery. We are table licensed and also have a range of wines to suit all budgets. Our restaurant offers an extensive menu which caters to all tastes and for private functions we are able to design menu plans to your requirements. We can also cater for any special dietary needs.

Cafe Mariner

South John St, The Pier, New Quay , SA45 9NP

T: 01545 560467

Café Mariners is located in the idyllic fishing village of New Quay. Serving traditional fish and chips, homemade specials, your usual favourites and all day breakfasts a good reputation has been gained for quality food. Recently voted the best Fish and Chips in Ceredigion for 2012 a warm welcome awaits you in Café Mariners and our take away fish and chip shop whether it's just a coffee, snack, ice cream or full traditional meal we cater for all.

Creme Pen Cei

The Pier/South John St New Quay SA45 9NN

T: 01545-561307

This bright and colourful Ice Cream parlour in my opinion helps to put New-quay on the culinary map. With an amazing and mind boggling selection of both Ice Creams & Sorbets, there is more than enough selection to satisfy anybody's palate. But that's not all Crème Pen Cei does well. They also have a wide selection of Panini's, baguettes, Salad boxes and the best coffee in town! We at Top 100 Attractions give a massive thumbs, and will stick our neck out and guarantee this food for thought selection will not disappoint!

Pennau Crafts & Coffee Shop

Rhydypennau, Bow Street, Aberystwyth, Ceredigion, SY24 5AA

T: 01970 820050 www.craftshopwales.co.uk E: Info@craftshopwales.co.uk

The Craft Shop in beautifully converted farm buildings, is bursting with exciting crafts and gift ideas for Christmas or for any occasion-preserves, slate crafts, Celtic Jewellery and much more...something for every one. The Coffee Shop. Enjoy traditional home made cooking in our award winning Coffee Shop. Call in for a morning coffee, a post of Welsh Brew Tea, sandwiches, jacket poatoes, mouth-watering sweets and cakes and home cooked ham, lasagne, Quiche Lorraine, savoury pancakes all serbced with our delicious and imaginative salad bar.

The Conrah Hotel & Park Restaurant

Chancery, Aberystwyth, Ceredigion, Wales SY23 4DF

T: 01970 617941 www.conrah.co.uk E: enquiries@conrah.co.uk

The Park Restaurant at the Conrah caters for all occasions, from relaxed meals with friends to larger special events. We pride ourselves on using home-grown, local and seasonal produce in our delicious meals. We also offer lighter meals in our bar area and our new "Little Dragons" menu for children, offers tasty, fresh and healthy food in smaller portions. Come and try our speciality home made afternoon teas or just call in for a drink to relax and take in the views.

The Cellar

8 Market Street Aberaeron, Ceredigion, SA460AS

T: 01545 574666 www.thecellar-aberaeron.co.uk E: cellaraberaeron@gmail.com

The Cellar is a restaurant for all occasions giving a warm welcome to everyone and serving coffee, lunch and evening meals.During the Summer months opening hours are extended as well as the menus, to include Tapas on the Terrace overlooking the Harbour for which Aberaeron is famous. Chef Daniel Evans' signature dishes include Mussels steamed in White Wine & Garlic, Trio of Lamb, Shin of Beef, Sea Bass with Shrimp, and a mouth watering selection of delicious desserts; all freshly made on the premises. The Menus change regularly to make the most of the wealth of wonderful, locally sourced produce.

Aberystwyth - Llanrhystud

Nestling at the base of the coastal plateau, Llanrhystud extends along the banks of the Afon Wyre about a mile from where the river reaches the sea. Situated on the edge of the fertile coastal plain, the village has long been a focal point of agricultural activity in the area.The extensive beach is composed of boulders and pebbles but during low water wide strips of flat sand become exposed.The now tranquil beach once resounded to the clatter of shipbuilding and, throughout the 19th century, four kilns at Craiglas were once the scene of a thriving lime industry.

The historical importance of Llanrhystud is emphasised by the number of ancient settlements in the vicinity.To the south of the village, two distinctly rounded hills; Castell Bach and the now wooded Castell Mawr were formerly both hill forts.They are separated by a gully traditionally known as the 'dell of slaughter', referring to an ancient battle, with the field below serving as a burial groundBy the 10th century Llanrhystud had become a religious settlement important enough to warrant the attention of marauding Danes who destroyed the village in 988 AD. The present parish church, dedicated to St Rhystud, a 6th century Celtic missionary, dates from 1854 but is of more ancient foundation.

Llanrhystud - Aberaeron

Following the beach southbound from Llanrhystud takes you to the vicinity of the twin-village of Llansantffraid Llanon. The Llansantffraid section lies on the low coastal apron whereas Llanon's terraced, stone-built houses extend along the old turnpike road. The mixed Welsh / Irish influence is again witnessed in this area. It is most unusual to have two churches in the same parish, both dedicated to female saints. Here we have one dedicated to a female Welsh saint, the second dedicated to an Irish saint.Tradition has it that St Non gave birth to the patron saint of Wales, St David, at Llanon around 500 AD: this is commemorated by the Non Stone, now in the Ceredigion Museum at Aberystwyth. St Ffraid (St Bridget), the patron saint of dairymaids was the daughter of an Irish chief; she founded the famous monastery at Kildare, where she died in 523 AD. South of Llanon you will encounter ancient strips of land called 'slangs'.The patchwork quilt effect produced by the division of the 'slangs' by furrows, stones and hedges is most striking. The southbound path climbs along the cliff top before descending towards historic Llanddewi Aberarth from where you can walk along the foreshore to Aberaeron or use the dedicated roadside path.

Aberaeron - New Quay

Descending towards New Quay, you first encounter the old shipbuilding beach at Cei Bach (the small quay). The earliest recorded sailing vessel built here was the 36-ton sloop 'Betsy' in 1805. Launching was ceremoniously conducted with all the craftsmen involved and the local population turning up to celebrate. The 291-ton three-mast barque 'Syren' which foundered en route from South America in 1887 was the largest ship built here. On the southerly extreme of Cei Bach, the headland of Llanina Point once extended further out to sea culminating in Carreg Ina, a large rock where, according to local folklore, a mermaid could be seen basking in the sun. She once became entangled in a fishing boat's nets and, on being released by fishermen, warned of an incoming stor enabling them to return safely to the shore.Ash and sycamore obscurea small stone church dedicated to Ina.The original church was lost to the waves but the existing structure, built in 1850, incorporates masonry from its predecessor. Dylan Thomas lived nearby during World War II.That period was Dylan's most prolific in terms of literary output. You will see from your OS map that you can walk to New Quay along the minor road from Cei Bach - rather than along Traethgwyn.

PEMBROKESHIRE

Pembrokeshire is one of Wales's most popular destinations, not only to the likes of us tourists, but for centuries now it has been a special location for artists, pilgrims and to many outdoor pursuits enthusiasts. Pembrokeshire is also famous for being home to Britain's smallest city (St Davids) this charming city was founded by St David, patron saint of Wales 1500 years ago and is still to this day, full to the brim of welsh charm! Pembrokeshire is also famous for the amount of blue flag beaches it has dotted around its coastline, a coastline that spans a vast 275 km! Not only has it won dozens of blue flag awards, but a huge number of green coast awards also! Just when you couldn't be blamed for thinking there were no more awards to be won, Pembrokeshire has deservedly won well over a hundred seaside awards too. Being the only coastal national park of its kind, and one of only three national parks in Wales, the others being the Snowdonia National Park and thirdly the Brecon Beacons, all of which are featured in this book. This section of the book features plenty of great places to visit, castles that have been the birth place to great kings, to theme parks, safari parks and animal farms alike. Pembrokeshire really is a unique setting, and certainly one to spend your holiday in!

Castell Henllys

t: 01239 891319 e: enquiries@castellhenllys.com
www.castellhenllys.com

Step back in time at Castell Henllys

Owned and managed by the Pembrokeshire Coast National Park Authority, Castell Henllys is an evocative Iron Age fort set within the rugged, magical landscape of North Pembrokeshire known as Gwlad Hud a Lledrith (Land of Magic and Enchantment). Today a visit to Castell Henllys is like stepping back in time. You can see how people lived in the Iron Age, what their houses were like, how they dressed and how they went about their daily life. Enter the roundhouses and step back into the past, soak up the atmosphere of a bygone era and imagine what life must have been like for our ancestors. Each of the roundhouses has been reconstructed on the original f oundation so you will be walking in the footsteps of the people who built Castell Henllys. There are daily guided tours during the season, events, an exhibition and a gift shop.

We have visited many different types of attractions during the course of our selection process and every single one has earned its right to be one of the Top 100 Attractions in Wales. None more so than Castell Henllys! Perched on a spur of land near the Pembrokeshire coast, this attraction has got everything you would require to make a great Welsh tourist attraction! Value for money, uniqueness, and great for all ages and that's just for starters. I have been to this attraction quite a few times and on every occasion I seem to spot something I hadn't noticed before. As you walk around the Iron Age fort it isn't hard to imagine what life would have been like on the west coast of Wales way back 2400 years ago. You get to smell the smells they would of smelt, you get to sample also the same harsh daily life that would have been their only form of survival, in what would have been very grim times for the human race. All this and more comes to life here and I feel the team at Castell Henllys have done an amazing job of recreating just how fundamental being a close knit community would have been to these early Celtic people.

Tenby

Pantglas, Crymych, Pembrokeshire, SA41 3UT

Folly Farm

t: 01834 812731 e: info@folly-farm.co.uk
www.folly-farm.co.uk

FUN, ZOO, FUNFAIR, ADVENTURE PLAY

Folly Farm Adventure Park and Zoo near Tenby is holder of The Best Family Day Out in Wales Award 2010-2012. With a friendly farmyard, indoor vintage funfair, its very own zoo and a whole host of indoor and outdoor play it reallyis true to say there's something for everyone whatever the weather. Jolly Barn and Farm - home to horses, pigs, sheep, goats, donkeys, chickens, turkeys, giant rabbits, ferrets, rats, mice and cockroaches and some fantastic farming play equipment. A land train tour of Follywood Country Park, a visit to Percy's Piggery and a stroll on the nature trail completes the fun in this area. Folly Zoo - home to over 200 animals and many endangered species including the only Giraffe in Wales, Tapir, Ocelot, Fossa, Camel, Lemur, Bongo and much, much more. Indoor Vintage Funfair - home to all the favourite old time rides such as the Golden Gallopers Carousel, the Caterpillar, The Coronation Speedway, Waltzer, Dodgems, Helter Skelter, Big Wheel and much, much, more. Adventure Play - home to Carousel Woods, the largest indoor playground in Wales and a whole host of outdoor play including CAT Diggers, a Formula 2 Go Kart Track and the Pirate Adventure playground.

We have featured several farm parks within this book and one that has to be amongst the best is Folly Farm Adventure Theme Park. Holders of the coveted Best Family Day Out in Wales Award, Folly Farm has all the makings of being one of the best family attractions located within the British Isles. As well as being a family friendly farm park the park also houses its very own zoo, indoor vintage funfair, and a wide array of indoor and outdoor adventure play areas. Folly Farm truly is an adventure park within an adventure park.

Tenby

Clerkenhill Adventure Farm

t: 01437 751227 e: dl@clerkenhill.orangehome.co.uk
www.clerkenhill.co.uk

COME ALONG AND ENJOY A GREAT VALUE DAY OUT FOR EVERYONE!

There is lots of indoor fun for those wet and windy days. Follow the safe adventure trail through the spooky woodland with lots of interesting swings and slides and sights along the way, watch out for giants, bears and spooks! There is even a beach, but beware of the sharks! Have a chat with the animals around the park. Watch the children laughing and playing in the numerous large play areas which include giant tube tunnel slides. Our 18 basket Frizbee Golf course is spread over 10 acres of a valley adjoining Clerkenhill Adventure Farm. You are surrounded by beautiful countryside with trees and streams surrounding the course.

Clerkenhill has what a lot of farm parks of its type doesn't, and that is uniqueness! The farm park plays host also to the very popular Frizbee Golf Course. I have to be honest before my visit to Clerkenhill I had never heard of Frizbee Golf, but soon got up to speed on the craze and can truly see why it is loved by so many people. As this attraction goes from strength to strength, If your looking for a truly fun day then I can seriously recommend Clerkenhill as one not to be missed.

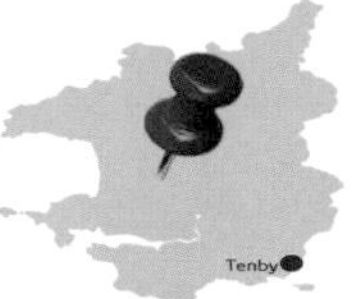

Clerkenhill Adventure Farm, Slebech, Haverfordwest, SA62 4PE

Picton Castle

t: 01437 751326 e: info@pictoncastle.co.uk
www.pictoncastle.co.uk

A Magical Day Out for all the Family!

Picton Castle and Gardens is a fairy tale castle with enchanting gardens, just a few miles from Haverfordwest. As well as being an important part of the county's history it, it is a popular destination for locals and tourists alike and attracts thousands of visitors each year. Picton Castle provides the perfect setting for a fairy tale wedding day with its fine entrance gates and long carriage drive sweeping up to the Castle forecourt.Situated close to the Cleddau Estuary, known locally as the 'hidden waterway', Picton Castle comprises 40 acres of some of the most beautiful woodland gardens and grounds in West Wales.Stroll beneath some of the largest and oldest trees in West Wales and discover woodland walks, ferns, a maze and abundant feasts of wild flowers that blend with unusual woodland shrubs from all corners of the world.Please note that castle tours may be restricted when wedding ceremonies take place in the Great Hall; please phone 01437 751369 to confirm tour times.

Picton Castle really is one of Wales's hidden gems. Despite being one of Wales's national treasures it still remains independently run which in today's economical climate is probably just as challenging as many other challenges that have faced the Castle in the past 700 years. What made me fall in love with Picton so much, was that the castle is steeped in history from the Norman invasion right down to the Cromwellian civil war, this castle has seen it all! Yet here it is, still standing as majestic and charming as it did when it was first built. Unlike many other properties in Wales, Picton offers tours seven days a week and are thoroughly enjoyable. If its just the gardens that your interested in you won't be disappointed! The gardens here at Picton are of a very high standard and in my opinion, add to the value of your ticket.

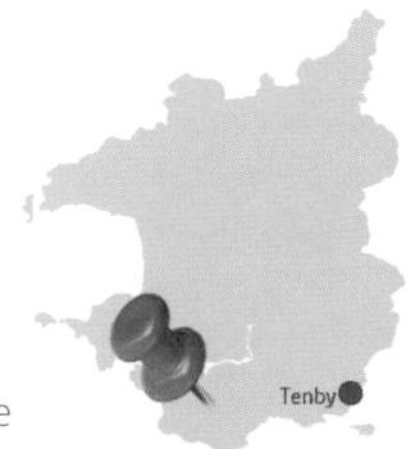

Haverfordwest, Pembrokeshire, SA62 4AS

Manor House Wildlife Park

t: 01646 651201
book online at www. manorhousewildlifepark.co.uk

OPEN EVERY DAY IN THE SEASON • OPEN WEEKENDS IN WINTER • OPEN OVER CHRISTMAS AND NEW YEAR

Four Zoonique Walkthroughs - get up close to endangered species

Manor House is Special - everybody loves this low-key and charming park. ITV's 'Anna's Welsh Zoo' is filmed at Manor House, and here you get to meet TV star Steve the Gibbon, his mate Lisa and their young son Bryn... watch this wonderful family as they swing through the trees in The Valley of the Apes. Zebra, Camel, Scimitar-horned oryx, Ostrich, Meerkats and so much more! Nothing beats the joy of hand-feeding a wallaby, especially when there's a joey in the pouch!You can wander freely in the Lemur Walkthrough with four endangered species of lemur, sit still and they'll come right up to you. And let's not forget Tommy the Tapir - everybody loves Tommy! Passionate about animals and want to get closer? Then the 'Shadow a Keeper Experience' is for you. Work with a keeper inside enclosures, feeding and caring for rare and endangered species - it's a life-enhancing, life-changing experience. People say our keepers should be bottled, they're so good, so knowledgeable. (Must be pre-booked on 01646 651201. Cost is £60 for one, £100 for two - this experience supports our conservation work.)

This conservation-led park has something for everyone. from the huge carved dragon on the front lawns and little scooters and cars for the young, the Hay Play Barn and Willow structures to Dolly and Macauley the world's naughtiest macaws! The real-food cafe is a special treat: with a seasonally-changing menu, everything is cooked in-house from scratch, real tea and the best coffee around! A great day out in Pembrokeshire! We especially loved walking with the animals in the African Village and Meerkat Mountain - see the new Meerkat Family close up.

Manor House

Tenby

Manor House Wildlife Park, St Florence, Near Tenby SA70 8RJ

Valley of the APES
THE African Village
LEMUR Walk-through
WANDER WITH THE Wallabies
a zoo for all seasons

PEMBROKESHIRE

Oakwood Theme Park

t: 01834 891373 e: info@oakwoodthemepark.co.uk
www. oakwoodthemepark.co.uk

Oakwood is Wales' BIGGEST day out!

Set in 80 acres of spectacular Pembrokeshire countryside, Oakwood is one of the UK's leading theme parks with more than 30 exhilarating attractions; including four world class rides to enjoy.
Don't miss Megafobia - famed as one of the wildest wooden coasters on the planet, it has been voted the best ride in the UK and the 3rd best ride in the world by coaster enthusiasts from the Roller Coaster Club of Great Britain.
The park is also home to Drenched the tallest, steepest and wettest ride in Europe, Speed with its awe-inspiring beyond vertical drop and Bounce where riders are shot into the air at up to 70kph in just two seconds!
Plus there's the added thrill of Vertigo* - the skydiver-designed extreme flight experience and the closest thing to flying like an eagle. (*subject to supplementary charge).
Oakwood's unique combination of attractions also includes spectacular family rides, children's themed play areas and so much more.

Oakwood has to be Wales's Premier Theme Park. With plenty of rides to keep you occupied all day, you are guaranteed not only value for money, but lots of great memories. After being recently taken over by Spanish theme park giants the Aspro Group, the management at Oakwood have got massive plans for the theme park and although it would be a far better place to visit on a non rainy day there is one thing that is for certain, that no matter the weather the fun goes on all day at Oakwood.

Tenby

Canaston Bridge, Narberth, Pembrokeshire SA67 8DE

OAKWOOD THEME PARK -25th ANNIVERSARY

Wales' most popular theme park celebrates its 25th anniversary this year with an action-packed programme of thrills and fun for all the family.

Exciting added attractions for 2012 include extended late-night opening in July and August including fireworks' finales* and the return of the hugely popular High Diving Show for the summer. The park is also planning a series of special events and celebrations to mark its 25th anniversary. Set in 80 acres of spectacular Pembrokeshire countryside, Oakwood is one of the UK's leading theme parks with more than 30 exhilarating attractions; including four world class rides to enjoy. Don't miss Megafobia - famed as one of the wildest wooden coasters on the planet, it has been voted the best ride in the UK and the 3rd best ride in the world by coaster enthusiasts from the Roller Coaster Club of Great Britain.

With a top speed in excess of 75 kph and 25 metre drops towards a lake combined with unique crossovers this twister has attained legendary status among coaster fans worldwide.

The park is also home to Drenched the tallest, steepest and wettest water ride in Europe, Speed with its awe-inspiring beyond vertical drop and Bounce where riders are shot into the air at up to 70kph in just two seconds! Plus there's the added thrill of Vertigo** – the skydiver-designed extreme flight experience and the closest thing to flying like an eagle. The ride provides awesome aerial views of the park and surrounding countryside and can accommodate one, two or three riders simultaneously (**subject to supplementary charge). Oakwood's unique combination of attractions also includes spectacular family rides, children's themed play areas and so much more. You can whizz around the watery slides of Snake River Falls, become a pilot on Plane Crazy or take a relaxing paddle on the Boating Lake. Seek out the spine tingling ghouls on Spooky 3D, plummet down the Waterfall slide, climb aboard the Pirate Ship or take on the hairpins of the Bobsleigh run. For smaller kids there's KidzWorld with its undercover adventure playworld The Fun Factory and the The Wacky Factory.

Thousand Islands Expeditions

t: 01437 721721 e: sales@thousandislands.co.uk
www.thousandislands.co.uk

WILDLIFE ADVENTURE BOAT TRIPS!

Exciting jet boat trips or traditional leisurely cruises with wildlife guides onboard. Witness some of the most powerful currents in Britain, pass beneath some of the highest cliffs in Wales, see spectacular breeding colonies of hundreds of nesting seabirds. Ramsey is home to one of the UKs largest Atlantic Grey Seal colonies, seal pups are on Ramseys beaches during September and October, look for our resident Harbour Porpoise feeding in the fast moving water in Ramsey Sound. Get the best of both worlds and see the RSPB Nature Reserve of Ramsey Island by land and sea, spend the day exploring the Island on foot and take guided cruise . Venture offshore on one of our jet boat trips searching for whales and dolphins and see the spectacular Gannet colony on Grassholm Island or an exhilarating jet boat trip across to Skomer Island to watch the Puffins and Shearwaters.

Thousand Islands really have got it all when it comes to making sure your trip to South West Wales is one not to be forgotten! They really do run a slick operation, from buying your ticket right down to embarking and disembarking their vessels. Every care is taken to make sure you are totally comfortable and safety is absolutely paramount! I personally feel the reason there are not more boats in this area popping up is because simply put, they have a hard act to follow!

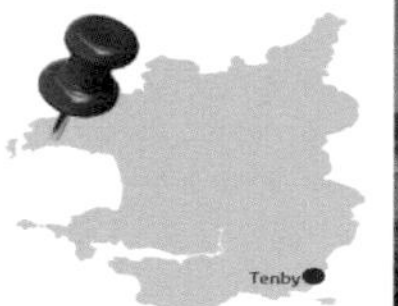

Cross Square, St Davids, Pembrokeshire, SA62 6SL

The Old Cross Hotel

Cross Square, St Davids, Pembrokeshire, SA62 6SP

T: 01437 720387 www.oldcrosshotel.co.uk E: enquiries@oldcrosshotel.co.uk

The Old Cross Hotel is situated in the centre of St Davids, right on the Cross Square. Our facilities include en-suite accommodation, a fully licensed restaurant and bar, both of which are open daily to residents and the public, and a parking space for each room. All our rooms have en-suite facilities, tea and coffee making equipment, TV, radio and hairdryer. There is one parking space per room in our private car park. All of our bedrooms are designated non-smoking rooms. Downstairs, feel free to relax in either of our two lounges, or on a sunny day sit out in the garden and watch the world go by.

Ty Coed DE - Bed & Breakfast

Roch Haverfordwest, Pembrokeshire SA6 6AW

T: 01437 711340 www.tycoedde.co.uk E: Julie@tycoedde.co.uk

Situated on the edge of the historic village of Roch, Ty Coed De has panoramic views of St Brides Bay and is only a mile away from the Newgale beach with its wide expanse of flat sand which is suitable for families and surfers alike. Ty Coed De offers first class accommodation in landscaped grounds, a haven for wild life, with views looking over farmland to the sea. There is plenty of private off road parking.

Gower Villa Caravan & Touring Park

Villa Lane, Clunderwen Pembrokeshire, SA66 7NL

T: 01437 562059 www.gvtp.co.uk E: relax@gvtp.co.uk

A simple straight forward park, providing an excellent base for touring West Wales. Our 4 star status means that you will find good facilities kept to a high standard.
A level site of both grass & hardstanding pitches set on the edge of the village of Clunderwen, near Narberth but only a 5 minute walk from the local Spar shop and pub. Fully tiled and heated toilet block with free hot water for the showers and washbasins. Centrally placed for touring Pembrokeshire with its wonderful beaches, castles, hills and varied towns and villages and the cathedral city of St Davids.

The Harp at Letterston - Restaurant with Rooms

Letterston, Haverfordwest, Pembrokeshire, SA62 5UA

T: 01348 840061 www.theharpatletterston.co.uk E: info@theharpatletterston.co.uk

Where can you get a really good pub lunch or entertain in style all under one roof? Try The Harp at Letterston. A family owned and run, family friendly pub and restaurant, where all are welcome. Originally a 15th century country inn, our recent renovations have brought this former coaching house bang up to date with the stylish Conservatory Restaurant where you can bring friends or family to be entertained. Choose from local favourites, Prime Welsh Fillet Steak, Welsh Mussels, Venison Roquefort, Whole Sea Bass, on the Menu featuring some superb local Welsh ingredients.

Coach Guest House

11 Deer Park, Tenby SA70 7LE

T: 01834 842210 www.coachhousetenby.co.uk E: Jackie@coachhousetenby.co.uk

The Coach Guest House is situated in Tenby, Pembrokeshire. Take a stroll along the beach or around Tenby town centre, both within 2 minutes walking distance from The Coach Guesthouse. All our bedrooms are en-suite with central heating, colour Free-View TVs Tea & coffee trays, hairdryer, shampoo, Bubble bath or shower wash. Clean towels are provided daily. Iron & Board are available in lounge on ground floor. The Coach has separate breakfast tables for each room.
Wifi available.

Caerhys Farm

Berea, St Davids, Pembrokeshire, SA62 6DX.

T: 01348 831244 www.organic-farm-holidays.co.uk E: caerhysbandb@hotmail.com

Caerhys Organic Farm a wonderful place to stay for bed and breakfast in Pembrokeshire Caerhys is on the picturesque coastline of north Pembrokeshire. We are just 1/2 mile from the coast and approx. 4 miles from St. David's. The farmhouse was built in 1864 and later extended and modernised in 1980. Bedroom 1 is a double and bedroom 2 is a twin / double bedroom, both are en suite and both have full sea views of Abereiddy. Bedroom 3 is a double room which has farmyard and country views, this bedroom has a private bathroom. All bathrooms have showers.

IvyBridge Guest House

Drim Mill, Dyffryn, Goodwick, Fishguard, SA64 0JT

T: 01348 875366 www.ivybridgefishguard.co.uk E: info@ivybridgefishguard.co.uk

Ivybridge is a friendly family run guest house offering comfortable accommodation. All of our 14 rooms are en- suite & provide free view television & hot drinks facilities and range from single & double rooms to triple and family suites. Our family suites comprise of a large ensuite bedroom with a bunk bedded room leading off from within the bedroom. We also welcome disabled guests and have a purpose built disabled suite available. Ground floor rooms are available on request. We also have a licensed Restaurant and Bar.

The Golden Lion

East Street, Newport, Pembrokeshire, SA42 0SY

T: 01239 820321 www.goldenlionpembrokeshire.co.uk E: hello@goldenlionpembrokeshire.co.uk

The Golden Lion is gloriously located in one the most attractive villages in North Pembrokeshire, a designated area of outstanding natural beauty. As family run Inn we put in extra care to ensure that every detail of your visit is of the highest standard and at the same time, creating relaxed and friendly atmosphere. We have 13 comfortable, light and airy en-suite rooms. All individually decorated, the style is clean simplicity – cool whites and creams, honey-hued oak, and original artworks come together to make a contemplative mix of the contemporary and the traditional. Relax in crisp cotton sheets, snuggly duvets and Welsh woolens.

The Royal Oak

West Street, Newport, Pembrokeshire,SA42 0TA

T: 01239 820 632

The Royal Oak is established as the CURRY HOUSE of Newport. We also specialise in fresh sea food and grills. Vegetarian and special diets also catered for. Take away service available. FROM the outside, it looks like a typical British pub, but inside the Royal Oak in the seaside town of Newport, Pembrokeshire, you can sample some fine Indian-style cuisine.For the pub specialises in home-cooked curries. However, those who aren't so keen on the spicy food, can choose from a wide selection of pub grub – from scampi to faggots in gravy.

The Lobster Pot Inn

Gaylane, Marloes, Nr Haverfordwest, Pembrokeshire, SA62 3AZ

T: 01646 636233

The Lobster Pot Inn is located in the the village of Marloes, Pembrokeshire West Wales. A warm welcome awaits you along with an excellent selection of real ales, locally caught fish, bar meals all day and traditional sunday lunches. For those wanting more than a bar meal we have restaurant with a range of starters, main courses and deserts. To keep the youngsters occupied we have games room and a garden area. Whether it's a Birthday Party, Christening or Wedding Reception, we can help. We offer excellent quality at a fair price, all in a friendly and relaxed atmosphere to create a memorable event.

The Golden Lion

East Street, Newport, Pembrokeshire, SA42 0SY

T: 01239 820321 www.goldenlionpembrokeshire.co.uk E. hello@goldenlionpembrokeshire.co.uk

The Golden Lion is gloriously located in one the most attractive villages in North Pembrokeshire, a designated area of outstanding natural beauty. Our mission is to deliver the absolute best in local cuisine and service in a relaxed and friendly atmosphere. Our team of talented and enthusiastic chefs prepare an evening menu based on seasonal local produce with our favorites being Welsh Black beef fillet, locally caught sea bass and carefully prepared lobster – fresh from the harbour just down the road. Polish off your feast with a posh pudding or one of our traditional familiars such as sticky toffee pudding or homemade crumble. Our spacious restaurant – recently refurbished in Welsh slate and oak – is perfect for families and groups, with plenty of cosy corners for the romantically inclined.

The Corner Piece Inn

Rudbaxton, Haverfordwest, Pembrokeshire, SA62 5PG

T: 01437 741460

Situated in the village of Rudbaxton, near Haverfordwest this cosy country pub offers a variety of drinks including a selection of real ales. The new management really have their fingers on the button when it comes to running a pub. But the reason why we have featured them in our 'Food for Thought' section is their amazing food. From tasty evening meals, to their famous Sunday lunches, the Corner Piece really does offer all you will need for your starving tastebuds.

The Old Cross Hotel

Cross Square, St Davids, Pembrokeshire, SA62 6SP

T: 01437 720387 www.oldcrosshotel.co.uk E: enquiries@oldcrosshotel.co.uk

Our chefs use mainly local produce for the home-cooked dishes served in our restaurant and bar. Start the day with a full cooked breakfast, cereal and toast. Fresh fruit and a selection of juices are always available. Our restaurant is open every evening, serving food freshly prepared on the premises, accompanied by a wine list that offers a good selection of European and New World wines. Children are welcome and we offer a range of homemade dishes both in the bar and restaurant for our young guests. Our restaurant is a non-smoking area at all times. We can cater for special diets such as vegetarian, gluten-free and dairy free provided that you notify us when you book. Advance booking is essential.

Restaurant at Nant-Y-Ffin Hotel & Motel

Llandissilio, Clynderwen, nr Fishguard, SA66 7SU

T: 01437 563423 www.nantyffin.co.uk E: info@nantyffin.co.uk

Our restaurant is open seven days a week offering a wide range of fresh and local produce. Our extensive menu has a variety of high standard dishes prepared by our qualified staff. Catering for all tastes and dietary requirements.

We are also open for Sunday lunches between 12pm-3pm.

Pre-booking is advisable to reserve a table.

LouLou's Cafe

Fountain House, Market Street, Newport, Pembrokeshire, SA42 0PH

T: 01239 820 777 www.loulouscafenewport.com E: mail@loulouscafenewport.com

Loulou's is a cosy and friendly café nestled below Carningli, Newport, in the beautiful Pembrokeshire Coast National Park. Using mainly local and organically sourced ingredients we offer a freshly cooked daily menu, along with take-out lunches and drinks, take-home frozen meals and outside catering service. Come and enjoy an organic morning coffee, lunch or afternoon tea and choice of cakes including gluten-free chocolate brownies, sugar-free orange daties, almond macaroons, fresh scones and much more! Our daily menu includes soups, homemade breads, filled wholemeal baguettes, savoury flan, houmous mezze, falafel and buckwheat pancakes.

Real Food Cafe

Manor House Wildlife Park, St Florence, Tenby, Pembrokeshire, SA70 8RJ

T: 01646 651201 www.manorhousewildlifepark.co.uk E: info@manorhousewildlifepark.co.uk

We cook proper food, from scratch in the kitchens, using fresh produce. We count our food miles, so local quality produce is important to us... some people come just for lunch! The Liverpool Echo agrees that we serve the best coffee in the UK! Our seasonal menu includes:Daily specials,Fruit scones and cakes - baked daily in our kitchens, Soup of the Day - always using fresh, local seasonal produce. All our sandwich fillings and dressings are made in-house to our own recipes Sit in or out with the birds.

CARMARTHENSHIRE

Carmarthenshire is to Wales as Kent is to England, the true garden of Wales. Before visiting this area of Wales, I truly thought that to be just a cliché that people come out with from time to time about places that had a lot of green landscapes in them. I couldn't have been more wrong! With breathtakingly beautiful mountains, fresh, green landscapes and hidden forests that take you all the way down to those enviable golden sandy beaches, Carmarthenshire truly is Wales's secret Oasis.

One can now see why they chose this idyllic location to play home to the National Botanic Garden of Wales. I spent a night in the Premier Inn in Llanelli, which at first I was wondering why someone would chose such a town to stay in as part of a Welsh holiday. I now know why! Being the largest town in Carmarthenshire this busy, bustling Welsh town truly is the epitome of Rural Welsh life. With the Millennium Coastal path nearby and the National Wetland Centre just a mile or so out of the town centre, there is just as much to do here as there is in any other Welsh town.

So on the face of it, Carmarthenshire really does get a huge thumb up from us all here at Top 100 Attractions. I also cannot wait to work on our next welsh book as there was an awful lot that I didn't get to see! The likes of Llanelly House, Pembrey Country Park, and of course the Millennium Coastal Path.

CARMARTHENSHIRE

Cenarth Adventure Centre

t: 01559 371621 e: fun@cenarth-adventure.co.uk
www.fun@cenarth-adventure.co.uk

FUN FOR ALL.....

Welcome to 'Cenarth Adventure Centre' ....West Wales' premier paintball and outdoor laser combat site!!
Open all year round, whatever the weather, this action packed site will ensure you have the time of your life!! Paintball can be played from 11 years old and Laser Combat from as young as 5 years old, so the whole family can join in on the action! You don't need to be in a group, you can just phone up and you can join in with other small groups and individuals. There are other activities on offer if you want to have a whole days fun....

Archery (7yrs+)
Off-road remote control buggies (6yrs+)
Paintball target range (8yrs+)
Woodland challenge course (10yrs+)
Cenarth Adventure Centre is the ideal place to have a fun day out!

CARMARTHENSHIRE TOURISM AWARDS 2011 GOLD VISITOR EXPERIENCE OF THE YEAR

Cenarth Adventure Centre is the only Paintball or Lasercombat games style attraction in our Top 100 Attractions list. The reason for that is a lot of combat games sites can sometimes fail when it comes to the 'Imagination Factor'. However the adventure centre here at Cenarth has certainly broken that old mould! It's imaginative, Hi-Tech and clear to see that no expense has been spared when it comes to making sure the game play experience is one that can't be rivalled. The site itself recently has been awarded the 'Visitor Experience of the Year' award for 2011 and after extensive research I would put money on it that it won't be their last! So as you can now see, that's why we just couldn't leave out Cenarth Adventure Centre, and neither should you!

Swansea

Allt Y Gelli, Cenarth, Newcastle Emlyn, Carmarthenshire, SA38 9JL

National Botanic Garden of Wales

t: 01558 667149 e: info@gardenofwales.org.uk
www.gardenofwales.org.uk

Come visit the National Botanic Garden of Wales!

Our mission to inspire, educate and conserve has not only made us a beautiful place to visit but a fascinating and relevant one too. We have an amazing collection of over 8000 different plant varieties, spread across 560 acres of beautiful countryside. We've developed a stunning range of themed gardens that appeal to a wide range of visitors, from those who just love the sight and smells of flowers to those who want to know about medicinal plants or the latest DNA research into plant evolution.We are very family friendly. There is always plenty of activities for families to do in school and bank holidays, and we have a year round diverse programme of events that appeals to a wide range of visitors. We have the world's largest single span glasshouse, designed by Lord Foster, that has the best display of mediterranean climate zone plants in the Northern hemisphere.

The National Botanic Garden is truly Wales's answer to England's Eden Project. I was in awe of the place when I first visited, I definitely wish I had more time to have seen everything, but at least now I have an excuse to go back! What we at Top 100 Attractions absolutely adore is attractions that help us to learn and understand our natural habitat, but with the slick way the team at the National Botanic Garden do it, is very hard to beat. There is always something happening here and you will truly need to set aside a whole day to see everything, which in our estimation is fantastic value for money. Also with a couple of cafes and a good food restaurant you needn't worry about what's for lunch?

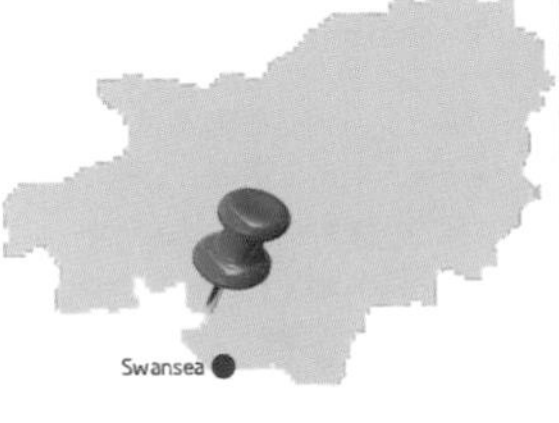

Llanarthne, Carmarthenshire, SA32 8HG

Ffos Las Racecourse

t: 01554 811092 e: info@ffoslasracecourse.com
www.ffoslasracecourse.com

For a Great Day Out - Come Racing!

Ffos Las Racecourse in Carmarthenshire is one of Wales's newest attractions, providing a hugely popular day out for families. The venue made history in 2009 when it became the first new turf racecourse to open in Britain in more than 70 years. Ffos Las is much more than a racecourse too – offering drive-in movies, gourmet and comedy evenings, wedding fayres, car boot sales and much, much more. The racecourse stages 26 racing fixtures throughout 2012 both on the flat and over jumps. Accompanied under 16s are always admitted free of charge, so a day or an evening at the races is very affordable. Highlights include William Hill Welsh Champion Hurdle day, five spring and summer evenings, a summer festival in August and Boxing Day. There's even racing at the climax to The Queen's Diamond Jubilee celebrations on Bank Holiday Tuesday 5 June.

Ffos Las racecourse, is a true Welsh success story that will be talked about for many years to come. The course was built at the site of an open cast coal mine after mining operations ceased, but as you visit the racecourse you would never even know it was there. Ffos Las, is Wales's third racecourse but by no means comes last. With state of the art everything, this modern racecourse has everything to offer the modern day punter. On the day I visited Ffos Las, I was allowed to walk around the course, and it was only then with no one else around, I realised just how much has been put into this site, and how every attention to detail has been focused on meticulously. With the new 26 race meeting itinerary now confirmed for 2012, now is the time to check your diary and make a definite date to visit, what is set to be a great racing year here in Wales.

Ffos Las Racecourse, Trimsaran, SA17 4DE

National Coracle Centre

t: 01239 710980 e: martinfowler7@aol.com
www.coraclemuseum.co.uk

Come visit Coracles from around the world

A Museum and Workshop of Coracles from around the world set in the grounds of a 17th Century Flour Mill beside the beautiful Cenarth falls famed for its Salmon Leaps and 200 year old Bridge over the Teifi River. The Museum, apart from its fine collection of coracles covers the history of coracles and the techniques and tools for building them. Also a section on the implements and methods used for the equally ancient art of poaching. The National Coracle Museum houses an international collection of coracles from as far afield as Vietnam, North America, India, Tibet and Iraq to complement the collection of coracles from around our home islands. The museum also incorporates a work shop to show the ancient craft of coracle making. Young children can also sit in a coracle and watch a video of how they are made.For organised parties a guided tour of both the museum and the 17th Century Flour Mill is available. From the Mill viewing areas and pathways provide wonderful views of the Salmon Leap and the 200 year old bridge.

The National Coracle Centre, is one of those attractions that I find so hard to find the words to say how great it is. With Coracles from all over the world on display, I was blown away to learn the history behind not only the Coracle, but behind the people that would of manned these strange vessels, not only many years ago, but still today. This attraction is most unique in the way that it is positioned right smack bang in the middle of two counties, not just one! Whether you're visiting Ceredigion or Pembrokeshire, it doesn't matter, as the only thing separating the two counties and this attraction is a bridge, which ironically crosses the very river that is home to many coracles even today. You will love it here, and the kids can even get taught how to sail one.

Cenarth Falls, Newcastle Emlyn, Carmarthenshire SA38 9JL

WWT National Wetland Centre

t: 01554 741087 e: info.llanelli@wwt.org.uk
www.wwt.org.uk/visit/llanelli

Fabulous days out!

The award-winning National Wetland Centre Wales (one of the world-famous WWT centres) is situated on the northern shore of the Burry Inlet, with stunning views over the estuary and Gower. Whether you're a serious bird watcher or just looking for fun and relaxation, you can enjoy a day of discovery, whatever the weather. Highly recommended for families. Wander amongst the beautiful, tranquil mosaic of lakes, pools, lagoons and reed beds, home to countless wild species as diverse as dragonflies and Little Egrets plus some of the world's most spectacular ducks, geese, swans and flamingos, many so tame they feed from the hand. Seasonal canoe safari and bike trails. Excellent access throughout, ample free parking for cars and coaches. Wheelchairs and mobility scooters available free of charge. Licensed café and gift shop. Group discounts and guided tours available on request. Room hire available.

The National Wetland Centre in Llanelli truly is one of the WWT's Jewels in the crown. Given a Site of Special Scientific Interest status and listed as a special protection area, it really becomes apparent why sir Peter Scott chose this very special site to play host to yet another of his wildfowl and wetland sites. As I was being shown around the Centre and site it quickly hit me how important the work WWT do. Not only do sites like this matter to the many species that call this home for various parts of the year but how important it is that we show our children how important it is to respect our environment that surrounds us. A yearly membership to all WWT's sites is available, and I'm sure as you visit some of the many sites it will soon become apparent how great value for money a yearly membership is.

Llwynhendy, Llanelli, Carmarthenshire SA14 9SH

Stradey Park Hotel

Stradey Park Hotel, Furnace, Llanelli, SA15 4HA

T: 01554 758171 www.stradeyparkhotel.com E: reservations@stradeyparkhotel.com

Tucked into the Welsh hillside, standing proud over our world famous Gower and Carmarthenshire coastline, the Stradey Park Hotel in Llanelli waits to welcome you into the family.
Prepare to be spoiled as we take great delight in making your visit the first of many. We take pride in our first class service, and have earned each one of our four stars by creating an art form out of our attention to detail. Whether you are joining us for a family break, romantic weekend or corporate event, you will find nothing is too much trouble to guarantee your comfort.

Kidwelly Farm Self-Catering Cottages and B&B

Penlan Isaf, Kidwelly, SA17 5JR

T: 01554 890 266 www.kidwellyfarmcottages.co.uk E: kidwellyfarmcottages@live.co.uk

Kidwelly Farm Cottages offer farmhouse bed and breakfast accommodation and self-catering cottages with en-suite bathrooms, wood burning stoves and exposed oak beams. Based on a beef, sheep and arable farm, the cottages overlook the ancient town of Kidwelly with its magnificent medieval castle and church. The farm has breathtaking views of the sea and countryside with a myriad of picturesque footpaths including one directly down to the town and castle. Our cottages are a perfect base to travel from to experience Carmarthenshire's many beauty spots.

Primrose Cottage

Bwthyn-y -felin, Llanqain, Carmarthen, SA33 5AH

T: 01267-236521 www.fbmholidays.co.uk/cottage-details/K000# E: millhouse.cottages@gmail.com

Primrose Cottage is idyllically situated within 6 acres of secluded meadow woodland in Dylan Thomas' Fernhill Valley, just south of Carmarthen and only 3 miles from the unspoiled estuary village of Llansteffan. The location is perfect for visiting many attractions on offer in south and west Wales, exploring castles, sea fishing, mountain biking, walking and enjoying beautiful sandy beaches. Carmarthen is a bustling market town with a good shopping centre and the friendly neighbourhood "taverns" of Llangain and Llansteffan offer excellent food. The nearest beach is at Llansteffan, 3 miles away, which is a long sandy beach with the Castle ruins on the hill above.

Jabajak Vineyard Restaurant with Rooms

Banc y llain, Llanboidy, Whitland, Carmarthenshire, SA34 0ED

T: 01994 448 786 www.www.jabajak.co.uk E: info@jabajak.co.uk

For unique bed & breakfast accommodation in West Wales, Jabajak is sure to delight - whether you are staying on business or for pleasure.
We offer friendly accommodation with wonderful food for visitors to Carmarthenshire, Pembrokeshire or Cardiganshire. Convenient to the main A40 route. Awarded Five Star status by Visit Wales & Wales in Style, Jabajak is listed along with other Welsh gems in the prestigious Welsh Rarebits collection. It is also a member of the Historic Hotels of Europe. Jabajak has a choice of ten rooms, all offering private bathrooms, comfort and relaxation at a range of tariffs.

The White Hart Inn

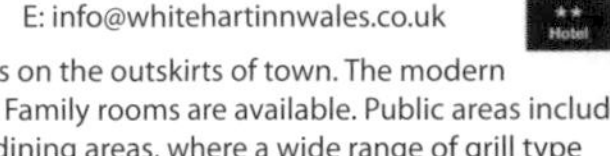

Carmarthen Road, Llandeilo, Carmarthenshire, SA19 6RS

T: 01558 823419 www.whitehartinnwales.co.uk E: info@whitehartinnwales.co.uk

This privately owned, 19th-century roadside hostelry is on the outskirts of town. The modern bedrooms are well-equipped and tastefully furnished. Family rooms are available. Public areas include a choice of bars and both smoking and non-smoking dining areas, where a wide range of grill type dishes is available. There are several function rooms, including a large self-contained suite. Local places of interest include Aberglasney Gardens and the Botanical Gardens of Wales at Middleton Hall, both of which are within 5 miles. We offer the ideal setting for a relaxing break away from it all or alternativley, overnight accommodation for that all important business trip.

The Castle Hotel

Kings Road, Llandovery, Carmathenshire, SA20 0AP

T: 01550 720343 www.castle hotel-llandovery.co.uk E: info@castle-hotel-llandovery.co.uk

Recently renovated, this traditional coaching Inn has been transformed into a stylish, warm, friendly bolthole at the heart of the thriving market town, Llandovery. The traditional bar has roaring fires and serves real ale, while the food, like the place, is simple and timeless, with a big emphasis on flavour and taste, using locally sourced quality ingredients. The 12 individually designed rooms feature rich colours, contemporary comfort and style. The original rustic charm and character of what was once a drovers inn has been fully restored with a fresh, modern touch.

The Ivy Bush Royal Hotel

Spilman Street, Carmarthen. SA31 1LG

T: 01267 235111 www.ivybushroyal.co.uk E: reception@ivybushroyal.co.uk

Commanding a spectacular position at the gateway to the Golden West, the Ivy Bush Royal has long welcomed leisure and business guests in considerable comfort and style. Once a favoured retreat for Lord Nelson and Lady Hamilton, the hotel has been sympathetically modernised to blend its old world charm with modern facilities. There are 70 comfortably furnished bedrooms, 2 family rooms and a suite. Fresh local produce is used extensively in our seasonal menus and beef from local farms feature prominently with succulent results. A comprehensive wine list complements the food with wines from all over the world and local beers are readily available.

Pant y Bas Cottage B & B

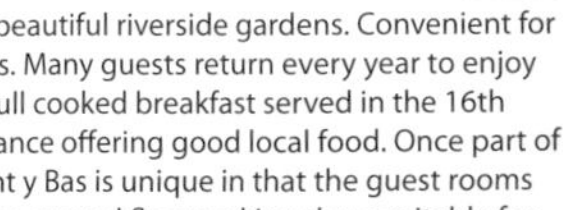

Llandeilo, Carmarthenshire, SA19 6SD

T: 01558 822809 www.southwestwalesbandb.co.uk E: annaandroy@btinternet.com

Separate ground floor quality accommodation situated in beautiful riverside gardens. Convenient for Aberglasney Gardens and national Botanic Garden of Wales. Many guests return every year to enjoy the hospitality of Anna and Roy at Pant y Bas. A generous full cooked breakfast served in the 16th century cottage.There is a friendly pub within walking distance offering good local food. Once part of the famous Dynevor Estate and now a family residence Pant y Bas is unique in that the guest rooms are purpose built in the delightful gardens and are all on the ground floor making them suitable for people with walking difficulties. Generous off road parking is situated at the back or the front of the premises. Pant y Bas has large landscaped grounds which are not overlooked. Family room available.

The Three Horse Shoes

6 High Street, Llandovery, SA20 0PT

T: 01550 721201 www.thethreehorseshoesllandovery.co.uk E: djwmorgan@hotmail.co.uk

The Three Horse Shoes sells traditional fish & chips of the best quality and offers the highest quality of service available. Our continued experience and commitment to excellence have earned us the reputation as one of the best restaurants available. At The Three Horse Shoes, you will receive the kind of quality and service in our restaurant and our take away that you would expect from such an experienced business. Our selection of food is always evolving as the needs of our customers change and you will regularly see our menu change over time. You can rest assured that you will enjoy the very best traditional local food at our premises.

Mansion House Restaurant & Rooms

Pantyrathro, Llansteffan,SA335AJ

T: 01792 894873 www. mansionhousellansteffan.co.uk info@mansionhousellansteffan.co.uk

The Tafarn Pantyrathro is the traditional Welsh Pub within Mansion House Llansteffan. The Tafarn Pantyrathro enjoys an excellent reputation as a popular eating place in Carmarthenshire, serving a delicious selection of locally sourced produce. Resident chef Anwen, prides herself on preparing and serving only the best in fresh Carmarthenshire food, served in a modern French style with a hearty dose of Welsh comfort food! Daily specials (lots of fresh local fish) feature alongside an extensive a la carte menu, children are welcome, they have a menu of their own, alternatively they may choose from the main menu at a reduced price.

Hamiltons Bar & Restaurant

11 Queen Street, Carmarthen, Carmarthenshire SA31 1JR

T: 01267 235631 www. hamiltonsbrasserie.co.uk E: info@hamiltonsbrasserie.co.uk

Established in 1960, Hamilton's is a family owned restaurant, where we have always tried to source our ingredients as locally as possible and cook your meals to order. Roast lunches are served daily, 2 course lunch & early evening menu, perfect for pre- theatre dining.Situated over two floors, there is ample room to accommodate parties, large & small. Why not have a drink in The Queens, next door – winner of CAMRA "Carmarthenshire Pub of The Year 2013"

Sosban Restaurant

North Dock, Llanelli, Carmarthenshire, SA15 2LF

T: 01554 270020 www.sosbanrestaurant.com E: reservations@sosbanrestaurant.com

Sosban, a 90 cover restaurant which serves a menu built on the best of Welsh produce in the relaxed style and dramatic surroundings of a building dominated by a 90ft stone tower that can be seen from miles around. Putting delicious things onto peoples plates and making them happy is what motivates us and the aim has been to create a restaurant which offers high standards of food but without pomp or unnecessary fuss. To eat, drink and be merry seems to us a fine and reasonable ambition and we are here to help you achieve just that.

Con Passionata

16 Nott Square, Carmarthen, Carmarthenshire, SA31 1PQ

T: 01267-243240 www.www.conpassionata.com/newsite/food-wine

In the heart of Carmarthen's old quarter, Con Passionata is a stylish brassiere. Our goal is to produce fantastic food, directly from our local producers straight to our customer's plate.The name Con Passionata comes from our passion for food, enjoyment and music. We are proud to be a Welsh restaurant with talented staff to transform your precious time into an unique dining experience. Open for lunch and dinner, Con Passionata is the right place for you.

Waverley Vegetarian Restaurant

23 Lammas Street, Carmarthen ,SA31 3AL

T: 01267-236521

Waverley Stores are an established health food shop that have been keeping their customers in and around the Carmarthen area healthy since 1847.Waverley Stores are a family run business that work as a team to cater for regular and new customers alike. We at Waverley Stores health food shop pride ourselves on offering all our customers in the Carmarthen area quality whole foods and have a regular supply of organic fruit and vegetables that help to keep you healthy. As well as our range of health foods, we can also provide our Carmarthenshire customers with various health supplements that combat everything from unwanted toxins in the system to stress.

Gwesty'r Emlyn Hotel

Bridge Street, Newcastle Emlyn, SA38 9DU

T: 01239 710317 www.gwestyremlynhotel.co.uk E: reception@gwestyremlynhotel.co.uk

Replenish in our elegant, comfortable and Michelin Recommended Bwyty'r Bont Restaurant which offers both lunch and evening menus. Lighter Bar Snacks can be enjoyed in either of our inviting bars or Lounge with a glass of wine from our extensive wine menu or a traditional pint of Real Welsh Ale. Vintage Afternoon Tea is also served throughout the afternoon in one of our stylish lounges. For larger groups of diners, Ty Nest provides an impressive setting to any social gathering or special occasion, happily seating up to 170 people.

Cafe Braz

3 King Street, Llandeilo, Carmarthenshire, SA19 6AA

T: 01558 822 034 www.cafebraz.co.uk

Cafe Braz is a great new edition to the Llandeilo high street. Serving only the best Lavazza coffee straight from Italy, fresh local produce and all cakes, pies and quiches are made either on site or locally. all that helps to make this coffee shop a great place, to either meet with friends, or if your just popping by a great place for lunch. The staff are friendly and it's easy to see why this little coffee shop is a big hit in the town.

SWANSEA & GOWER COAST

If I was writing this introduction page a few years ago you can be rest assured that it wouldn't be as many words as what it is today! Swansea over the past ten years has gone through somewhat of a facelift. With buildings going up almost every few months, this small city in Wales has now been transformed into a city that could give any city in the UK a run for its money. Now throw the Gower coast into the mix, and that is a recipe that even Gordon Ramsey or Delia could not of come up with. These areas ten years ago were nice places to visit, now ten years on, they are fabulous places to visit. Why could that be you may ask yourselves? Well let me enlighten you. The county council in Swansea along with the Gower rural district council, really have had a great vision of what is needed to bring tourists to the locality. Together with every business within the tourism sector of those areas, they have transformed that stretch of coastline into somewhere that is able to attract people from all over the world.

The area can now, not just be known for being home to notable people such and Catherine Zeta Jones and Dylan Thomas, but now be known for being one of the best places in Wales to spend your valuable holiday time. Speaking of Catherine Zeta Jones, no trip to Swansea or the Gower coast is complete until you visited the Mumbles. I have some fond memories of my time in Swansea and the Gower coast and I hope I am responsible for the fond memories your going to have once you've been there too.

Perriswood Country Pursuits

t: 01792 371661 e: info@perriswood.com
www.perriswood.com

Enjoy a day out at the Perriswood Archery and Falconry Centre!

Overlooking Oxwich Bay, under the expert tuition of qualified instructors;
Perriswood offers archery for adults and children from the age of 6 of all abilities, in a fun, safe, and interesting way. Lessons are available for 15 minutes, half an hour, or an hour. The Centre has indoor and outdoor ranges for all weather conditions. There is also a small animal park for members of the family/party who do not wish to shoot.Also popular is the 'Arrows, Talons and Tea' offer, which consists of a taster session of archery, refreshments in the coffee shop, followed by a bird of prey display where you can hold and meet these magnificent birds.
Booking for this package is essential. Half and full day bird of prey experiences are also available. Please telephone 01792 371661 for times, availability and prices. New activities are planned for 2012.
visit www.perriswood.com for details.

No trip to the Swansea area is complete without a visit to the Gower!.. Complete with blue flag beaches, unique coastlines and Catherine Zeta Jones's hometown 'The Mumbles' you'll have no time to get bored!.. But one place that needs to be on your itinerary is Perriswood Country Pursuits! Whether your looking for an indoor or an outdoor attraction, Perriswood simply has it all! From Archery to Shooting and not forgetting the Falconry Centre there is always something to keep you busy! 2012 is set to be a great year for Perriswood Country Pursuits and with their weekly pass available to everybody, you don't have to cram it all into one day.

Swansea

Perriswood Farm Penmaen, Gower, Swansea, SA3 2HN

1940's Swansea Bay

t: 01792 458864 e: mail@1940sswansea.co.uk
www.1940swanseabay.co.uk

GO BACK IN TIME AND EXPERIENCE THE 1940's!

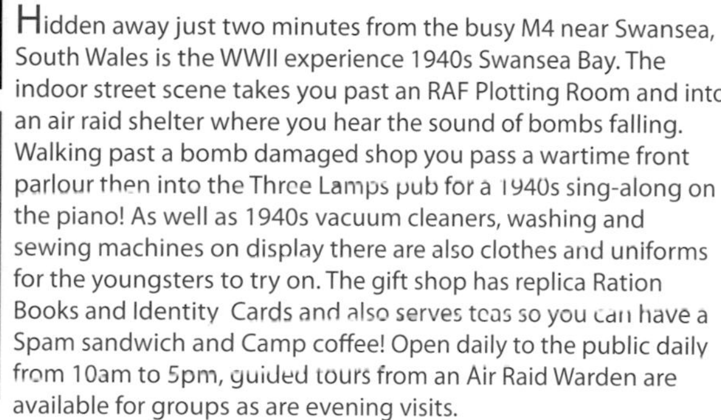

Hidden away just two minutes from the busy M4 near Swansea, South Wales is the WWII experience 1940s Swansea Bay. The indoor street scene takes you past an RAF Plotting Room and into an air raid shelter where you hear the sound of bombs falling. Walking past a bomb damaged shop you pass a wartime front parlour then into the Three Lamps pub for a 1940s sing-along on the piano! As well as 1940s vacuum cleaners, washing and sewing machines on display there are also clothes and uniforms for the youngsters to try on. The gift shop has replica Ration Books and Identity Cards and also serves teas so you can have a Spam sandwich and Camp coffee! Open daily to the public daily from 10am to 5pm, guided tours from an Air Raid Warden are available for groups as are evening visits.

Here at the 1940's Swansea Bay Museum you get to taste life and soak up the atmosphere of how life in Swansea and the rest of the UK would have been way back in the 1940's. At first when I arrived at this attraction, I was a little bit unsure of what to expect with this attraction being smack bang in the middle of an industrial estate, but the museums location really is quite fitting to the message the museum is trying to give. Complete with its own set of trenches and guard posts it is very easy to allow yourself to be transported back in time where Vera Lynn would have been at number one in the top 40 and ration books would have been just as important to you as your Gas Mask! The owners of this attraction have put everything they can into making your experience here one never to be forgotten and for that we here at Top 100 Attractions applaud them. It goes to show that it's not just money you need to create an attraction of this nature but devotion, patients and in this attractions case a love for all things 40's!

Swansea

Elba Crescent, Crymlyn Burrows, Swansea, SA1 8PT

Dynamic Rock Adventures

t: 01792 474555 e: info@dynamicrock.co.uk
www.dynamicrock.co.uk

Swansea Indoor Climbing Centre

If you're new to climbing we have a number of options to get you started. Why not book onto a taster session with one of our experienced, qualified instructors for a gentle introduction to rock climbing in the safe and comfortable environment of the indoor wall.

Indoor climbing is a fun activity for all the family, and will provide a new and exciting experience when visiting South Wales and the Gower. We also offer corporate events/team building and a great birthday party experience for kids of all ages!

Situated in Clydach, the centre is easily accessible to the whole of South Wales and is only a 4 minute drive from junction 45 of the M4. The centre has ample parking and a bus stop on its doorstep. For the more energetic of us, cycle route 43 goes directly past the centre and can be picked up at Swansea bay and on a summer's day makes a pleasant walk or run along the river Tawe.

Dynamic Rock Adventures really does live up to its name. What I liked about this attraction was its diversity. Whether you're a beginner climber visiting for a taster session or a seasoned climber looking for that next challenge, this attraction definitely has it all. But what really swung it for me and was the deciding factor in choosing Dynamic Rock for this edition of the Wales book, was the outdoor aspect to this attraction. From a wide range of outdoor activities you really are spoilt for choice. Whether it's Coasteering, Gorge Walking or in fact Abseiling, there is plenty to do for everyone. The facilities are also of a very high standard and with the inclusion of a well stocked cafe, you can leave the packed lunch at home. All in all I found Dynamic Rock Adventures to be a very slick operation indeed and certainly worth a visit.

Swansea

16-18 Hebron Road, Clydach, Swansea SA6 5EJ

Gower Coast Adventures

t: 07866 250 440 e: info@gowercoastadventures.co.uk
www.gowercoastadventures.co.uk

Join us aboard the Sea Serpent to discover the unspoilt beauty of the Gower Coast!

A family run business established in summer 2003, our aim is to provide a breathtaking, interactive tour of the South Gower Coast, leaving our passengers with unforgettable memories. Guided by professional qualified crew with excellent local knowledge, you will encounter a wealth of marine wildlife, fascinating local history (from prehistoric bone caves to tales of smugglers) and a unique thrill as we skim across the open water. With Gower being the UK's first designated Area of Outstanding Natural Beauty, the coast affords many chances to stop and take it all in. Whether to talk, take photos, watch birds and seals at play in their natural habitat or just to pause and admire the scenery that inspired Dylan Thomas in some of his most renowned poems.

There are a number of companies running boat trips around the coasts of the UK, and we have featured a couple within this book. However what makes Gower Coast Adventures one of the special ones is their modern approach to the way they run their tours. With many years experience you couldn't be in safer hands. They are also helped along by some of Wales's first class coastlines and I think they have been very clever in the locations they choose for their itineraries. From the calm waters of Port Eynon Bay to the dramatic cliffs along the Gower coast you can't help notice that Gower certainly has the 'Wow Factor'!

Swansea

Departs From: Knab Rock, Mumbles & Port Eynon Beach

Patrick's with Rooms

638 Mumbles Road, Mumbles, Swansea, SA3 4EA

T: 01792 360199 www.patrickswithrooms.com E: patrickswithrooms.com

Time is one of the most precious commodities we have so why not spend it wisely at Patricks with Rooms …in one of our 16 beautiful sea facing and individually designed en suite bedrooms which aim to offer so much more than just a night away.….relieve the stress of modern day life in our well equipped resident's gym – just packing your sports bag makes you feel so much fitter!….eat in our restaurant for a sensory explosion.….indulge in our lounge with time to sit and read the papers with your favourite tipple ….or all of the above which ever you choose we look forward to giving you…… "Seriously good food, wine, service and sleep"……

The Alexander

3 Sketty Road, Uplands, SWANSEA, SA2 0EU

T: 01792 470045 www.alexander hotel.co.uk E: reception@alexander-hotel.co.uk

At the privately owned Alexander Guest House we offer a friendly welcome to all our guests. Service is efficient with special attention given to the comfort of all guests. We have a good knowledge of the local area and can advise about the many local places of interest. The Guest House is situated on the edge of Uplands where a good range of local amenities are at hand including take-away outlets, restaurants, hair and beauty salons, a launderette, bars - everything you could possibly need for a comfortable stay. The Alexander is on the bus route to the Gower Peninsular and offer a frequent service to the city centre just 1 mile away. A prompt and reliable taxi service operates in the area and can be ordered in advance by our staff.

Fairyhills

Reynoldston, Gower,Swansea, Wales SA3 1BS

T: 01792 390139 www.postbox@fairyhill.net E: postbox@fairyhill.net

Fairyhill. A contemporary country house hotel. With an award-winning restaurant. Your comfort, our absolute priority. Sumptuous, old world surroundings, outstanding natural beauty. It's in the detail. The little things that matter. Bigger beds. Softer pillows. Crisper sheets. Warmer lighting. Way too many cushions. Luxury toiletries. Fluffy towels, changed twice daily. You want the comforts of home. But more than home. Here, there are people to do that for you. This is leisure time, play time, down time, your time. Don't live to work, work to live a little. Sleep in. Snuggle down. Kick back. Put on a CD, or a DVD or plug in your iPod. Take a long shower. Or a deep bath. Just be.

Tide Reaches Guest House

388 Mumbles Road, Mumbles, Swansea, SA3 5TN

T: 01792 404877 www.tidesreachguesthouse.com E: info@tidesreachguesthouse.com

Situated in a prominent position, overlooking the promenade, Mumbles Head and Swansea Bay. Tides Reach Bed and Breakfast is an ideal base from which to explore the village of Mumbles, the Gower and the City of Swansea and surrounding areas. All of the rooms at our bed and breakfast are decorated with a Victorian influence in keeping with this 1855 Bath House. Rooms are equipped with televisions, DVD players, broadband internet access, iron, hairdryer, alarm clock, hospitality trays and pampering kits. We offer a full Welsh breakfast to set you up for the day, or should you wish you can simply have a selection of fresh organic fruit. We cater for vegetarian and vegan breakfasts and all of our breakfast produce is sourced locally.

The Dragon Hotel

The Kingsway, Swansea, SA1 5LS

T: 01792 657100 www.dragon-hotel.co.uk E: info@dragon-hotel.co.uk

The Dragon Hotel is a Swansea landmark, centrally located and within walking distance of the city's key attractions, shops, theatre, restaurants, marina and vibrant night-life. It's also popular with golf visitors, with over 70 courses within an hour's drive of the hotel to choose from.This 4 star property offers 106 en-suite bedrooms, an award-winning restaurant and leisure facilities which include an indoor 18m pool, sauna, gymnasium and a beauty treatment room.Renowned for its friendly, helpful team, we are here to help you make the most of your visit and look forward to welcoming you during your stay in Swansea, Wales.

The Old Manse B&B

West End, Penclawdd, Swansea, SA4 3YX

T: 01792 850519 www.oldmansebandb.co.uk E: cb.manse@gmail.com

At The Old Manse Bed and Breakfast we aim to make you comfortable in our beautiful house which has original features dating back to it's origins as the minister's house for Tabernacle chapel. We aim to provide a beautiful home to stay in, with lovingly prepared food, In the beautiful area of the Gower Peninsula. The Old Manse is over one hundred years old and has retained some interesting original plasterwork, engraved glass and marble fireplaces. However it has also been updated with super new bathroom and ensuite, and new heating system providing plentiful hot water to the luxury showers We will serve you food cooked with love and care, help you to relax, and enable you to enjoy beautiful Gower.

The Windsor Lodge Hotel

Mount Pleasant, Swansea, SA1 6EG

T: 01792 642158 www.windsor-lodge.co.uk E: reservations@windsor-lodge.co.uk

Windsor Lodge Hotel offers good sized rooms with free wireless and broadband, each room is en-suite and has tea & coffee as well as a tv. We have single, double and family rooms available.There is a licensed lounge bar in the hotel for guests to relax in. Full breakfast is served in the dining room at the Windsor Lodge Hotel, and light snacks are available throughout the day. We offer a simple menu of home cooked food which guests can enjoy in a relaxed atmosphere. We have a free spacious car park and the hotel is within 5 minutes walk of the train and bus stations, making the Windsor Lodge Hotel easily accessable for most visitors to Swansea.

The Towers Hotel & Spa

Jersey Marine, Swansea, SA10 6JL

T: 01792 814155 www.towershotel.co.uk E: reception2@towershotel.co.uk

Cymru Wales Gwesty Hotel ★★★★

Our 70 en-suite bedrooms are all air conditioned with SKY TV and internet access. Three of our executive suites have private lounge areas, ideal for a small meeting or just simply a quiet, private place to relax in peace. Our award-winning Tower houses three bespoke suites, ideal for romantic getaways and special occasions such as weddings and anniversaries. Each is individually decorated with beautiful views of the expansive hotel grounds. Our Annex has 26 luxury en-suite rooms, full leisure facilities including an indoor swimming pool, sauna, steam room, jacuzzi, gymnasium and a Spa offering a full-range of treatments.

Patrick's with Rooms

638 Mumbles Road, Mumbles, Swansea, SA3 4EA

T: 01792 360199 www.patrickswithrooms.com E: reception@patrickswithrooms.com

The excitement for Patricks with Rooms food is not only the customers, it is equalled by that of the teams. Flavour, freshness and innovation are what you can expect from our menus. Early mornings you may see our team of chefs out on a field trip picking sloe berries for the Christmas menu, six months down the line, or scrambling across the rock pools for that secret location of laverbread. We have even invested in a green house and raised beds to ensure that the pea shoots are picked as and when they are needed, micro herbs are plentiful and so that the chefs can experiment with new flavours for the up and coming menus.

Billy Suttons Coffee Shop

86 Sterry Road, Gowerton, Swansea, SA4 3BW

T: 01792 873310 www.billysuttons.co.uk E: billysuttons@gmail.com

We as many over the years have sought a good, consistent coffee and during our research visited many coffee shops and coffee suppliers in South Wales and west country before deciding on our beans. Our coffee is freshly ground everyday using beans supplied by the world's leading Italian coffee producer Segafredo Zanetti. We offer a range of coffees, hot and cold beverages which can all be complimented by our cakes and savouries which are also available to take away, but why not stay with us and enjoy our hospitality and relax by the fire. We aslo offer free wifi internet connection with download and upload speeds of up to 3.6mbps and should you need to plug your laptop in to keep you working and enjoying our hospitality then we have power outlets conveniently sited throughout.

The Greyhound Inn

Oldwalls, Llanrhidian, West Glamorgan, SA3 1HA

T:01792 391027 www.thegreyhoundinnoldwalls.co.uk E: TheBar@thegreyhoundinnoldwalls.co.uk

The Greyhound is a traditional 19th century inn with a welcoming atmosphere. There is a well-stocked bar offering three or four real ales from our very own Gower Brewery. An extensive bar menu is served from noon until 9pm Monday to Saturday and 3pm to 9pm Sundays. From 12.00 until 2.30pm on Sundays a traditional roast dinner is served, with the option of a vegetarian alternative.

The food is home-cooked and, wherever possible, locally sourced. Specials at the Greyhound regularly include locally caught sea bass and Gower saltmarsh lamb.

Our two function rooms are available for hire for a range of events. Please ask for Chris or Emily and they will provide you with further details.

Fairyhills

Reynoldston, Gower,Swansea, Wales SA3 1BS

T: 01792 390139 www.postbox@fairyhill.net E: postbox@fairyhill.net

The recipe is straightforward. Imagination. Inspiration. The finest local ingredients. Welsh beef, salt-marsh lamb, sea bass and lobsters from the bays are all used when available and in season. Vegetables and herbs from our walled garden. Much from within 10 miles. A highly-skilled kitchen. Careful preparation. Perfection in execution. White linen, fine china, crystal glass. Warmth. Hospitality. You can even taste the anticipation. One of the ten best restaurants outside London, said the Daily Telegraph. Acclaimed by the Good Food Guide. Bestowed with rosettes by the AA. And no jacket required.

The Dragon Hotel

The Kingsway, Swansea, SA1 5LS

T: 01792 657159 www.dragon-hotel.co.uk E: info@dragon-hotel.co.uk

Our award-winning Dragon Brasserie, located at street level in the heart of Swansea, offers an informal and leisurely dining experience and serves a contemporary mix of European style cuisine and light bites – for which we are the proud recipients of an AA Rosette in recognition of our food.
Open daily, The Dragon Brasserie offers an impressive selection of wines, many of which can be enjoyed by the glass and which provide a perfect accompaniment to any dish. Light and airy with floor to ceiling windows, it is an ideal place to watch the world go by as you dine with friends, family or business colleagues.

The Grand Hotel

Ivey Place, High Street, Swansea, SA1 1NX

T: 01792 645898 www.thegrandhotelswansea.com E: info@thegrandhotelswansea.com

The Grand Hotel, Swansea has been a landmark hotel since the 1930's, largely due to its ideal location and unique design. In 2004 the hotel was subject to a complete re-furbishment and reopened as one of Swansea's leading independent hotels, Great attention to detail was given to insure guests are offered the very best in accommodation. The Grand Hotel Swansea offers its residents and walk in guests full breakfast service in our private dining room on the first floor over looking Swansea's historic central rail station. Our breakfast service includes an extensive cold buffet featuring fresh fruit platters, cheeses, salami's & smoked salmon. We serve an extensive bar menu from 12 – 9pm Monday through to Saturday and until 4pm Sundays.

The Towers Hotel & Spa

Jersey Marine, Swansea, SA10 6JL

T: 01792 814155 www.towershotel.co.uk E: reception2@towershotel.co.uk

We love food. And we certainly don't mind the odd drop of good wine. We are equally at home creating a sophisticated, discreet ambience and gourmet dinner for two, as we are with serving up a healthy dinner for a top sports team or a sumptuous five-star buffet for a wedding or conference. Open for breakfast, lunch and dinner seven days a week, our skilled chefs specialise in new European cuisine and traditional Welsh Fayre, using the very best in local seasonal produce delivered fresh each day. We can also confidently and creatively cater for vegetarians and those with other dietery requirements.

Gower Kitchen

39 Uplands Crescent,Swansea, SA2 0NP

T: 01792 476344 www. gowerkitchen.com E: gowerkitchen@mail.com

The Gower Kitchen is a place to meet, eat and relax, we offer a relaxed dining experience from brunch through to dinner. Open from 11am until 11pm, we offer a fantastic brunch menu, coffee and cakes all day, and lunch and dinner from our seasonal chalkboard menu using the finest local fresh produce. The retro inspired style of The Gower Kitchen ensures it is a place where you will love to hang out, the bold wallpaper, exposed brick and original features are a feast for the eyes and the quirky artwork makes sure you'll never tire of things to look at.

Oldwalls Gower

Oldwalls, Swansea, SA3 1HA
T: 01792 391468 www.oldwallsgower.com E: info@oldwallsgower.com

Oldwalls Gower offers newly renovated, luxury accommodation nestled within 50 acres of stunning grounds. Perfectly situated to explore everything Gower has to offer with an abundance of welcoming pubs, first class restaurants and beautiful beaches just minutes away, including Rhossili Bay, recently voted Britain's best beach.
The resort boasts various room types comprising of standard double/twin, superior suites and the stunning Rose suite. Rose suite boasts a private garden, balcony, hot tub and sauna.
Each room is complete with luxury en-suite facilities, flat screen TV, dressing table, tea/coffee making facilities and underfloor heating. Select rooms have their own private gardens with views of the lake. All rooms come with a fridge and free WI-FI.

SOUTH WALES VALLEYS

When one hears the words 'South Wales Valleys' the first words that always spring to everyone's minds are Rugby and Coal Mining, but the valleys are so much more than that. It is true to say that Rugby and Mining does play a part in so many lives within the valleys, but if you were to take a good look at the area, you would see that the place has so much more going for it. Rolling hills, quaint Welsh villages and some great tourist attractions really do make this part of Wales a great place to visit.

I was taken aback at how friendly people really are round there. Not that I have heard any different, but you could be forgiven for thinking, that because most people who live in the valleys are strong charactered working class people, that they could be guilty of being gruff and bad tempered. But, after visiting the area, speaking with the people who live there, it really couldn't be further from the truth. I found the people here to be absolutely fantastic and there is so much to see and do here, it wouldn't be hard at all to plan your week's holiday around all the attractions open for you to visit. With some great places to visit, some lovely accommodations to stay in, a visit to the South Wales Valleys is a must. I am already planning my next visit to the area, as not only did I visit some fantastic places that could be visited time and time again, but I also made some great friends along the way!

Llancaiach Fawr Manor

t: 01443 412248 e: info@llancaiachfawr.co.uk
www.llancaiachfawr.co.uk

History and Hauntings,Ghosts and Gardens,Celebrations & Commiserations,Weddings, Wildlife & who knows what else...

Llancaiach Fawr Manor stands proudly, as it has done since c1550, overlooking the Glamorgan uplands. It is set within a restored period garden which provides the perfect opportunity to enjoy the passing of the seasons in this tranquil location. It is where the past and the present meet.

This superbly restored gentry manor house is no ordinary heritage attraction. History here is tangible. The costumed servants of the house are living and working in 1645 and allow you to share and engage in their world. Fires crackle, candles flicker and the sounds and smells of domestic life make your visit a memorable experience of the past. It takes a moment to attune your ear to the unfamiliar speech within the Manor itself, but within seconds of your warm welcome you become immersed in the time of the Civil Wars and the cares and concerns of ordinary people living in extraordinary times.

This attraction is very unique indeed. All though It is true to say there are houses of this nature dotted all across the UK, however, very few houses exist where there past inhabitants actually come to life and are free to walk around the house as if they would have done 300 years ago. Now don't be put off when I use the term past inhabitants! Although this house is one of the 10 most haunted houses in the UK, the historic interpreters are there to give you a taste of what life would of been like back then, but what occurs during the hours of darkness is a different matter! I couldn't get over how much in character the interpreters were! The minute you walk through the door you really would think you had just stepped back many years in time! It was fascinating to hear them speak just the same type of language that would have been spoken way back in William Shakespeare's time. I loved every minute of my tour of Llancaiach Fawr and cannot wait till I return.

Caerphilly

Llancaiach Fawr Manor, Gelligaer Road, Nelson, Treharris, CF46 6ER

Big Pit

t: 01495 790311 e: bigpit@museumwales.ac.uk
www.museumwales.ac.uk

Big Pit is a real coal mine and one of Britain's leading mining museums.

Big Pit transports you back to an age when coal was king and the south Wales valleys echoed to the sound of collieries working. The centre-piece of your visit will be a trip 300ft underground on an authentic tour with an authentic miner as your guide – ask them about their experience, they all have very personal stories of working 'at the face'.
You can also get a feel for the atmosphere by taking a tour through the Mining Galleries, where a 'virtual' miner transports you forward to more modern times, and explains how a mechanised colliery works – complete with all the flashes, bangs and crashes you could expect to find underground.
Don't be fooled though, this isn't some twee romanticised view of the industry. In our award-winning exhibitions, we talk about the downside of the industry – disasters, dust, and strikes, and what does the future hold for coalfield communities and the industry.

Mining in Wales has been the biggest form of employment Wales has seen for not only decades but centuries also. Big Pit has to be one of Wales's iconic tourist attractions. Probably one of the only coal mine attractions that actually make you believe you are one of the many thousands of miners that go off to work, still to this day. You get to not only tread where they once trod, but get to don the same gear and use the same equipment that would have, and could have, saved many of hardworking lives throughout the years. Combining fun, and education, Big Pit has got it all! Allow at least half a day to visit Big Pit and the rest!

Merthyr Tydfil

Big Pit, Blaenafon, Torfaen NP4 9XP

Cheeky Monkeys

t: 01633-867578 e: info@cheekymonkeyscwmbran.co.uk
www.cheekymonkeyscwmbran.co.uk

Come and have fun at Cheeky Monkey's!

The newest & biggest soft play centre in Torfaen South Wales welcomes children for exciting indoor and outdoor play! Cheeky Monkeys is a Children's Softplay Centre situated in Fairwater, Cwmbran that has been open since January 2009. The building is newly renovated and covers a massive 9000sq ft. Cheeky Monkeys aims to provide a superior entertainment venue, with the opportunity to enjoy the adventure of play, in a relaxed family atmosphere. Cheeky Monkeys offers structured and unstructured play in a safe and stimulating environment with separate play areas for different age groups. There are 4 play zones, a toddler area, a junior area, a massive sports area and an outside play area- which includes a sand pit and paddling pool. All in all, Cheeky Monkeys offers a great opportunity for the FAMILY to interact, parents/carers can join in with their children or take the opportunity to unwind.

There are only two Children's adventure play centres featured within this book and Cheeky Monkeys has every right to be one of them. Even though the building wasn't originally built to house such a facility, it wears it like a glove. We liked Cheeky Monkeys as soon as it was put forward to us and without a doubt the children and parents that frequent the play centre on a regular or a one off occasion like it even better. The owner has put everything into this place with only one thing in mind and that is the children's enjoyment, that in her eyes always comes first. Colette the proprietor of Cheeky Monkeys and her manager Kate, have put together not only the right equipment and facilities but the right team of staff to make sure that all your precious bundles of joy are not only catered for in the right way but also kept amused for hours on end, big thumbs up from us.

Merthyr Tydfil
Cwmbran

105 Fairwater Way, Fairwater, Cwmbran, NP44 4PS

Brecon Mountain Railway

t: 01685 722988 e: enquiries@breconmountainrailway.co.uk
www.breconmountainrailway.co.uk

ONE OF THE MOST POPULAR RAILWAYS IN WALES !

Travel in one of our all-weather observation coaches behind a vintage steam locomotive through beautiful scenery into the Brecon Beacons National Park along the full length of the Taf Fechan Reservoir to Dol-y-Gaer on one of the most popular railways in Wales. At Pontsticill you can alight from the train and visit the Cafe, admire the view across the water to the peaks of the Brecon Beacons, and go for a ramble alongside the reservoir. There is a play area here for children. On your return to Pant, visit our workshop where old steam locomotives are repaired - follow the footpath to a picnic site which has an amazing panoramic view of the valley. Visit our Licensed Tearooms and buy a souvenir of your visit in our shop.

The Brecon Mountain Railway is another one of those great railways that we have featured within our book. With amazing views and stunning locations you will be spoilt for choice when pointing that camera. Obviously it would be far better to be on the train when it's a sunny day but with the route being so spectacular it really is an all-weather railway. Whether you want to start your journey in the Brecon Beacons or its main station in Merthyr Tydfil depending of course where your accommodation that evening is and coupled with the fact that the car parking facilities are so good at Merthyr, it probably makes more sense to start there, the choice is yours. But whatever you decide be sure not miss out on this great little railway line.

Merthyr Tydfil

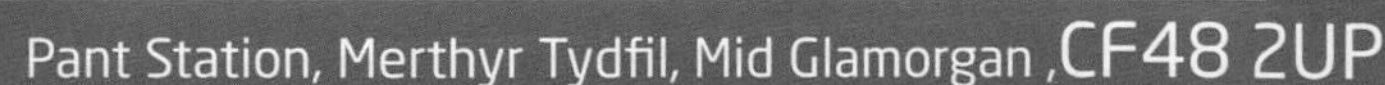

Greenmeadow Community Farm

t: 01633 647662 www.greenmeadowcommunityfarm.org.uk

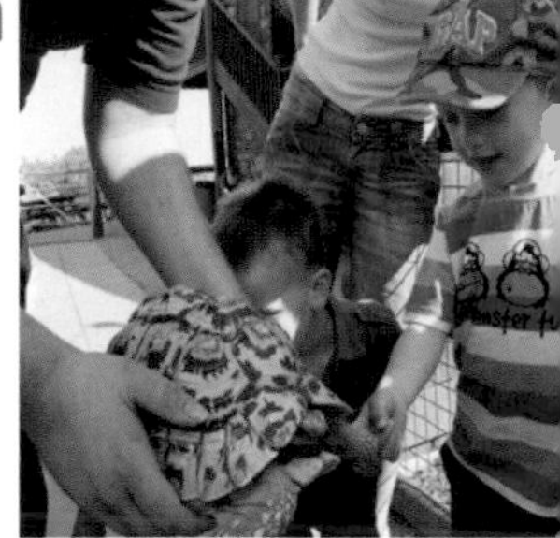

Come and explore farm life and meet some of your favourite farm animals!

Greenmeadow Community Farm has been a working farm for over 250 years. Set in over 120 acres, we have a wide range of pedigree and rare breed animals which you can come and meet up close.

We are open every day from 1st February – 23rd December, with daily tractor and trailer rides, undercover hatchery, activity room and much more! Just off the M4, nestled in the heart of Cwmbran, we are truly a Community Farm in every sense of the word, working closely with and serving the local community and welcoming visitors from far and wide.

We have a cosy farmhouse café offering kids' favourites and homemade specials. The farm shop is full of tractors and animals to take home after your visit. There really is something for everyone so come along and enjoy a fun day out with all the family.

Greenmeadow is one of those types of attractions that you think you're only going to spend a couple of hours at and then end up staying most of the day! The fact that it is a working farm as well as a popular tourist attraction really impressed me as the two things normally are not easy to combine. There is literally something always going on at Greenmeadow, whether it is a school group, children's party or one of the great community events that take place throughout the year, there's always something to get involved with and that said, it's easy to see why Greenmeadow so aptly gets its title Greenmeadow Community Farm. As I watched all the staff going about their business, it dawned on me that to the staff this isn't just a job to them they actually care so greatly for the animals and the land that surrounds them.

Merthyr Tydfil

Cwmbran

Greenforge Way, Torfaen, Cwmbran, NP44 5AJ

Caerphilly Castle

t: 029 2088 3143 e: cadw@wales.gsi.gov.uk
www.cadw.wales.gov.uk

The fortress sprawls over a huge area making it the largest castle in Wales.

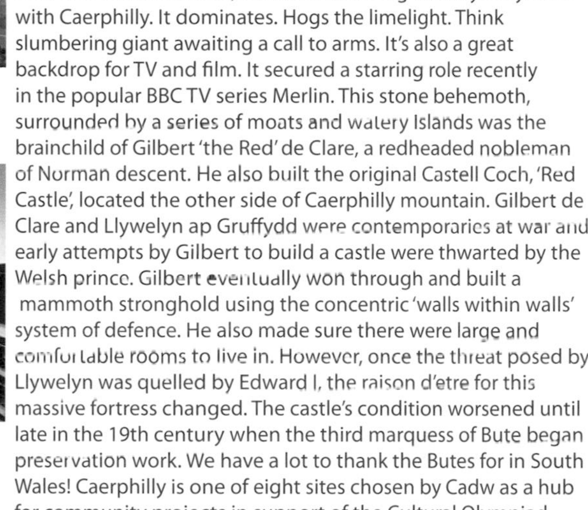

Like the famous cheese, the castle has long been synonymous with Caerphilly. It dominates. Hogs the limelight. Think slumbering giant awaiting a call to arms. It's also a great backdrop for TV and film. It secured a starring role recently in the popular BBC TV series Merlin. This stone behemoth, surrounded by a series of moats and watery Islands was the brainchild of Gilbert 'the Red' de Clare, a redheaded nobleman of Norman descent. He also built the original Castell Coch, 'Red Castle', located the other side of Caerphilly mountain. Gilbert de Clare and Llywelyn ap Gruffydd were contemporaries at war and early attempts by Gilbert to build a castle were thwarted by the Welsh prince. Gilbert eventually won through and built a mammoth stronghold using the concentric 'walls within walls' system of defence. He also made sure there were large and comfortable rooms to live in. However, once the threat posed by Llywelyn was quelled by Edward I, the raison d'etre for this massive fortress changed. The castle's condition worsened until late in the 19th century when the third marquess of Bute began preservation work. We have a lot to thank the Butes for in South Wales! Caerphilly is one of eight sites chosen by Cadw as a hub for community projects in support of the Cultural Olympiad celebrations in Wales.

Although Caerphilly castle is the second largest castle in Great Britain, second to Windsor, I personally feel, this castle has the largest character. Out of all the castles I have ever visited, I have to say, this one truly makes you feel that you have stepped back over 700 years to when this huge fortification was at its peak. You'll have to allow yourself a good few hours to see everything, making this attraction total value for money.

Caerphilly

The Twyn, Caerphilly, Mid Glamorgan CF83 1JL

Heritage Park Hotel

Trehafod,Rhondda,CF37 2NP

T: 01443 687057 www.heritageparkhotel.co.uk E: reservations@heritageparkhotel.co.uk

Rhondda people are renowned for their warm and friendly welcome. This is mirrored by Emma Jones, the General Manager of the hotel, who, together with her team constantly strive to ensure that you and your guests are made to feel comfortable when you visit their hotel and restaurant.
Unwind and Relax - The hotel offers forty-four spacious and tastefully decorated en suite bedrooms. We also offer bedrooms with interconnecting doors for families, and several larger bedrooms where an extra bed can be accommodated.

The Coach House

2 Twyn Sych, Rudry, Caerphilly, CF83 3EF

T: 029 2088 4772 www.coachhouserudry.co.uk E: enquiries@coachhouserudry.co.uk

Set in the heart of the country, with idyllic views and breath-taking scenery we have greeted travellers from around the world. For some 15 years people have enjoyed a warm welcome with comfort & value... in short - the country way. Bed & Breakfast with all the comforts of home. Continental style or Full English - the choice is yours. Our accommodation options include: Single Room (en suite/shared bathroom)- Double En-suite - Twin Rooms En-suite - Family Rooms En Suite - Private parking facilities - Pet friendly at management discretion (policy on request/pets at owners discretion after consultation)- Access policy on request.

Tai'r Bull Inn

Libanus, Brecon, Powys LD3 8EL

T: 01874 622600 www.tairbull.com E: helen@tairbull.com

As you can see, we are lucky enough to be situated in the breathtakingly beautiful Brecon Beacons National Park, an area of outstanding natural beauty in the heart of Mid Wales. We offer you a warm friendly atmosphere, five newly decorated en-suite bedrooms, delicious home-cooked food in our dining room and a great selection of refreshments, including real ales, in the Tai'r Bull bar. We offer you a warm friendly atmosphere,five newly decorated en-suite bedrooms, delicious home-cooked food in our dining room and a great selection of refreshments, including real ales, in the Tai'r Bull bar.

Blaen-Nant-Y-Groes Farm Cottages

Cwmbach, Aberdare, South Wales, CF44 0EA.

T: 01685 881457 www.bnygfarm.com E: harpers@runbox.com

On the edge of the Brecon Beacons, these 4-star stone cottages have free internet and private balconies. Blaen-nant-y-Groes Farm Cottages have a scenic location in Cwmbach, just a 15-minute drive from Merthyr Tydfil. The cosy cottages feature flag-stone floors and exposed beams, and each has a real wood-burning stove. All cottages have a private entrance and BBQ area with wonderful countryside views. Each cottage has a modern kitchen with a refrigerator, microwave and dishwasher. All Blaen-nant-y-Groes cottages feature a dining area, comfortable leather sofas and a TV. Set in 15 acres of grounds, the Blaen-nant-y-Groes Farm Cottages are a 30-minute drive from Cardiff. The Brecon Mountain Railway is a 20-minute drive away and Aberdare can be reached in a 10-minute drive.

The Blueberry Inn

6-8 Market Street, Pontypridd, South Wales, CF73 2ST

T: 01443 485 331 www.blueberryinn.co.uk E: bookings@blueberryinn.co.uk

The Blueberry Inn is a unique hotel based in the centre of Pontypridd In South Wales. Only a stones throw away from Cardiff there is great access to the Capitol of Wales by Car or Train. The Blueberry will blow you away with it's attention to detail and design. All the room are fully equipt with all the mod cons and have all the comfort's you would expect from a top end hotel. The building itself is host to a superb bar and kitchen, along with a lounge function room. On the whole the Blueberry Inn is a real gem in the heart of the Valley's.

Nant Ddu Lodge Hotel, Bistro & Spa

Cwm Taf, Merthyr Tydfil, CF48 2HY.

T: 01685 379111 www.nant-ddu-lodge.co.uk E: manager@nant-ddu-lodge.co.uk

Welcome to our 3-Star country hotel nestled in the heart of the Brecon Beacons. Use us as a base to enjoy the beauty of the local area and make yourselves at home. Treat yourself to a pampering experience in our spa and enjoy the freshest local food in our bustling bistro or bar. Nant Ddu is an informal, yet professional retreat in which to relax, unwind and enjoy the best South Wales has to offer. Our hotel is unfussy and has a friendly, inviting atmosphere. We think that our down to earth approach combined with comfortable surroundings creates a special, memorable place to stay.

Bessemer Hotel

Hermon Close,Dowlais, Merthyr Tydfil, CF48 3DP

T: 01685 350780 www.bessemerhotel.co.uk E: sales@bessemerhotel.co.uk

the Bessemer Hotel, a new and vibrant establishment that looks to set new standards in the hotel industry. Whether you are a carefree traveller or business-person with a tight schedule the Bessemer can cater for your every need and offer you that 'little extra'. Our Carvery and Grill lets you choose the size of your meal. The bedrooms here at the Bessemer Hotel are among the finest to be found in Hotels anywhere and we can assure you that your stay with us will be a pleasant one. The Bessemer Hotel can offer you outstanding facilities that are second to none. Free WIFI is now available!

The Bunk Barn

Pantcefnyffordd, Church Road, Penderyn, CF44 9JR

T: 01685 811789 www.thebunkbarn.com E: info@thebunkbarn.com

The bunkbarn is located in the village of Penderynwithin the Brecon Beacons National park. The barn is an ideal base for exploring the Brecon Beacons & South Wales, and is in within easy reach of Brecon, Swansea and Cardiff.Four Star accommodation is available for small and large groups (including disabilities). The old granary has been completely renovated to the highest of standards. It has been awarded four stars by the Wales Tourist Board and provides accommodation for up to 16 people. (larger groups may be possible - please contact us) Pantcefnyffordd is a working Welsh Hill farm. We mainly farm sheep and cattle but also have horses, chickens, ducks, dogs, cats and even peacocks!

The Bunch of Grapes

Ynysangharad Rd Pontypridd, Mid Glamorgan CF37 4DA

T: 01443 402934 www.bunchofgrapes.org.uk E: info@bunchofgrapes.org.uk

We like to think the Bunch of Grapes is how a great pub should be, a friendly welcoming bar serving award winning ales ciders and bottle beers in front of a roaring log fire with a restaurant attached that also serves award winning food. Using locally sourced seasonal produce with creativity and flair but without pretence.A pub where you are likely to walk in to beer festival one day with a Welsh choir in full voice and return another to find a Welsh cheese and cider festival in the main bar. Where you can enjoy a home made pie and mash in the bar with a pint of Welsh ale while cheering on the Welsh rugby and then return with friends to a fine dining meal in the restaurant .

Alfred's Bar & Grill

3/4 Market St, Pontypridd, CF37 2ST

T: 01443 404060 www.alfreds-bar-and-grill-pontypridd.co.uk E: alfredsgrill@yahoo.co.uk

Alfred's is a spacious complex set over two floors. The style is modern Manhattan with exposed steel beams, strip-oak flooring and bespoke contemporary artwork. A large atrium with glass balcony welcomes you, adorned with sofa lounge and fireplace. In Alfred's the main focus of the design was to create an enjoyable, stress-free environment. The downstairs bar has a plentiful array of beers, wines and cocktails, along with the 'Deli Menu' lunchtime option.Upstairs opens out into a large dining area with a central, open-plan grill kitchen. Customers are able to choose from the great selection fish and meat at the counter, even down to the size and weight.

Bella Capri Italian Restaurant

25 Ton-y-Felin, Caerphilly, CF83 1PA

T: 029 20869612 www.bellacapri.co.uk E: info@bellacapri.co.uk

We opened the Bella Capri in June 2002 and have worked hard to provide fine cuisine in a warm, informal and family friendly atmosphere. Our restaurant is perfect for romantic meals, noisy get-togethers or more formal business meetings. We are able to cater for large parties and we are a popular location for a wide variety of occasions. We can cater for engagement & wedding parties, company functions, birthdays etc. In fact, we can make any occasion special for you.

You will be able to choose many dishes inspired by our homeland, the beautiful Island of Capri as well as popular Italian dishes from other parts of Italy.

Heritage Park Hotel

Trehafod,Rhondda,CF37 2NP

T: 01443 687057 www.heritageparkhotel.co.uk E: reservations@heritageparkhotel.co.uk

Rhondda people are renowned for their warm and friendly welcome. This is mirrored by Emma Jones, the General Manager of the hotel, who, together with her team constantly strive to ensure that you and your guests are made to feel comfortable when you visit their hotel and restaurant. The Loft Restaurant is not typical of a modern hotel but once again reflects tradition and heritage. The intimate atmosphere, enhanced by the beamed features, provide an ideal setting for that 'Special Occasion' or quiet romantic meal. Many of the timbers originated from an old wharf warehouse on the waterfront of Cardiff docks.

The Maenllwyd Inn

Rudry, Caerphilly, Mid Glamorgan, CF83 3EB

T: 02920 882372 www.chefandbrewer.com E: paulburwood@aol.com

A charming, traditional pub restaurant in a contemporary style. We are proud to offer freshly prepared pub food and high quality drink at great value, served by our welcoming and friendly staff.
Whether you are a cask ale fan, love a chilled glass of white wine or a freshly ground cup of coffee, we will serve you in comfort. Great for a meal with family or friends or a romantic meal for two, our menu and daily changing specials will delight all palates and appetites.

The Irish Tymes Bar & Restaurant

Cardiff Road, Caerphilly, CF76 8LD

T: 029 20876543 www.theirishtymes.co.uk E: info@theirishtymes.co.uk

The Irish tymes was established in June 2008 when opened by Terry and Tracey Burton, predominantly as a music and sports bar for the over 25's. The Irish Tymes has a large bar area, resturaunt, live bands & events, a function room, and is fully Wi-Fi enabled.
Whether its a light Lunch, a hearty dinner, a celebration or get together, the Irish Tymes menu caters for all. We are now also open at 9am for breakfast.

Tai'r Bull Inn

Libanus, Brecon, Powys LD3 8EL

T: 01874 622600 www.tairbull.com E: helen@tairbull.com

As you can see, we are lucky enough to be situated in the breathtakingly beautiful Brecon Beacons National Park, an area of outstanding natural beauty in the heart of Mid Wales. We offer you a warm friendly atmosphere, five newly decorated en-suite bedrooms, delicious home-cooked food in our dining room and a great selection of refreshments, including real ales, in the Tai'r Bull bar. We offer you a warm friendly atmosphere,five newly decorated en-suite bedrooms, delicious home-cooked food in our dining room and a great selection of refreshments, including real ales, in the Tai'r Bull bar.

Nant Ddu Lodge Hotel, Bistro & Spa

Cwm Taf, Merthyr Tydfil, CF48 2HY.

T: 01685 379111 www.nant-ddu-lodge.co.uk E: manager@nant-ddu-lodge.co.uk

We are incredibly proud of our produce, food and customer care here at the Lodge. The team in the kitchen & restaurant strive endlessly to provide the best possible cuisine and service which have guests & locals coming back time and time again. You'll find the freshest ingredients cooked with simplicity and style. The result is a mouthwatering menu of local foods bursting with natural flavours. Our vibrant and down-to-earth bistro is a hit with guests and locals alike. Our relaxed, informal style sets the perfect tone for a night of good food, fine wines and a fun, enjoyable atmosphere.

Ogmore Valley Waterfall Walk

Directions

From Cardiff, take the A470 to the Pontypridd junction, and follow signs for the Rhondda Valleys and Rhondda Heritage Park. This should take you through the mess of the A4058. Once past Pontypridd, ignore signs for the Rhondda Heritage park, and just stick with the A4058, all the way to Treorchy. From Treorchy, at an understated junction by The Stag pub, turn left onto the A4061, signposted to Bridgend. Not long after passing the station, turn left onto the A4061 again. Not far along here, turn right, again onto the A4061, again signposted to Bridgend. The road climbs up the ridge via some impressive hairpin bends. Just as you approach the top, at a junction with the A4107, parking is on the left. SS 9394 9459. If needed, there is additional parking slightly further on, and some more on the A4107.

If you are only planning on viewing the waterfalls from the road, continue along the A4061 past the next sharp bend, down into the next valley. As the road does one of the most extreme hairpin bends in Wales, the waterfalls are on the crags above the road. SS 9271 9471.

Route

For the walking route, take the path heading up the grassy bank on the left side of the A4107, and follow it to pick up the path running along the top of the Craig Ogwr cliffs, above the continuing A4061 (not the off-roader tracks that head away from the cliffs). Follow the path to the end of Craig Ogwr, where the Tarren Rhiw-maen Falls can be seen tumbling down the Tarren Rhiw-maen cliffs. After the path crosses a stream, it heads away from the cliffs, crossing fields to arrive at a dirt track (or if you arrive at the A4107, you went too far to the right - follow the A4107 to reach the dirt track). Turn left and follow the dirt track. When it splits, take the left-most branch, and follow it to a corner, then turn right. This gives some good views over Blaengarw.

The track ends and a path continues to reach another path running along the ridge, where you can continue onwards to the next hill if desired. Turning right leads via the masts on the top of Werfa back to the track junction. Follow the track back to the road. Turn right and follow the road back to the parking area, passing superb views over the Graig Fâch and Graig-fawr scarps. (Optionally, as the road passes at its closest to the scarp edge, you may be able to use the off-roader tracks on the right to head back to the parking areas.)

GLAMORGAN'S COAST & COUNTRYSIDE

Home to the most Southerly point in Wales, people have been visiting and living in the Vale of Glamorgan and its surrounding areas for 200,000 years now, once visited, it's not hard to see why! Still, not without seeing its fair share of hard times however, that hasn't stopped this area becoming a fantastic tourist destination. I think the fact that the BBC has filmed its present two series of its hit show 'Being Human' coupled with 'Gavin & Stacy' also being filmed in the seaside town of Barry, only goes to show that this area of Wales really has got what it takes to pull the tourists in from further and now wider areas.

The outstanding yellow-grey cliffs on the Glamorgan Heritage Coast which stretches in-between Llantwit Major to Ogmore by the Sea are unique only to the Celtic seaboard (Cornwall, Wales, Ireland and Brittany) as they are formed of Liassic limestone - totally unique for a Celtic nation. They were formed 200 million years ago when Wales (as well as Cornwall and Ireland) lay below a warm, shallow, equatorial sea during the start of the Jurassic period. In the present day the cliffs contain elements of Jurassic age sea-creatures (although not land dinosaurs - the Celtic nations were all underneath the sea), such as ammonites.

I do not think you need any more convincing that the Vale of Glamorgan has its fair share of stories, places to see and things to do than any other place in Wales. What makes this place so unique however is its versatility to be a great place of history, an amazing outdoor pursuit's area, or just simply somewhere to unwind and take it all in! Whatever you choose to do, Glamorgan has to be on your itinerary of places to visit whilst visiting the great country of Wales.

GoApe - Margam Country Park

t: 0845 643 92 15 e: info@goape.co.uk
www.goape.co.uk

LIVE LIFE ADVENTUROUSLY!

Go Ape is the UK's number one tree-top adventure. Head to Go Ape!
Margam, nr Port Talbot for two to three hours in the trees, taking on zip wires, Tarzan swings, rope ladders and a variety of high-wire crossings, all set in the UK's most beautiful forests. There are now 27 Go Ape courses dotted around the UK, which means there's one near you. No two courses are the same so if you've been before, check out another site for a whole new adventure. And bring your Tribe!

We've talked about Margam Country Park in this book before, as the park is also featured as one of the Top 100 Attractions, but nestled perfectly between the trees at Margam is 'Go Ape' This popular nationwide phenomenon is enjoyed by people of all ages, and once you've actually visited there, it becomes ever so apparent why! A state of the art rope works course is what you'll find, with an intricate network of Crossings and Zips, and the longest zip wire (167m) to contend with and that's just for starters. If you haven't got a head for heights like me then do not worry! Go Ape's team of trained staff are always on hand to guide you through the course and get you safe to the other side!

Margam Country Park,Port Talbot, South Wales ,SA13 2TJ

Gavin & Stacey Tour

t: 0844 2471 007 e: info @britmovietours.com
www.britmovietours.com

Come and see what's occurring in Barry Island

Come and see what's occurring in Barry Island with Dave's Coaches on the Official Gavin and Stacey Tour. Tour the locations in the original vehicle used by Dave's Coaches in the TV show and visit the home of Stacey, the arcade where Nessa works at and the church where she nearly gets married to Dave and much more. The tour is a great way to see the Island and its surrounding areas as our guide shows you the sites from the hugely popular TV show. As tour guests you will have an exclusive opportunity to sit in Nessa's chair in the Amusement arcade when making a purchase, sit in Dave's seat on the Dave's Coaches bus and get discounts at some of the vendors on the seafront. You'll also have opportunities to stop, take pictures and see the locations up close.

I personally love the series of Gavin & Stacy as do millions of people in not only this country, but many countries over the world. So when I heard about this tour, I thought I would sceptically investigate more! Boy was I in for a shock! I learned that this tour coach has changed the face of tourism in Barry for ever and no trip there would be complete without taking this tour. They take you round all the favourite locations and you will learn many things you didn't already know about the show! In my opinion this tour is one of the best TV tours out there and on that basis worth every penny! But the Gavin & Stacy tour isn't the only tour they do, so check out their website above, for information about their complete itinerary.

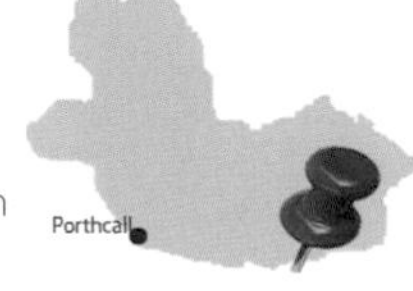

Brit Movie Tours Ltd, 18 St James Road, Sutton, Surrey, SM1 2TP

Fonmon Castle

t: 01446 710206 e: fonmon_castle@msn.com
www.fonmoncastle.com

Magical heritage property in Vale of Glamorgan!

Fonmon is one of the few mediaeval castles which are still lived in as a home. Since it was built by the St. John family c1200, it has only changed hands once. In 1656, during the English Civil War it was bought by Colonel Philip Jones, a direct ancestor of Sir Brooke Boothby, the present owner.

Today Fonmon welcomes visitors in many different ways both as a wedding and events venue and through Public opening and tours:

The Castle is open to the Public from April to September. There is no need to book. Public opening times for individuals, families and groups of less than twelve are on Tuesdays and Wednesdays between midday and 5pm. Public guided tours are at 2pm, 3pm and 4pm. Access to the garden and grounds is free.

Last entrance to the garden is at 4pm.

Assistance dogs only allowed.

Wales is one of those one of countries that has an abundance of natural tourist attractions as well as many great man made attractions. But in amongst all of them are some hidden gems to uncover, that's where my book comes in very handy as I have already done the job for you. One of those hidden gems that I speak so much about is Fonmon Castle. Usually in the UK, castles of the thirteenth century are in ruins and are being cared for by CADW or the English Heritage, not Fonmon though! One of the many amazing things about this property is the fact it has remained in the same family for over 700 years. Tours around this property only take place on Tuesdays and Wednesdays ordinarily, however for groups of twelve or more, arrangements can be made. I really loved my tour here at Fonmon, you will to!

Porthcall

Fonmon, Nr Barry, Vale of Glamorgan, CF62 3ZN

The Welsh Hawking Centre

t: 01446 734687 e: Jamie@welsh-hawking.co.uk
www.welsh-hawking.co.uk

Why Don't You Pop Down! For a Super Day Out!

Situated in 25 acres of scenic parkland, with ample car parking, a souvenir shop, and light refreshments available in the Cafe during the Summer Season. Visitors are welcome to picnic on our tables in the large mown grass areas of the park. At the Welsh Hawking Centre you will see over 200 Bird of Prey including Eagles, Owls, Hawks, Falcons and Buzzards. They can be seen and photographed in the mews, weathering ground, breeding and if you are fast enough, flying! We also have rabbits, chickens and chicks for the young and not so young to touch, smell and feed. This is very important for children to learn to love animals in latter life. We pride ourselves on the personal contact we have with our visitors, so please ask any of the staff any questions or help you may need.

Sitting on the site that was once the great Cardiff Zoo, is the Welsh Hawking Centre. Don't be deceived by the name though as Hawks are not all you will find here! This attraction has gone from housing many famous animals from all over the world to now being the home of just over 200 birds of prey. But it doesn't just stop there as there are many other animals running around from rabbits to guinea pigs, ducks, geese and rabbits all roaming around and very friendly. As I was being shown round this great attraction it was so clear to see the love the owners have for all of their birds and animals. But with bigger plans and new things being added all the time a visit here is worth every penny.

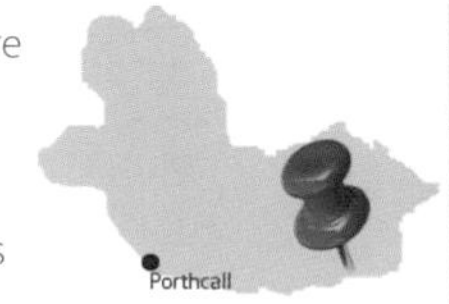

Weycock Rd, Barry, Vale Of Glamorgan, CF62 3AA

Margam Country Park

t: 01639 881635 e: margampark@npt.gov.uk
www.margamcountrypark.co.uk

ENJOY A GREAT DAY OUT!

Margam Country Park is an historic country estate which offers outstanding countryside with breathtaking views, heritage features and a range of visitor attractions. Our Fairytale land brings nursery rhymes alive, the adventure playground is a must for children of all ages. Jump aboard the Margam Train for a trip through the Parkland. Discover the rare breeds on the farm trail. Spot the famous Margam Deer, the largest herd of Fallow Deer in South Wales.
Admire the eighteenth century Orangery and the impressive mansion house or enjoy a picnic by our tranquil lake.

Margam was the original site for a cistercian monastery, then being acquired after the dissolution of all monasteries in the UK in 1540 became the family seat of Sir Rice Mansell. Its now however home to Margam Country Park, and plays host to another one of our Top 100 Attractions 'Go Ape'. As I walked around the estate I could easily of been walking round the grounds of Hogwarts of 'Harry Potter' fame. With Deer walking within yards away from where I stood its easy to see why this park has made it into our Top 100 list. With remains of the abbey still intact it's no wonder why people like to spend all day here. Entrance into the park is totally free but there is a small car parking fee. But no matter what, a visit around the park for the day is priceless.

Porthcall

Margam Country Park,Port Talbot, South Wales ,SA13 2TJ

The Fairways Hotel

West Drive, Porthcawl, Glamorgan, CF36 3LS

T: 01656 782 085 www.thefairwayshotel.co.uk E: reception@thefairwayshotel.co.uk

All rooms have king size beds which can be adapted to suit families or twin rooms.Recently redecorated, the rooms, all en-suite, ensure comfort as well as practicability.
Each room also has access to high-speed Broadband Internet allowing you to keep in touch with families and friends at the click of a mouse. Each room is equipped with a TV and Tea and Coffee making facilities. You will find our accommodation is ideal for a golfing weekend break, call us to book in your touring party or golfing society as we have access to some of the best golf courses in South Wales.

Y Bwthyn Bach Self Catering Cottage

Welsh St. Donats, Cowbridge, Vale of Glamorgan, CF71 7ST

T: 01446 774451 www.bydd.co.uk E: enquiries@bydd.co.uk

Stay at the holiday cottage Y Bwthyn Bach lying in the heart of beautiful Vale countryside where peace and tranquility abound. The ground floor accommodation comprises of an open plan lounge, well equipped kitchen, spacious bathroom and a bedroom (twin or double bedded). The rear door leads to a patio and attractive garden. Located 11 miles from Cardiff and 3 miles from the historic town of Cowbridge it makes an ideal touring base for Southern Wales. Short breaks available.

Stockwood Apartments

63 High Street, Cowbridge, CF71 7AF

T: 01446 774814 www.bearhotel.com E: enquiries@bearhotel.com

Combine the comfortable surroundings and friendly atmosphere of the privately owned 3 star Bear Hotel with the privacy of our luxurious Stockwood Apartments and exclusive Two-bedroom Stockwood Cottage. Situated a short walk from the hotel in the centre of Cowbridge with easy access Into Cardiff City Centre, these exceptional properties are ideal for a long stay or for a relaxed 'home from home' feeling. Although these properties are fully equipped for a self-contained and self-sufficient stay, guests are still more than welcome to use the Hotel's Restaurant and Bar Facilities. Breakfast is also served in the Hotel Restaurant as an optional extra.

Hazelwood Guest House

Tondu Road, Bridgend, South Wales, CF31 4LJ

T: 1656 647780 www.hazelwood-house.co.uk E: info@hazelwood-house.co.uk

Purpose built in 2008 our luxury guest house, minutes from Bridgend town centre, has received the highest reviews on Tripadvisor by our guests. Designed with the guest in mind, and offers the highest standard of accommodation in Bridgend similar to you would expect to find at a quality hotel.
Built to Gold Business Standard and having received our four star rating, our guest house offers accommodation in eight spacious en-suite bedrooms, a discrete dining room and a lounge area housed in the conservatory. Residents also have access to the carefully tended garden which is set in 2.5 acres of natural parkland alongside the river.

Blanco's Hotel & Restaurant

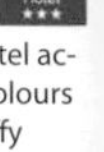

Green Park,Port Talbot, SA12 6NT

T: 01639 864500 www.blancoshotel.co.uk E: info@blancoshotel.co.uk

Blanco's Hotel offers spacious and inviting surroundings, designed to offer guests the best in hotel accommodation. All 65 rooms are beautifully appointed, tastefully decorated in muted, relaxing colours and heavenly beds are adorned with crisp, fresh, white bed linen. Generous bathrooms with fluffy towels all combine to create a real feeling of a luxurious home from home. Whether your looking for comfortable accommodation for the night or a sophisticated venue for a meal or wedding function Blanco's Hotel and Restaurant, is Port Talbot's smartest place to eat, drink, relax and stay.

The Bear Hotel

63 High Street,Cowbridge,CF71 7AF

T: 01446 774814 www.bearhotel.com E: enquiries@bearhotel.com

The Bear has origins as far back as the 12th Century. Probably best known as being the inn where they changed the horses on the mail run from Cardiff to Swansea. During the 18th Century Napoleon's troops were held in the ëBear Pití en route to London after a failed invasion at Fishguard!! This famous Coaching Inn is steeped in history. Nowadays, this privately owned 3 star hotel is famed for itís fine home cooked food, friendly atmosphere and really good ale. The Bear Hotel Cowbridge is just 20 minutes away from Cardiff city centre and the Cardiff Bay development, making it an ideal base to visit Europe's fastest growing city for art, culture, shopping and entertainment.

Foam Edge Guest House

9 West Dr, Porthcawl, Bridgend, CF36 3LS

T: 01656 782866 www.foam-edge.co.uk E: hywelandhelen@aol.com

Located prime position on seafront, overlooking the Bristol Channel, North Devon & Swansea Coastlines. Easily accessible from junction 37 of the M4. Cardiff International Airport 35 mins. drive. Ideal location for golfers, walkers, cyclists, fishing, surfing, masses of local history.
A place to relax and enjoy yourself. Established in 2000, the house has been refurbished to a high standard. All rooms offer en suite facilities, Private off-road parking on forecourt. We have an extensive breakfast menu with most dietary requirements can be catered for.

Bryn-Y-Ddafad Guest House

Welsh St. Donats, Cowbridge, Vale of Glamorgan, CF71 7ST

T: 01446 774451 www.bydd.co.uk E: enquiries@bydd.co.uk

Bryn-y-Ddafad is set in a peaceful rural location surrounded by rolling countryside 5 minutes from the M4 and within easy reach of Cardiff. Comfortable, flexible accommodation suitable for the needs of tourists and business travelers. Ground floor annex with self catering option. Scrumptious breakfast with vegetarian options. Free off road parking and free Wi-Fi. Walkers, golfers and cyclists welcome. Laundry service. Lovely NGS approved garden. Visit our website for availability, a video and special offers where you may book on-line.

Poco Poco Mediterranean Restaurant

14 Wyndham Street, Bridgend CF31 1EF

T: 01656 667999 www.pocopoco.co.uk E: info@pocopoco.co.uk

Poco Poco Tapas Bar and Continental Restaurant offers an unrivalled dining experience with a European atmosphere. Friendly and relaxed, the Mediterranean ambience provides the perfect setting for a romantic meal or a get-together amongst friend. A fusion of continental flavours can be found in our tapas selection, a la carte menu and daily specials. Our range of vibrant and sumptuous Tapas draw influence from around the globe. Alternatively, the a la carte menu boasts an array of delicious dishes, such as chargrilled sea bass with chilli infused butter and a pesto dressing. We are sure Poco Poco offers a dining experience unlike any other in Bridgend.

The Huntsman Restaurant

Station Road , Dinas Powys, Vale of Glamorgan, CF64 4DE

T: 029 2051 4900 www.thehuntsmanrestaurant.co.uk E: info@thehuntsmanrestaurant.co.uk

The restaurant is stylish and comfortable with modern original canvas artwork as well as an intriguing collection of stoneware hot water bottles along the beams in the dining area.This charming barn conversion can be found in old Dinas Powys, tucked away behind the Star Inn, sharing the ample car parking facilities.Chef, Hilary changes the menu every couple of months and always features Welsh meat and game, simply prepared with a variety of sauces, all freshly cooked to order. Evenings: Wednesday through to Saturday from 6.30p.m. Lunch Times: Thursday to Saturday from 12p.m - 2pm Sunday - 12 - 2.30pm. Closed all day Monday and Tuesday. Closed Sundays through July, August and September.

The Prince of Wales Inn

Ton Kenfig, Bridgend, CF33 4PR

T: 01656 740 356 www.princekenfig.co.uk E: prince_of_wales@btconnect.com

Set on the edge of the beautiful Kenfig Nature Reserve on the South Welsh coast, this magnificent 16th Century family run Pub is steeped in history, character and charm.

With panoramic views of the Bristol Channel and Gower Peninsula, The Prince Of Wales Inn is open throughout the year and is the ideal place for great food, great beer and good times. The upstairs room at the Prince of Wales is available to hire for all functions: Birthday parties / Christenings Funerals (sympathetically arranged), Theme Nights, Hog Roasts ,Video Horse racing ,Charity Raising Events, Conference Meetings, Hot or Cold buffet available.

Cefn Mably Hotel

1 Lavernock Road, Penarth, Vale of Glamorgan, CF64 3NW

T: 02920-706473 www.cefnmablyhotel.co.uk E: info@cefnmablyhotel.co.uk

Cefn Mably Hotel is easily reachable from M4 and Cardiff Airport. The Hotel is located very near Penarth center and just 10 minutes drive to Cardiff City Center, Millenium Stadium as well as Cardiff's biggest shopping centre John Lewis.

If you wish to visit Millenium Opera or relax and enjoy a chic, cosmopolitan atmosphere at Cardiff Bay Mermaid Quay it is also 10 minutes drive from the Cefn Mably Hotel.

You can enjoy tranquility sea views from Penarth Pier or just stay behind for a drink and a meal at Cefn Mably Pub.

Blanco's Hotel & Restaurant

Green Park,Port Talbot, SA12 6NT

T: 01639 864500 www.blancoshotel.co.uk E: info@blancoshotel.co.uk

Whether your looking for comfortable accommodation for the night or a sophisticated venue for a meal or wedding function Blanco's Hotel and Restaurant, is Port Talbot's smartest place to eat, drink, relax and stay. Blanco's may be one destination, but the cuisine you'll sample here will take your taste buds on a trip around the world. The spacious contemporary restaurant, with its intimate booths, is perfect for enjoying a simple, informal lunch, an afternoon tea away from the town just outside the door, or a relaxing post-work drink. Seasonal and innovative menus blend British & European cuisine. Succumb to a mouth-watering Traditional Sunday Roast, home cooked to perfection.

Isabella's Restaurant

9-10 Well Street, Porthcawl, Bridgend, CF36 3BE

T: 01656 782330 www.braseria-isabellas.co.uk

Recently refurbished and with the addition of new wheelchair friendly access and bathroom faciities. Isabella's Tapas Bar and Spanish Restaurant offers an unrivalled dining experience with a European atmosphere. Friendly and relaxed, the Mediterranean ambience provides the perfect setting for a romantic meal or a get-together amongst friend.A fusion of continental flavours can be found in our tapas selection, a la carte menu and daily specials. Our range of vibrant and sumptuous Tapas draw influence from around the globe. Seafood lovers can take their pick from a daily selection of fresh fish, while meat eaters enjoy an impressive choice of sauces to compliment their fillet or sirloin steak, that includes creamy dolche late to spicy piccante for the more adventurous.

The Market Place

66 The High Street, Cowbridge, CF71 7AH

T: 01446 774 800 www.the-marketplace.co.uk E: enq@the-marketplace.co.uk

Our restaurant is set in one of the most historic buildings in Cowbridge which exudes a timeless atmosphere. The original house was built onto the medieval town walls adjacent to the West Gate, which is now our restaurant. The log fire still burns on those cold winter nights.
We look forward to welcoming you to our restaurant to enjoy our food and excellent wine selection in a special atmosphere.

The Watermill Country Pub

Ogmore-By-Sea, Nr Bridgend, Vale of Glamorgan, CF32 0QP

T: 01656 650562 www.watermillogmore.com E: watermill@sabrain.com

Our restaurant is set in one of the most historic buildings in Cowbridge which exudes a timeless atmosphere. The original house was built onto the medieval town walls adjacent to the West Gate, which is now our restaurant. The log fire still burns on those cold winter nights. The Watermill menu changes regularly using the finest seasonal ingredients to create interesting and comforting dishes. Our wide ranging and ever changing menu features dishes such as Roast ham hock & sticky cider sauce with caramelized apple and Chicken breast wrapped in pancetta. We also have an excellent choice of wines available to accompany your meal ñ and wide choice is also available by the glass.

WYE VALLEY & VALE OF USK

I have to be totally honest with you when writing this piece, that before going to visit some of the great places within this section of the book, I had never visited the Wye Valley area before. I knew of and had heard about the places that make up both the Wye Valley and the Vale of Usk but didn't know that collectively that that's what they were called. But I can honestly say with true conviction that once visited, these places are certainly not places to be forgotten in a hurry. There are so many historical connections with this area of Wales and that can be readily seen in our selection of tourist attractions for this section of the book. From museums to castles, magical gardens to stately homes and a historical ship thrown in for good measure, this area is steeped in that much history, you'll begin to forget which year your now in.

Although they are not mentioned as one of the Top 100 Attractions in Wales, Chepstow racecourse is a huge pull to the area, along with its sister racecourse Ffos Las in Camarthenshire they make up most of the Welsh race meetings. I mention this only because for decades this racecourse has continued to bring people from all over the UK to its race meetings, and I didn't want you to think that it was only historical events or places that the Wye Valley was renowned for. For centuries now people have seen the Wye valley as a very special place, they have taken to boating holidays and trips up the Wye river in their millions so much so, that now the Wye river has been given the status nationally as a Special Area of Conservation.

Abergavenny Museum

t: 01873 854282 e: abergavennymuseum@monmouthshire.gov.uk
www.abergavennymuseum.co.uk

FROM PREHISTORIC TO THE PRESENT DAY!

Abergavenny Museum is set in the grounds of a 'ruined' Norman Castle, where you can enjoy a picnic during the summer and spectacular views on colder days. The collections are of local significance, with particular emphasis on costume, rural life, agriculture, domestic and working life.
We have six display areas. The Keep Gallery which tells the History of Abergavenny from Prehistory to the present day. A World War II Air Raid Shelter, Saddlers Shop, Welsh Kitchen and Basil Jones' Grocery Shop. Our temporary exhibitions which change three or four times per year, take place in our recently refurbished gallery.
You can discover more about the castle using our family backpacks, which are free to use. In addition we run a program of events and educational activities to suit all interests. Please visit our website for up to date details. 'Follow' us on Twitter and 'Like' us on Facebook.

Abergavenny and its surrounding areas are fantastically steeped in history and atmospherically fantastic! As far as small towns go, this one simply has it all. It has charm, character, and with it only being positioned 6 miles from the border between England and Wales, you can easily see why it gets tens of thousands of visitors every year. Medieval Abergavenny is a little town with a big personality. What I like so much about the castle and museum is, it too shares that same personality. So no matter whatever the weather, you can be rest assured there is something for everyone here no matter what age. In short, I think a trip to both the castle and museum should be on everybody's to do list.

Newport

Castle Street, Abergavenny, Monmouthshire, NP7 5EE

Newport Wetlands

t: 01633 636363 e: newport-wetlands@rspb.org.uk
www.rspb.org.uk/newportwetlands

Experience a special place for wildlife and for you

Come and explore our vast reedbeds, enjoy wonderful views of the Severn Estuary, or stroll through shady woodland on one of our many trails. Whether you're looking for a quiet walk in tranquil surroundings, a day out with the kids, a bit of retail therapy or a chance to relax with a cup of tea in our coffee shop, Newport Wetlands is the place for you. We have a variety of wildlife spectacles for you to see, from the elusive bearded tit to wading birds like avocets scouring the mudflats, from breath-taking starling flocks in autumn to the cacophony of birdsong in spring. Newport Wetlands boasts a unique play area for children and a wide range of events to suit all ages from pond dipping to crafts, guided walks to photography and bird identification workshops.

The Visitor Centre is open 9.00am to 5.00pm and the Coffee Shop
10.00am to 4.00pm. We are open every day of the year except Christmas Day.

Newport Wetlands National Nature Reserve is an incredibly special place. Despite being situated right next door to a power station, thousands of birds call this home, along with a huge variety of other wildlife. Otters, water voles and stoats, as well as dragonflies, damselflies, moths and butterflies all live here. There is also a huge diversity of flora, including several species of orchid, which fill the reserve with colour throughout the spring and summer. So whatever time of year you visit, there will be something to get excited about!

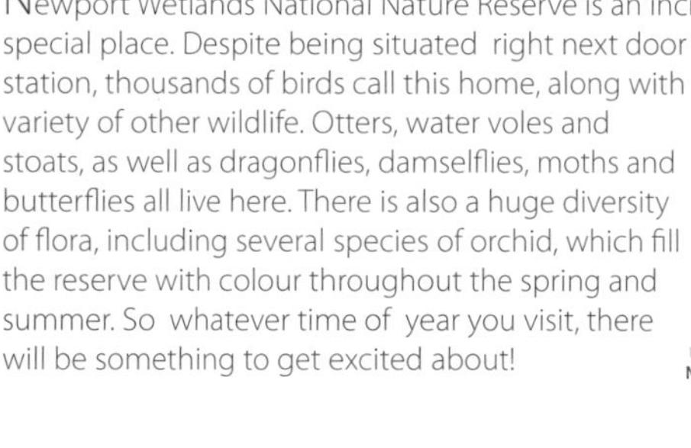

West Nash Road, Nash, Newport, Gwent, NP18 2BZ

Newport Medieval Ship

t: 01633 215707 e: newport.ship@newport.gov.uk
www.newportship.org

Explore the Newport Ship Project!

The Newport Medieval Ship is a truly remarkable archaeological discovery made in 2002 on the banks of the River Usk. This 15th century merchant ship is one of the best preserved and most complete examples ever discovered and raised. The vessel is currently undergoing conservation at the ship centre in Newport. Whatever the weather our themed open days are fun for all the family. With guided tours of the facility we tell you the tale of the project, from the discovery and world-wide campaign to save the ship, to the detailed recording process and what it has taught us about medieval life. Families can dress as knights and ladies, take part in craft activities and trails, sail in a coracle and if the children misbehave then send them to the stocks! Delve into the past with re-enactors and prepare to be entertained. All events are free! Please see the website for more details!

The Medieval Ship in Newport, is a truly unique attraction. For those who have never been lucky enough to see archaeology up close and personal, then you will absolutely love this place. In the unusual setting of a huge warehouse, the team are working on the recording and conservation of this fantastic find. Go to one of the four open days in 2013 (July 27 and Sept 7) to see for yourself the hard work that is taking place to care for this important vessel. The ship centre staff and volunteers are extremely knowledgeable, full of interesting facts and bursting with enthusiasm. The re-enactors present on open days, bring the medieval experience to life. Take the family and enjoy a fun filled journey through the past.

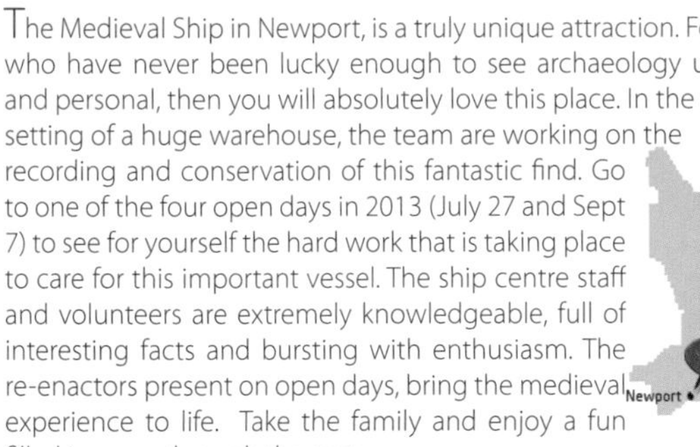

Unit 22, Maesglas Industrial Estate,Greenwich Road, Newport, NP20-2NN

Llanvihangel Court & Gardens

t: 01873 890217
www.llanvihangel-court.co.uk

A Tudor Manor House with landscaped gardens.

Llanvihangel Court is an historic 16C Tudor Manor House with landscaped gardens. The house contains fine 17C panelling and plaster ceilings, with an important yew staircase, stables and large barn. Among other historic associations, it was a reputed hideaway for Charles 1 during the Civil War.
Weddings: An ancient and beautiful private family home with romantic gardens which provide the perfect venue and photographic opportunities for your wedding. The ceremony takes place in the 17th century Great Hall, seating up to 100 people. Receptions can be held in a marquee on a lawn in the grounds with the caterer of your choice.
Open to the public on a daily basis during May & August and as well by appointment & for groups.

Over the years I have investigated and visited many old houses, castles and stately homes. Once visited, many of them found a way into my heart; Llanvihangel Court & Gardens was indeed one of them. Room after room of pure history is what you will find once on a tour of this house. Once I had been shown round by its owner I just wanted to go round and round again. It's very strange how a house can do this to you, and to be honest it is hard to explain. But we knew choosing this house to be in our book was a must, and when you make a visit here you'll know exactly why! Because this house is so fragile, the house isn't open all the time, so It is very important that you phone ahead to find out tour times and assure a place on a tour, but I guarantee once visited never forgotten.

Newport

Llanfihangel Crucorney, Abergavenny, NP7 8DH

Dewstow Gardens

t: 01291 430444 e: gardens@dewstow.co.uk
www.dewstow.co.uk

Discover a lost garden with tunnels and underground grottoes!

Dewstow Gardens is one of the least known of all the attractions in southern Wales, but also one of the most interesting. The gardens are a wonderful place to wander in themselves, with beautifully landscaped paths and decorative beds, artificial waterfalls and man-made pools, but it's Dewstow Grottoes that make this place really fascinating. It's astonishing to think that, only 10 years ago, this strange and wonderful garden was buried beneath thousands of tons of soil, lost and forgotten for over half a century. Built around 1893, Henry Oakley created a garden – his own personal wonderland – that was described by the few who visited as a "magical and wondrous place". When Oakley died in 1940, the gardens fell into disrepair, and were eventually buried and returned to farmland just after ww2. After a huge excavation and renovation project beginning in 2001, the gardens are now open to visitors during the summer months.

If I didn't know better I could of easily been forgiven for thinking that Dewstow was the setting for Lewis Carroll's ' Alice in wonderland' Dewstow House was built before I804, when John Proctor (d. I837) lived there. Dewstow Gardens were built after 1895 and buried after World War II. Rediscovery and large scale restoration of the gardens began in 2000. There is a labyrinth of tunnels interconnecting underground grottoes, ponds, tropical glass houses, rock garden and an alpine garden that help to make this attraction not one to be missed. If I'd of had time I could easily of spent hours at this very special place! So if I were you, I'd pack a flask! You could be there for sometime!

Newport

Caerwent, Monmouthshire, South Wales, NP26 5AH

The Nelson Museum

t: 01600 710630 e: nelsonmuseum@monmouthshire.gov.uk
www.monmouthshire.gov.uk

Admission Free to all!

Horatio Nelson was born in Norfolk, died at sea and is buried in London. However, Monmouth is home to one of the best collections about the famous admiral in the world. Find out about Nelson's life, loves, death and commemoration. The Nelson Museum was founded in 1924, following the bequest to Monmouth by Lady Llangattock of her Nelson collection. The museum moved to the current premises (a market hall complex built in the 1830s) in 1969, at which time the local history collections for the town were incorporated. The Local History centre deals with Monmouth and its people, including Charles Rolls of Rolls Royce fame and Henry V. The Nelson collection includes both personal and commemorative material, and is particularly noted for the large number of personal letters. Star exhibits include Nelson's fighting sword, and a selection of outrageous forgeries, including Nelson's 'glass eye'.

Open daily all year: Monday to Saturday (incl Bank Hols) 11-1, 2-5; Sunday 2-5 (close at 4pm daily November to February inclusive)

The Nelson Museum, is neatly located in the centre of Monmouth. Although this museum isn't one of the largest museums in the UK, it certainly reveals the truth into the statement, 'size isn't everything'. The staff here are so friendly and I liked the way they were on hand at any point to answer any question. The Museums main focus is Lady Llangattock's large collection of Nelson memorabilia. There is also an amazing collection of historical items pertaining to Lady Llangattock's famous son 'Charles Stewart Rolls' of Rolls Royce fame. But just when you think that's it, upstairs in the museum, houses an amazing local art collection. Now you can see exactly why the Nelson Museum has earned its place as one of Wale's Top 100 Attractions.

Newport

New Market Hall, Priory Street, Monmouth, NP25 3XA

Chepstow Museum

t: 01291 625981 e: chepstowmuseum@monmouthshire.gov.uk
www.chepstowmuseum.co.uk

ADMISSION FREE!

Chepstow Museum's atmospheric displays reveal the rich history of this once important port with all its associated trades and busy market town, the working life of its people, their pleasures and pastimes. The importance of the river Wye for trade, industry, salmon fishing, and for the first ever package holiday – the Wye Tour boat trip fashionable with tourists over two centuries ago, is explored with exciting new touchscreen interactives. A growing collection of paintings illustrates the inspirational quality of the Wye Valley that continues to attract artists and tourists alike. Home of this award winning museum is an elegant 18th century town house, just across the road from Chepstow Castle, the building's own fascinating history as private house, school and Chepstow's hospital is also vividly recreated. Special activities for young visitors include drawers to explore, things to make. Programme of exhibitions, talks, workshops and children's holiday activities.
Open Mon-Sat 11-5, Sun 2-5
(close 4 Nov-Feb, open 10.30-5.30 July-Sept)

Monmouthshire has a rich and varied history and one of the main reasons we decided that three of its museums should be crowned 3 of the Top 100 Attractions in Wales. One of those museums is Chepstow Museum. Here you will find a museum within a museum with many different themes within its displays. Once being a girls boarding school and an old hospital amongst many other things, this building has seen its fair share of history. The museum is always adding new displays and themes, which can be seen with the new outdoor ancient fishing boat display which is set to bring even more visitors flocking in.

Chepstow Museum
Newport

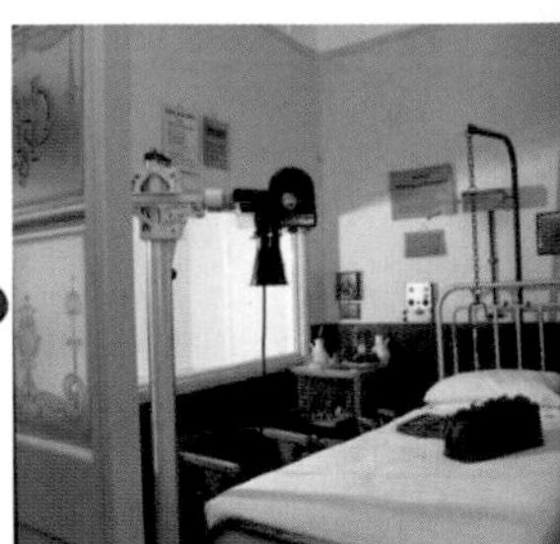

Chepstow Museum, Bridge Street, Chepstow, NP16 5EZ

Kings Arms Hotel & Restaurant

29 Nevill Street, Abergavenny Monmouthshire. NP7 5AA

T: 01873 855074 www.kingsarmsabergavenny.co.uk E:enquiries@kingsarmsabergavenny.co.uk

The Kings Arms Hotel is a late sixteenth century coaching inn located in the heart of the bustling Welsh market town of Abergavenny, the gateway to Wales. We offer something for everyone, comfortable, well-appointed guest accommodation, delicious restaurant food from chef, Jim Hamilton, and a versatile function space for all manner of events up to a 100. Whatever your reason for visiting , a getaway break or a lazy lunch, we'd like to extend you the warmest of welcomes. Come in and take a look around.

West Usk Lighthouse

Lighthouse Road, St.Brides, Newport, NP10 8SF

T: 01633 810126 www.westusklighthouse.co.uk E: info@westusklighthouse.co.uk

The West Usk Lighthouse is a cosy bed and breakfast plus a small wedding venue situated near the City of Newport, Gwent, at the junction of the Severn and the Usk Estuaries, overlooking the Bristol Channel. All rooms are wedge-shaped and there is a stone spiral staircase in the centre, right above a collecting well, which is now our wishing well! The entrance hall is slate bedded and we have a Dalek at the bottom of the stairs and a Tardis on the roof, which is an added bonus for Dr Who fans and those visiting the new Dr Who Exhibition in Cardiff. The lighthouse has had a long history of being in the media. Cosmopolitan magazine once named it as "one of the 'Most Romantic in Britain".

The Swan Hotel

Cross St, Abergavenny, Monmouthshire NP7 5ER

T: 01873 852829

The Swan Hotel stands prominently at the entrance to the historic market town of Abergavenny known as the Gateway to Wales.The hotel is a family run business and they pride themselves on good value for money especially their locally sourced, homecooked food served in both cozy bar and restaurant. The Swan hotel offers 11 en-suite bedrooms at competitive prices and two versatile function rooms that offer facilities for small weddings,christenings or parties.
The Swan is within easy reach of all local tourist attractions.

Hardwick Farm Bed & Breakfast

Hardwick, Abergavenny NP7 9BT

T:01873 853513 www.hardwickfarm.co.uk E: carol@hardwickfarm.co.uk

Cymru Wales
Ffermdy Farmhouse ★★★★

We are a family run farm; Mother and daughter, Carol and Anna, run the bed and breakfast and father and son, Cyril and Dave, run the dairy farm; complete with self-milking cows! Upon prior arrangement we can also provide tours of the farm and show you how the cows use the self-milking equipment, it's fascinating! Rural setting, family atmosphere.Staying with us is like a home from home for our guests, with all the welcome features you would expect to see. We have LCD TVs in all our bedrooms and we are also a WiFi enabled farm. If you require access during your stay, please let us know.

The Riverside Hotel

Cinderhill Street, Monmouth, Monmouthshire, NP25 5EY

T: 01600 715577 www.riversidehotelmonmouth.co.uk E: info@riversidehotelmonmouth.co.uk

The Riverside Hotel is a family run business and we pride ourselves on providing efficient, friendly service and good value for our guests. We have 17 en-suite bedrooms, an excellent restaurant, conservatory lounge and the Agincourt Suite; our versatile and spacious banqueting room which offers facilities for weddings, conferences or parties. We are committed to our guests. Whether you visit us for business or pleasure, you can be sure of our personal attention and a warm welcome. We look forward to making your stay as comfortable and enjoyable as possible.

The Coach House

St John's Street, Monmouth, NP25 3EA

T: 01600 775517 www.riversidehotelmonmouth.co.uk E: bookings@thecoachhousemonmouth.co.uk

A traditional, family run restaurant offering quality food and fabulous bed and breakfast accommodation.Situated in the heart of the rural market town of Monmouth, the 16th century Coach House Inn provides a great base to explore the beautiful Wye Valley and Forest of Dean, where you can discover world famous attractions like Tintern Abbey or the ancient Offa's Dyke path. Our recently renovated rooms offer fantastic 4 star en-suite bed and breakfast accommodation with a choice of double or twin/superking beds and includes traditional English or Continental breakfast.

The Beaufort Raglan Coaching Inn & Brasserie

High Street, Raglan Village, Monmouthshire NP152DY

T: 01291 690412 www.beaufortraglan.co.uk E: enquiries@beaufortraglan.co.uk

The Beaufort Arms is in the village of Raglan, historically connected with nearby Raglan Castle, close to both Monmouth and Abergavenny. It's owners and their welcoming staff offer very good service combined with excellent food and drink in a relaxed informal atmosphere with bedrooms to match. All rooms at the Beaufort are individually decorated all with crisp white cotton sheets, duck down duvets and throws. Complimentary water as well as tea/coffee and hot chocolate making facilities. Irons and ironing boards are available plus flat screen TVs, direct dial telephones and internet.

Bistro Prego (With Rooms)

7 Church Street, Monmouth, NP25 3BX

T: 01600 712600 www.pregomonmouth.co.uk E: enquiries@pregomonmouth.co.uk

Bistro Prego offers mouth-watering cuisine and has eight rooms with en-suite bathrooms and all this right in the heart of Monmouth's old town. Bistro Prego opened at the turn of 2006/2007 and offers not only an excellent range of fine food and wine but also eight well-appointed rooms all for people visiting Monmouth. For these reasons alone it would be a welcome addition to the town. Prego has eight rooms, all with TV's, coffee and tea-making facilities, en-suite bathrooms, hairdriers etc and offers guests a pleasent lounge lit during the day by a lovely roof skylight.

Gentle Jane Tea Room

Grosmont, Monmouthshire, NP7 8EP

T: 01981 240902 www..gentlejane.co.uk gentlejane@mac.com

We hope that you will enjoy the friendly atmosphere of Gentle Jane, a beautifully restored building in the centre of Grosmont village. Light lunches, cakes and drinks are all freshly prepared to order, and where possible, ingredients are fresh, seasonal and locally sourced.There is a large range of loose-leaf teas, and our excellent coffee is roasted by a local supplier, before being freshly ground in Gentle Jane. Cakes and baked goods, always an important element in a tea shop, are all freshly baked on the premises, with a wide, changing selection.

La Brasseria Italiana

The Stables Mews, Lewis Lane, Town Centre, Abergavenny NP7 5BA

T: 01873 737937 www. brasseriaitaliana.org.uk E: brasseriaitaliana@btconnect.com

We, at La Brasseria Italiana in Abergavenny are proud to be The Traditional Italian Rstaurant in town and our aim is to provide great food, locally sourced and simply cooked capturing the true essence of Italian Cuisine, and for All our customers to have a great time enjoying a comfortable enviroment with a friendly but professional service.

We are pleased to welcome all of You in our Restaurant , hoping You will enjoy the experience and have You back always.

Harry's Sandwich Bar

3 St. Johns Street, Town Centre, Abergavenny NP7 5RT

T: 07759 449 077

Whether you want a cooked breakfast, a tasty sandwich or a filling meaty baguette, Harry's is the place for a light takeaway snack or something more substantial. Our carvery baguettes are famous in the area, and where possible we source all local produce and where possible we always try to keep our prices as affordable as possible and give excellent value for money.

Restaurant 1861

Cross Ash, Abergavenny, NP7 8PB

T: 0845 388 1861/ 01873 821297 www.18-61.co.uk

Restaurant 1861 is a family run venue for appreciating the very best of fabulous local produce, cooked to perfection and presented with a delicate and imaginative touch.

With its rural location, it offers a fine alternative to country pubs while providing a sophisticated ambience with friendly attentive and highly professional service.

Opening times from 12pm & 7pm.Parties large and small can be easily accomodated and sometimes even have a spare table available for passers by, so don't hesitate to call in if you're passing.

The Crown at Pentygelli

Old Hereford Road, Pantygelli, Abergavenny, NP7 7HR

T: 01873 853314 www.thecrownatpantygelli.com E: Crown@Pantygelli.com

The Crown at Pantygelli is a thriving pub and restaurant, situated in this quiet spot between the Sugarloaf and Skirrid mountains, catering for both the modern traveller and local populace whilst still retaining the charm and hospitality of a bygone age. The Crown at Pantygelli offers a selection of first class meals which are freshly cooked and served throughout the premises, including our fine patio and terrace in the warmer weather.Such is the popularity of the food that at weekends you would be well advised to phone and reserve a table a few days in advance.

Deli Delicious

16 Nevill Street, Abergavenny, NP7 5JX

T: 01873 850022 www. deli-d.co.uk enquiries@deli-d.co.uk

At Deli Delicious we pride ourselves on the great selection of local Welsh and worldwide produce available. From Artisan breads to Zebra Steaks, if it's delicious, we stock it! So if you are looking for a Welsh gift for a loved one or a delicious takeaway sandwich or pasty from our fresh counter, cheeses, charcuterie, pickles or preserves, we have it all and if it's not in stock we will try our best to source what you need. A lot of time and care goes into all items that we stock, so all that's left to do is come and see for yourself.

Bistro Prego

7 Church Street, Monmouth, NP25 3BX

T: 01600 712600 www.pregomonmouth.co.uk E: enquiries@pregomonmouth.co.uk

Bistro Prego offers mouth-watering cuisine and has eight rooms with en-suite bathrooms and all this right in the heart of Monmouth's old town. Bistro Prego opened at the turn of 2006/2007 and offers not only an excellent range of fine food and wine but also eight well-appointed rooms all for people visiting Monmouth. For these reasons alone it would be a welcome addition to the town. "Prego is all about using quality locally sourced produce to create great flavours but with no over-the-top frills or overly complicated knick-knacks," explains Head Chef Steve Robbins. "We have a daily menu which changes on a weekly basis depending on what locally sourced seasonal produce is available". People can feel free to come in for a quick snack or indulge in a three course meal".

The Swan Hotel

Cross St, Abergavenny, Monmouthshire NP7 5ER

T: 01873 852829

The Swan Hotel stands prominently at the entrance to the historic market town of Abergavenny known as the Gateway to Wales.The hotel is a family run business and they pride themselves on good value for money especially their locally sourced, homecooked food served in both cozy bar and restaurant. The Swan hotel offers 11 en-suite bedrooms at competitive prices and two versatile function rooms that offer facilities for small weddings,christenings or parties.
The Swan is within easy reach of all local tourist attractions.

CARDIFF & AREA

When we selected all of our Top 100 Attractions, we had a lot of things to take into consideration, such as, value for money, disabled facilities, food outlets, visitor experience, just to name but a few. Not one of our attractions have paid an advertising fee to be selected, and each one is in here on merit. As far as tourist attractions in Wales are concerned, Cardiff's are all very compact and certainly if you don't have transport, still very easy to get to. Cardiff has millions of visitors a year on just weekend visits alone, without including people visiting as part of their holiday break. So as you can imagine, accommodation at times can get very scarce. It's always a good idea when planning to visit Cardiff to check your accommodation availability first, that way you don't end up staying somewhere that ordinarily wouldn't suit you, or at worst end up disappointed that you didn't get any accommodation at all. Having said all that, Cardiff now has twice the amount of hotels, guesthouses and other accommodation types that it did ten years ago, so you should be able to find something to suit both yourself and your pockets. I couldn't get over how cosmopolitan Cardiff now is, and the people are so friendly and they genuinely love to have so many people visiting their great city every year. Whether it be rival rugby teams, people there for concerts or even if you are just visiting for the day, you will be very surprised how geared up the Cardiff people are to accommodate your every needs.

Bay Island Voyages

t: 01446 420692 e: nicholasbiv@hotmail.com www. bayisland.co.uk

WAVE BOUNCING BUZZ IN THE BAY!

If you are looking for a quick fix of adrenalin or want to have a fast adventure experience, thrill seekers everywhere will love our Bay Island Voyages tours.

Based in the lock keepers cottage right outside the welsh assembly building we offer regular trips to the Holm islands and Bristol Channel. After donning waterproofs and lifejackets its all aboard our all weather 9 meter RIBS, purpose built for tackling the huge tides found in the channel and around the islands. Powered by two massive engines the boats can cover great distance at speed and we keep everyone entertained with a lively commentary at points of interest.

The two hour tour is best for offshore islands and the coastal cruise is great for groups, stag n hen, or birthday parties. Family run and geared towards children's needs we also offer shorter duration trips within the bay for smaller kids or those who just want a fast speedboat ride.

Bay Island Voyages offer a very unique boating experience. Wether it's a fun bay cruise, or a fast and exhilarating trip out to some of the best scenery Cardiff Bay has to offer, you won't be disappointed with Bay Island. The owners of the company have got some fantastic and innovative ideas coming to fruition for the 2012 season and if you keep checking their website you can keep up to date with those plans. I was very impressed with not only their professionalism but in their approach to making sure that every person that takes a trip with them, is left with long lasting memories.

CARDIFF

Lock Keepers Cottage,Harbour Drive, Cardiff, CF10 4PA

Cardiff Castle

t: 029 2087 8100 e: cardiffcastle@cardiff.gov.uk
www.cardiffcastle.com

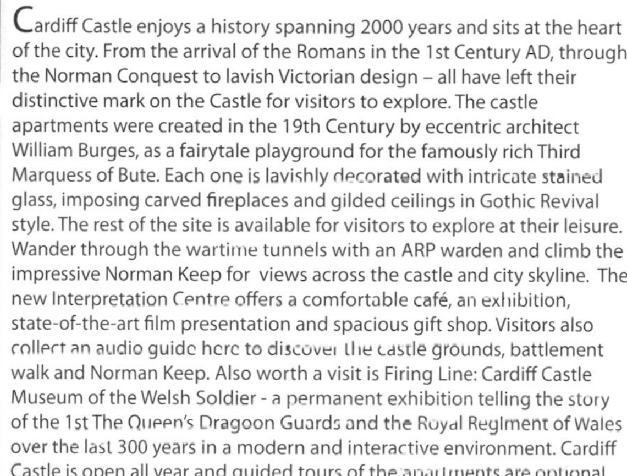

Discover 2000 years of history in the heart of the city!

Cardiff Castle enjoys a history spanning 2000 years and sits at the heart of the city. From the arrival of the Romans in the 1st Century AD, through the Norman Conquest to lavish Victorian design – all have left their distinctive mark on the Castle for visitors to explore. The castle apartments were created in the 19th Century by eccentric architect William Burges, as a fairytale playground for the famously rich Third Marquess of Bute. Each one is lavishly decorated with intricate stained glass, imposing carved fireplaces and gilded ceilings in Gothic Revival style. The rest of the site is available for visitors to explore at their leisure. Wander through the wartime tunnels with an ARP warden and climb the impressive Norman Keep for views across the castle and city skyline. The new Interpretation Centre offers a comfortable café, an exhibition, state-of-the-art film presentation and spacious gift shop. Visitors also collect an audio guide here to discover the castle grounds, battlement walk and Norman Keep. Also worth a visit is Firing Line: Cardiff Castle Museum of the Welsh Soldier - a permanent exhibition telling the story of the 1st The Queen's Dragoon Guards and the Royal Regiment of Wales over the last 300 years in a modern and interactive environment. Cardiff Castle is open all year and guided tours of the apartments are optional .

Cardiff Castle, truly is the great bastion of all Welsh castles. I had been here on a couple of occasions before my latest visit, and thought I knew what to expect, I was totally wrong! There is even more to see and do, than the last time I was here, and the new Caffi'r Castell is the perfect setting to break your visit before making your way downstairs to the Cardiff Castle Museum of the Welsh Soldier. Whether it's lunch you require or just a simple cake and coffee there is something on offer to satisfy any pallet. I would easily set aside three hours to see everything here within the castle, but, if you're like me and love to read everything you might want to make that four hours.

CARDIFF

Castle Street,Cardiff CF10 3RB

Cardiff International White Water

t: 029 2082 9970 e: info@ciww.com
www.ciww.com

Dive straight in!

Winner of 'Best Visitor Experience' at the Visit Wales awards, CIWW is an on demand white water rafting facility in the International Sports Village, Cardiff Bay.
The course has variable river flows so adventurers at all levels can enjoy the thrill of white water rafting.
Why not try Canoeing, Kayaking or even Stand Up Paddle Boarding? The flat water area offers a range of paddle sports, from the mild to the wild, which the whole family can enjoy!
Or grab a drink in the café bar and relax on the balcony while watching the rafters take on the water.

All training and equipment is provided (age 8+).

Ideally located within Cardiff's high tech sports village, it's no wonder Cardiff International Whitewater is one of Europe's leading whitewater centres. Whether your an experienced rafter or a novice kayaker, Cardiff International Whitewater has it all from Rafting, Hydrospeeding, and Kayaking, you take your pick! What I was so impressed with, was how versatile the centre is, whether your an olympic athlete or part of a stag party the same level of professionalism is shown across the board. If you've never tried anything like this you really need to give it a try! Chris, Ben and the team are always on hand to make sure you get the most out of your visit.

CARDIFF

CIWW, Watkiss Way, Cardiff, CF10 1NS

Cefn Mably Farm Park

t: 01633 680 312 e: mail@cefnmablyfarmpark.com
www. cefnmablyfarmpark.com www.moodysow.com

ALL WEATHER FAMILY FUN!

Cefn Mably Farm Park is a huge all weather family farm attraction & soft play in one. Set in rolling countryside close between Cardiff and Newport. We offer a unique mixture of farm animals and soft play areas - the ideal place for action packed days out with the kids, birthday parties, schools, and groups. The park is designed for families with toddlers to teens. The fun begins as you enter the indoor soft play barn where the children can let off steam and relax using wifi with a coffee and a slice of home made cake on a comfy leather couch. once you and the kids are worn out from feeding the animals on the farm and playing on the electric go-carts and real diggers, you can visit our new farm shop and butchery to pick up a good old fashioned 28 day matured stake for your tea and some home made smoky bacon for your breakfast!!!.

Children have been enjoying the farm park at Cefn Mably for many years now, and is now seeing the children that were, bring their children that now are, to enjoy this great attraction. Recently redeveloped by Rhys Edwards and his wife Alyona, Cefn Mably has been transformed into a children's farm park wonderland that even adults can enjoy. With a newly introduced play barn and farm shop selling local produce within a few miles of the farm park, Cefn Mably really is the epitome of all farm parks and it's great to see they've stuck to their original ideals and more.

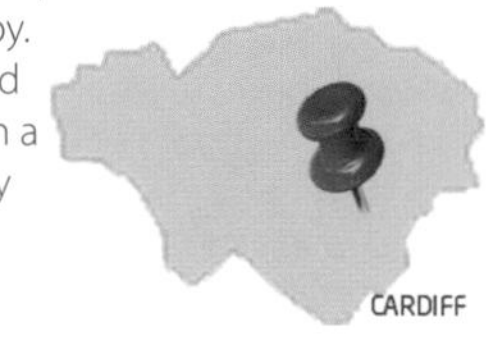

Cefn Mably Farm Park, Began Road, Cefn Mably, Cardiff. CF3 6XL

Millennium Stadium Tours

www.millenniumstadium.com/tours
t: 029 2082 2228 e: tours@millenniumstadium.com

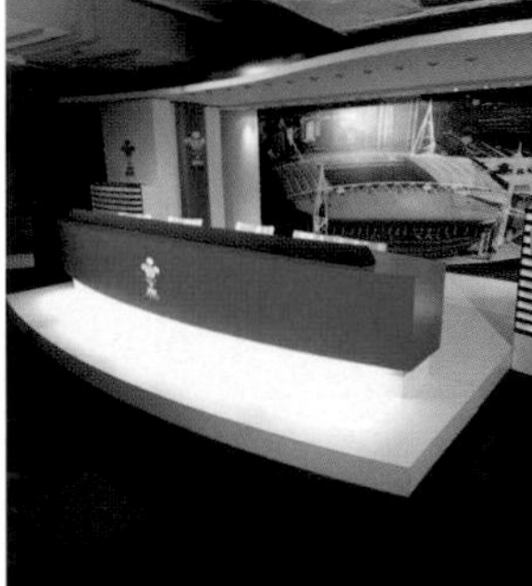

Millennium Stadium Tours

Walk in the footsteps of Ryan Giggs. See where Madonna stood. Where Shane Williams laced his boots and where all the action takes place on event days. Come and explore the magnificent facets and features that make the Millennium Stadium one of the most impressive icons of modern Wales. Join one of our experienced tour guides and visit the Press Conference Suite where the worlds of rugby and journalism meet. Experience the build up before the match in the Dragon's Lair, Wales's team dressing room. Hear the roar of 74,500 fans as you walk down the players' tunnel towards the hallowed turf. Learn about the only palletised pitch system and fully retractable roof in the UK, which allows the entire playing surface to be removed to create one of the world's largest indoor arenas. Take in the view of the pitch from a VIP hospitality suite, and finally lift the trophy to the skies like a sporting superstar in the President's Box, an area normally reserved for royalty.

On the original site where once stood the Cardiff Arms Park, the Millennium Stadium emerges gracefully up from the busy streets of Wales's capital city. Not only is the stadium capable of hosting all the top rugby and football games but is also one of the UK's top concert venues. From great stars such as Tina Turner, The Stereophonics, Manic Street Preachers not forgetting the recent Michael Jackson Tribute concert, which was shown in many countries worldwide. So as you can see, taking a tour around the stadium is not only awe inspiring but breath taking. As you walk through the same corridors and dressing rooms that have played home to some of the worlds sporting giants to the press conference room that graces our TV's every year. Then to be able to stand near the great pitch that's hosted many a great sporting battle. A Millennium Stadium tour is worth every penny.

CARDIFF

Millennium Stadium,Gate 4, Westgate St,Cardiff, CF10 1NS

ParcPlay Cardiff

t: 029 20345696 e: parcplay@googlemail.com
www.parcplaycardiff.com

PLAY,PICNIC,PARTY!

We are a one-of-a-kind children's play centre, you won't find any dark whiffy ball pits at Parc and thats a promise! Instead we have top of the range German made timber play equipment spread in a seamless transition from outdoor to undercover to indoor play areas so you can bask in the sunshine or shelter from the showers.. the fun literally continues whatever the weather! The kids will discover a pirate ship, timber fort, zip wire, climbing wall, a huge double slide, a grass toddler land and much more! For adults we provide refreshments, a range of seating from deck chairs to picnic benches (picnics welcome!) and free wifi. All this is located along the banks of the River Taff just a stone's throw from Cardiff city centre and other great attractions such as the Millennium Stadium, Cardiff Castle and Cardiff Bay!

There are only two children's play centres within this book, so what you may be asking yourselves is why did these two stand apart from all the rest? Let's start with Parc Play! Not only is this play centre indoor, but uniquely outdoor too! Parc Play hasn't only captured the hearts and imaginations of many youngsters within Cardiff, but also pulls children from miles around. I wondered why? But when I visited the play centre it all became apparent, this all weather play centre has it all! Slides, a zip wire, timber castle and toddler land...not to mention the pirate ship...Enjoy!

CARDIFF

Unit 4, Curran Embankment, Cardiff, CF10 5DX

National Museum Cardiff

t: 029 2039 7951 e: post@museumwales.ac.uk
www. museumwales.ac.uk

Discover art, archaeology, natural history and geology!

National Museum Cardiff houses amazing collections of art, natural history, geology and archaeology – all under one roof! Wales's National Museum of Art, on the first floor, spans 500 years and includes Old Master paintings, one of Europe's best collections of Impressionist works, and new galleries for the display of Modern and Contemporary art, which opened in July 2011.

Downstairs the Natural History galleries are home to dinosaurs, woolly mammoths, a real piece of moon rock and a huge variety of plants, insects and animals from Wales and across the world. The Archaeology gallery Origins: in search of early Wales, traces life in Wales from the very earliest human remains 230,000 years ago through the Stone Age, the invasion and conquest of the Romans and to the end of the Middle Ages. A changing programme of temporary exhibitions and events takes place throughout the year. Details are on the website.

Whether you're into art, archaeology, natural history or geology, National Museum Cardiff has the lot! The Museum is unique in the UK in its range of arts and science displays and the world-class art collection includes work by Poussin, Turner, Monet, Van Gogh, Picasso and Hockney to name a few. Origins, in search of early Wales, the Evolution of Wales and Natural History galleries are all here waiting for you to discover. Then there's the Clore Discovery Centre, where you can get hands on and explore the collections up close. You'll need a full day here and it's all totally free! Now that's what we call value for money!

Cathays Park, Cardiff, CF10 3NP

Doctor Who Cardiff Bus Tour

t: 0844 2471 007 e: info@britmovietours . com
www.britmovietours.com

Prepare yourself for an intergalactic adventure!

Prepare yourself for an intergalactic adventure as we take you on a tour of Cardiff locations featured in Doctor Who where much of the show has been filmed since its return in 2005. The Doctor Who Cardiff Bus tour is a great way to see the Welsh capital and its surrounding areas as we visit areas such as Penarth, Llandaff and Cardiff Bay where some of the most memorable Doctor Who locations seen in the show are situated. You will get a chance to wander through Amy Pond's village, locations from the Xmas 2012 episode and see sites from Doctor Who spin offs – The Sarah Jane Adventures and Torchwood, plus many other interesting Doctor Who locations and landmarks along the way. You'll learn how the show is made, get trivia about some of the stars from the show and you'll have the chance to stop on several occasions, stretch your legs, take pictures and see the locations up close.

We have featured another Brit Movie Tour in this Wales book, which is the close by Gavin & Stacey tour, being so impressed with this company and the tours they do, we just had to feature this Doctor Who tour. These tour guides really know their stuff, whether you're a fan or not, you'll have so much fun along the way! Being three and a half hours long, means you will get absolute value for money, and to be able to see these filming locations up close and personal, really does leave you with some long lasting memories. You would think it might be just as easy to go on your own to these places, well firstly you'd have to know about them, then you'd have to get there, that's before you even start thinking about bus and taxi fares! Knowing the accommodation situation in Cardiff, the accommodation package is also worth a look.

CARDIFF

Wales Millennium Centre, Tour Meeting Point inside the main foyer.

Cardiff Cycle Tours

t: 07500-564389 e: info@cardiffcycletours.com
www.cardiffcycletours.com

DISCOVER EUROPE'S YOUNGEST CAPITAL WITH OUR TOURS!

Truly the best way to explore this beautiful and fascinating young city is by bike. Cardiff is rapidly becoming a great cycling city, it is mostly flat - a great advantage - and there is a growing network of cycle routes. The Taff trail is the backbone which connects the Bay with the centre and further afield to Castell Coch. Cardiff CycleT ours offers you the unique combination of discovering the major attractions in the city with a leisurely bike ride.

From Cardiff Bay right down to Bute Park and the heart of the city, you will have a unique experience of time and place, discovering a Cardiff not accessible by car or bus. The Bute dynasty, the docks, the wetlands, hidden churches, and much more.

The tours are on the fantastic Pashley Bikes, made in Britain, which guarantee a comfortable and leisurely ride. No sweat, just pure enjoyment and relaxation, and history to flavour the trip. Cardiff Cycle Tours start daily in front of the Wales Millennium Centre in Cardiff Bay, check our calendar on the website for tour times, reservation recommended.

With two tours currently to chose from, Cardiff Cycle Tours in my opinion is not only the best, but the only option when it comes to looking around this great Welsh Capital. With humour and a vast knowledge of the city and its history the owner and tour guide Pol Van Steelant really has fine tuned his tour guide craft and offers amazing value for money. The Bay tour is a leisurely ride around "new Cardiff", whilst the Bute tour is firmly steeped in the history of this city. With the fees not being too huge this option is all the more doable. However if you want to just hire a bike and see the city at your own pace then that also can be arranged. A trip to Cardiff is made better by taking one of these tours!

CARDIFF

Cardiff Cycle Tours, BHAC, Bute Street, Cardiff

Techniquest

t: 029 20 475 475 e: info@techniquest.org
www.techniquest.org

THE EDUCATIONAL CHARITY OF CARDIFF BAY!

Enjoy a great family day out at Techniquest, Cardiff Bay - the UK's longest established science centre. You can fire a popgun, sink an oil rig or launch a hot air balloon as you play with our 120 interactive exhibits. Friendly staff are on hand to make sure you get the most from your visit. See the stars in the Planetarium or watch live demonstrations in our Science Theatre. Take a break in Cafe TQ with a range of hot and cold drinks, sandwiches, snacks and hot meals. To complete your Techniquest experience visit our shop with its quirky gift ideas, toys, books and souvenirs. Everything is under one roof with easy wheelchair access, disabled toilets and a lift to all parts of the building. Throughout the year we run special events including star gazing evenings, animal weekends as well as science and engineering weekend plus rockets, dinosaurs and more.

Techniquest in Cardiff really made a lasting impression on me. Not only were the staff really knowledgeable about everything to do with science, but they were quite slick in the way they put it across. I liked the way none of the staff talked down to those who may not know all there is to know about science. This attraction isn't just for school children, or those wishing just to learn about science. The team at Techniquest (Cardiff) have really gone out of their way to make this an attraction for all ages, and for that very reason we were unanimous that both Techniquest (Cardiff) & Techniquest (Glyndwr) made it into the Top 100 Attractions in Wales line up.

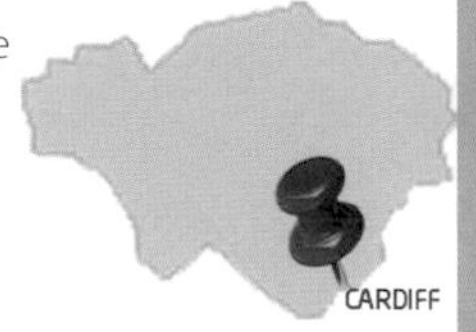

Castell Coch

www.cadw.wales.gov.uk
t: 029 2081 0101 e: cadw@wales.gsi.gov.uk

The beautiful fabled home of a very wealthy man.

While resting on ancient foundations, Castell Coch (Red Castle) is relatively modern, the by-product of a vivid Victorian imagination, assisted by untold wealth. The Middle Ages fascinated the Victorians as much as the Victorians fascinate us today. High Gothic was the order of the day. The 'eccentric genius' William Burges was given free rein by his paymaster, John Patrick Crichton-Stuart, the 3rd marquess of Bute, to create a rural retreat to complement the opulence of his main residence, Cardiff Castle. He didn't hold back. Dazzling ceilings, over-the-top furnishings and furniture were liberally applied. Detailed architectural drawings still survive today and following Burges's death in 1881, colleagues faithfully continued work on the interiors for another ten years. The castle was not suitable for, nor was it intended to be, a permanent residence and the family's visits were infrequent. We think Burges would approve of our conservation efforts to date and like him, we are not afraid either to embrace the latest technologies. Multi-sensory resources allow easy exploration of the site using touch screen technology which are of particular benefit to our visitors with sensory or physical disabilities.

We have featured a number of castles within this book, and each as magnificent as the other. Castell Coch on the other hand is dazzlingly different, not only in its architecture, but also in its interior. This gothic style structure stayed more or less with the same family until around 1950, and once visited it's not hard to see why! Well I wouldn't want to leave this fairy tale castle, would you?

Tongwynlais, Cardiff, CF15 7JS

The Jolyon's Boutique Hotel

Bute Crescent, Cardiff, CF10 5AN

T: 02920 488775 www.jolyons.co.uk E: info@jolyons.co.uk

This premier Cardiff Hotel offers superb luxury accommodation in Cardiff opposite the Millennium Centre. Since its opening in October 2004 Jolyons Hotel has proved to be a very popular addition to this vibrant area of Cardiff. The Jolyons Boutique Hotel Cardiff has six individually-designed bedrooms, lavishly furnished, with king-sized beds, Wi-fi facilities, free-to-view television, beverages, some with views of Cardiff Bay. Sumptuous en-suite bathrooms, including one with a whirlpool bath and one with a wet room appointed to the highest standards, with extra large fluffy towels, bathrobes and toiletries.

Jolyon's at No10

10 Cathedral Road Cardiff CF11 9L J

T: 02920 091900 www.jolyons.co.uk E: reception.city@jolyons.co.uk

Jolyon's is an exquisite new boutique hotel in the heart of Cardiff. Whether you're visiting for a week or a couple of hours, for work or for pleasure, our 21 individually designed lavish rooms, personal service and tastefully created menus are sure to impress. Everything at Jolyon's at No. 10 is unmistakably boutique. Our furnishings are bespoke, handmade and lovingly restored to create a warm, comfortable and relaxing place to stay. Whether you're looking for a bedroom, to meet, to hold an event or good quality food – Jolyon's at No. 10 is your perfect location!

Lincoln House Hotel

118-120 Cathedral Road, Cardiff, CF11 9LQ

T: 02920 395558 www.lincolnhotel.co.uk E: reservations@lincolnhotel.co.uk

The Victorian hotel in the heart of Cardiff Imagine all the benefits of Victorian splendour in a hotel just minutes from Europe's youngest, most vibrant capital. Welcome to Lincoln House Private Hotel in Cardiff, South Wales.Whether you are visiting the Welsh capital for business, sport, culture, relaxation or for the city's busy nightlife, our traditional bed and breakfast offers some of the best-placed accommodation in Cardiff. Full Welsh breakfast . Luxury beds . Full en-suite facilities . Free Wi-Fi . Free parking. Laundry service . Flat screen digital Freeview television . Tea and coffee facilities . Email, fax and photocopying facilities.

Maltsters

42 Cardiff Road, Llandaf, Cardiff,CF5 2DS

T: 029 2033 3096 www.maltstersllandaff.com E: Maltstersllandaff@sabrain.com

Maltsters is a pub that once visited, you won't forget in a hurry! Situated in the heart of Llandaff village on the North-Western outskirts of central Cardiff, Maltsters is a combination of traditional British inn and contemporary style. We have five, stylish, individual and highly appointed bedrooms. Each room has a state of the art Apple media and entertainment 'Maltsters media' system to ensure your stay is as enjoyable as possible. Whether you want to play music, surf the net, download a film or even play one of your own DVDs, it's all there at the click of a mouse! All rooms are ensuite with a bath and rain shower and we have even thought about the ultimate comfort; you can even enjoy watching the plasma TV while relaxing in the bath!

Dexby Town House

126 Cathedral Road, Cardiff, CF11 9L

T: 029 2034 0882 www.dexbytownhouse.co.uk E: info@dexbytownhouse.co.uk

Dexby town house is a family run bed and breakfast on cathedral road which is a 10 minute walk from the centre of cardiff. Attractions within walking distance of the guest house include the Millenium Stadium, Swalec stadium, Cardiff City football ground and the world renowned Cardiff castle and the Cardiff International Arena. The rooms have been recently refurbished and now has 6 individually designed rooms, beautifully furnished with king sized beds, sumptuous en suite bathrooms, free wi-fi connection, flatscreen tv's, tea and coffee facilities, toiletries, hair dryers and white fluffy towels. At Dexby town house all guests will receive a very high standard of service.

The Angel Hotel Cardiff

Castle Street, Cardiff , South Glamorgan, CF10 1SZ

T: 02920 649 200 www.pumahotels.co.uk E: stay@pumahotels.co.uk

One of the favourite historical hotels in Cardiff, The Angel Hotel Cardiff is a beautiful Victorian landmark in the capital of Wales. Ideally located near the centre of Cardiff, the hotel is perfect for holidays and short breaks in Cardiff and South Wales. The hotel itself is neatly positioned between the Millennium Stadium and Cardiff Castle, with many of the bedrooms offering views of the castle. This Cardiff hotel boasts modern, air conditioned bedrooms, a restaurant and cocktail bar. With great hotel offers, deals and breaks in Cardiff, The Angel Hotel Cardiff is the perfect place to stay in this vibrant city.

Maldron Hotel Cardiff

St Mary St, Cardiff ,CF10 1GD

T: 02920 668866 www.maldronhotelcardiffcity.com E: info.cardiff@maldronhotels.com

Maldron Hotel in Cardiff City Centre opened in May 2011 and is built to a 4 star standard. Located in the heart of the city on St Mary Street, the Maldron Hotel is one of the most conveniently located hotels in Cardiff City Centre. The Hotel is adjacent to Cardiff Central Railway Station. The Millennium Stadium is only a short walk from the hotel. Mill Lane is right around the corner from the hotel boasting some of the most famous names in food including, Jamie's Kitchen, and some of the big names in Italian, French, Spanish and Indian cuisine, you will be spoiled for choice making us one of the most sought after Cardiff City Hotels.

Owl Manor B&B

29 Plymouth Road, Barry Island, Vale of Glamorgan, CF62 5TY

T: 01446-621909 www.owlmanor.co.uk E: i cherylsangels@hotmail.co.uk

Owl Manor is a great stop off point for both a relaxing break or busy nightlife break. We are close proximity to Cardiff & Cardiff Bay, Cardiff Airport and within easy walking distance of the beaches of Barry Island. Great place for all the events in Cardiff but a peaceful nights sleep! Owl Manor Guesthouse is not only a warm friendly environment with comfortable rooms, lovely breakfasts, great location we also offer a unique opportunity for you to experience Angelic Healing. If you want to know more then simply ask or book an appointment. This is available to everyone. Angelic healing courses are also available.

The Kings Arms

Church Road, Pentyrch, Cardiff, CF15 9QF

T: 02920 890202 www.kingsarmspentyrch.co.uk

The Kings Arms is a traditional Welsh longhouse pub situated in the leafy village of Pentyrch on the outskirts of Cardiff. Offering fresh locally sourced food and Welsh ales, this late 16th century grade II listed building is bursting with character. Cosy snug bar with original flagstone floor and open fire-place, large lounge bar with limewashed walls and log burning fire and intimate restaurant opening onto large landscaped gardens. Enjoy seasonal lunch time or supper menus, our epic Sunday roast or just pop in for a pint and a friendly chat.

The Potted Pig

27 High Street (underneath Zizzi), Cardiff CF10 1PU

T: 029 2022 4817 www.thepottedpig.com E: info@thepottedpig.com

Opened in 2011 The Potted Pig has made its home in a former bank vault underneath the city. We serve a varied and constantly changing menu of modern British food with a few French and New-York grill inspired influences. The menus are based on food we love cooking and eating rather than a single concept. At The Potted Pig we make every effort to keep our menus seasonal, which means using as many locally sourced products from independent and local suppliers as possible. Our wine and drinks menu has been carefully selected to match our menus and we carry an excellent range of independently sourced wines as well as a fantastic array of bottled lagers, ales and ciders.

The Pancake House

Unit 18, The Old Brewery Quarter, Cardiff, CF10 1FG

T: 02920 644954

Situated in the heart of the old brewery quarter is The Pancake House. A perfect place for break-fast, lunch, dinner, dessert or even just a snack. We serve freshly made sweet and savoury pancakes and theres a lot to chose from! We also serve coffees, teas, cold drinks, milkshakes and icecreams. There's also a lovely outdoor seating area to enjoy. We are open from 10am - 10pm during the week and from 9am - 11pm weekends.

The Corner House

Caroline Street, Cardiff, CF10 1FF

T: 02920 228 628 www.cornerhousecardiff.co.uk E: enquiry@cornerhousecardiff.co.uk

Our menu changes with the seasons and is modern British, comfortably interwoven with some Mediterranean influences. It ranges from traditional favourites such as fish and chips and steaks to freshly made pizzas and pastas with the chef's daily specials showcasing the finest market fresh ingredients. There's something for everyone and for all occasions too. You don't have to go for the full works if you don't want to, just have a snack and a lovely drink in the bar with your friends. We are also very proud of our beers and we have a great selection of cask ales, super chilled draft and bottled beers to quench your thirst.

The Fig Tree

The Esplanade, Penarth, Vale of Glamorgan, CF64 3AU

T: 029 2070 2512 www.thefigtreepenarth.co.uk E: enquiries@thefigtreepenarth.co.uk

Set in a beautifully restored Victorian beach shelter, the fig tree has the best views in the Vale. Whether you sit in the Restaurant, on the Veranda or the Roof Terrace you can look out across the Bristol Channel to Somerset, Flat Holm and Steep Holm.
The award winning fig tree offers affordable traditional and contemporary fresh food for all the family.
Lunch Tuesday to Sunday from 12pm
Dinner Tuesday - Saturday 6.30 - 9.30pm

Wally's Delicatessen & Coffee House

38-46 Royal Arcade Cardiff Wales CF10 1AE

T: 029 2022 9265 www.wallysdeli.co.uk E: steve@wallysdeli.co.uk

Wally's is the premier delicatessen in Wales and the South West of Britain, specialising in fine foods from around the world.We have been trading from our premises in Cardiff for nearly 60 years now, and have recently developed our own website, which we believe to be the most comprehensive Online Delicatessen on the Internet today! When you visit Wally's Delicatessen why not pop upstairs to Wally's Kaffeehaus, our recently-opened Viennese-style Coffee House, where we aim to offer a taste of Vienna in the heart of Cardiff. If you are planning a visit to Wally's Delicatessen, please note that we are normally open from 8.00 am to 5.30 pm from Monday to Saturday and from 11.00 am to 4.00 pm on Sundays.

The Old Cottage Free House

Cherry Orchard Road, Lisvane, Cardiff, CF14 0UE

T: 02920 765 961 www.oldcottagecardiff.co.uk

Our menu changes with the seasons and is modern British, comfortably interwoven with some Mediterranean influences. It ranges from traditional favourites such as fish and chips and steaks to freshly made pizzas and pastas with the chef's daily specials showcasing the finest market fresh ingredients. There's something for everyone and for all occasions too. You don't have to go for the full works if you don't want to, just have a snack and a lovely drink in the bar with your friends. Just stop by for a pint of ale, read the papers and chill out or book a table and enjoy simple food prepared with care.

Valentinos Restaurant

5 Windsor Place, Cardiff, CF10 3BX

T: 029-2022-9697 www.valentinocardiff.co.uk e: valentinocardiff@btconnect.co.uk

Valentino's Restaurant is a place for fine Italian dining to grace any occasion. Our freshly prepared food, using daily deliveries of meat, fish and vegetables plus only the very best Italian olive oil, helps the chef create a superb Italian cuisine which captures the essential flavours of traditional Italian food. Here at Valentino's Restaurant we keep you warm and cosy in the winter and provide air conditioning in the summer, ensuring that dining with us is always a pleasant experience. Our ground floor can accommodate up to 75 covers, we also have a function room which can accommodate up to 45 covers and has its own private bar.

Bosphorus Turkish Restaurant

Mermaid Quay, Cardiff, CF10 5BZ www.bosphorus.co.uk e: hakan@bosphorus.co.uk
Tel: 029 2048 7477

The Bosphorous Turkish Restaurant is unique in its cuisine, and its location commands a spectacular position in Mermaid Quay, Cardiff Bay, as you sit on its stilts over the water.

Enjoy your meal inside or outside in the sunlight, the choice is yours. We specialise in Modern Turkish Cuisine, such as traditional dishes taken from the Ottoman Empire and is complimented by exclusive european seafood. Selections of our dishes are also suitable for vegetarians.

Try our delectable Turkish wines, there's a selection of red and white such as,Yakut, Buizbag and Dolucia to enjoy with your meal. Then perhaps a glass of the traditional Turkish spirit, Raki, to savour with a cup of Turkish coffee. Whatever your taste, an evening spent in the warm and hospitable atmosphere of the Bosphorus will certainly be a memorable one.

Top 100 Review

We think we all know Turkish food because we may of at some time in the past, eaten a kebab from a Turkish takeaway? Or because we may of holidayed in Turkey at some point. But let me tell you, you've not really tasted Turkish food until you've eaten at Bosphorus Restaurant at the very trendy Mermaid Quay on the new Cardiff Bay. The menu here at Bosphorus is a trendy take, on a very traditional Turkish menu. I have always associated turkish food with the likes of local take aways, and for that very reason, I have never really ventured near a Turkish or Greek restaurant for that matter, but do that at your peril, as every tasty dish that came to my table, just blew me away! I couldn't believe how much I was enjoying the food that was being brought too me, and would highly recommend this restaurant as being one of the best in Cardiff.

Newborough Beach and Llanddwyn Island

Route 263-002

From the A55 continue over the bridge onto Anglesey and take your first left to Llanfairpwllgwyngyll (abbreviated) and then take the A4080 to Newborough via Brynsiencyn. When you arrive in Newborough village take the first left at the Crossroads (convenience store on the corner) along Church Street and follow signs for the beach. You will arrive at an automatic toll barrier which allows you access to the Newborough forest. Follow signs for the beach and car park.

Now walk in a westerly direction along the forest path which runs parallel to the beach. When you arrive at the beach you will see Llanddwyn Island which can be cut off at high tide for about 1 hour. Continue towards the island and the information building which explains the history of the island and how the volcanic eruptions took place billions of years ago. You will be drawn to a collection of ruins and artefacts including a celtic cross, a ruined 16th century church and a modern Latin cross which commemorates St. Dwynwen who in the 5th Century was the patron saint of Welsh lovers.

The views around the island take in rock spurs, quiet sandy coves and views of the Snowdonia mountains. You will also see many seabirds including Oyster Catchers, Cormorants and Shags so don't forget your binoculars. On a warm day the beach is one of the finest in the UK and has Blue Flag status. Dogs are not allowed on part of the beach from May to September (from the car park to Llanddwyn Island - including the island) - dogs can be let off the lead in the forest areas. This a beautiful walk and mostly fairly flat and one that should not be missed if you are visiting North Wales or Anglesey.

Courtesy of Walk North Wales
www.walknorthwales.co.uk

Trefriw to Llyn Geirionydd & Crafnant

Route OL17-018

Trefriw can be accessed from Conwy along the B5106. Trefriw is famous for the Woollen Mill which still weaves cloth today and exports all over the world.- well worth a visit!

The twin lakes of Llyn Geirionydd and Llyn Crafnant are easily accesible to walkers from Trefriw. The trail takes you through woodlands and then as you climb up above Trefriw some breathtaking views back down the Conwy valley. You will then descend to a farm at Penrallt where you may see some unusual breeds of sheep. Continue along the public footpath and the walk will soon bring you to the now derelict Klondyke Mill which was a lead ore and zinc ore processing factory built in 1900. Just a short walk brings you to Llyn Geirionydd which is the only lake in the Snowdonia National Park which allows power boats and water skiing. There are few if any fish in the lake due to water poisoning as a result of the lead from the adjacent metal mines although I do believe it is safe to swim in the lake.

Following trail No. 5 from Llyn Geirionydd takes you on the path to Llyn Crafnant. Once at the Llyn Crafnant you can follow Forest Enterprise circular trail around the lake or shorten the walk by about 2.6 miles by missing out the lake walk. You then follow the road downhill towards Trefriw for about 0.8 miles and take a path to your left along a forest trail which provides a more interesting route back to Trefriw.

This walk is 8.1 miles or 5.5 miles if you miss out the lake walk. It should take around 4 hours or 2.5 to 3 hours for the shorter route. Walking boots are advisable as there is a total ascent of 1615 feet which makes it a challenging walk.

Courtesy of Walk North Wales
www.walknorthwales.co.uk

Cwm Idwal and Y Garn

Route OL17-011

A short walk to Cwm Idwal followed by a demanding ascent to a high peak on the Glyders known as Y Garn. The descent passes just below the notorious Devil's Kitchen and then meanders through mountain formations noted for their rock climbing, rare plants and wild mountain goats.
The walk starts from Ogwen Cottage which you can approach from Capel Curig or Bethesda on the A5. There is a Pay and Display car park, toilets and refreshments. Take the path to Llyn Idwal which can be picked up from just behind the toilet block. After arriving at the lake turn right following the beach. Ascend the broad north-east shoulder of Y Garn by a zig-zagging path and continue by the exposed and steepening ridge above to a junction with the main ridge between Y Garn and Foel Goch. Turn left for the summit.

Descend south then south-east to Llyn y Cwn. Follow a path north-east from Llyn y Cwn and down through a stone filled runnel on to a broad ramp and with the Devil's Kitchen cliffs on your left carry on the descent on stoney paths to a better path diagonally across the hillside to the foot of the Idwal slabs. Follow the path around the lake and return to the start along a stone track.
This walk should not be undertaken without the right walking equipment, map and compass. It is not advisable to do this walk on misty, windy or frosty days unless very experienced.
(4.2miles – allow at least 4 hours)

The short walk around Cwm Idwal is a pleasant alternative for those not wanting to include the ascent. There is a well constructed path which takes you around the perimeter of the lake and offers some magnificent cliff scenery.

Courtesy of Walk North Wales
www.walknorthwales.co.uk

Shell Island

t: 01341 241453 e: enquiries1@shellisland.co.uk
www. shellisland.co.uk

CATERING FOR ALL THE FAMILY & WITH EXCELLENT FACILITIES!

Based in North Wales and boasting stunning views of the unspoilt Welsh countryside, including Cardigan Bay and the Snowdonia National Park, Shell Island is one of Europe's largest Campsites. Catering for all the family and with excellent facilities Shell Island will make your camping experience one to remember. From Shell Island on a clear day, you will have fantastic views of the North Cardigan Bay. Looking out across the bay is the Llyn Peninsula, with Abersoch, Pwllheli and Criccieth on the facing shore. To the North lies Snowdon (3559ft), the highest mountain in England and Wales. With its snow capped peak in the,spring, walkers from all over the UK ascend it throughout the year. Harlech castle, stood prominent on the hill at Harlech is clearly visible, and to the right of it, the Rhinogs Mountain range. Looking south towards our sand dunes lies Cader Idris, and the Cambrian mountain range, with the coast extending all the way down to Pembrokshire.

I went to visit Shell Island at the height of the season, and towards the end of the season, and the place was a hive of activity on both occasions. The island itself has lot's to offer all ages and all walks of life. Shell Island has got great facilities and all at affordable prices to. I just couldn't get over the atmosphere of the place, everybody speaking to each other like they were all part one big family. I was astonished to find the management at this site doing the types of jobs you wouldn't see management at a lot of resorts doing! Shell Island is certainly a one off and gets a massive thumbs up from us all here at Top 100 attractions in Wales.

Cae Gethin, Llanfair, Harlech, Gwynedd, LL46 2SA

Waterfalls Walk

(National Park Authority, Forestry Commission)

Location: Pontneddfechan,near Glynneath

Distance: 2-4miles/3-6kma,pprox 1-2 hour walk

Initially, a gentle walk beside the River Neath to see spectacular falls.The path is in relatively good condition all the way to the left hand waterfall and is easy walking. The other falls are up the right hand fork of the river where the path deteriorates and it climbs high above the river,so is unsuitable for young children or weaker walkers.
In spring and summer the air is thick with the scent of ramsons(wild garlic).This grows everywhere but is most evident near the entrance, where it forms a thick carpet under a large rocky overhang.
The beauty of this wooded valley belies its long industrial history, but the past remains in the shape of abandoned mines and mills along the path. Once hives of activity,these are now moss-covered and silent.
There is plenty of bird life throughout the year. Watch out for grey wagtails hunting along the river banks for insects. Despite their name, these birds have bright yellow undersides. There is no mistaking the second part of their title, as they wave their long tails up and down in a constant semaphore message to partners and potential rivals.
Wood Anemone Dippers are also distinctive, with dumpy bodies, dark brown backs and upstanding tails, reminiscent of an oversized wren. They have a large white bib that makes them stand out against the dark waters and constantly duck as they stand on rocks amidst the rushing torrent. They hunt aquatic insect larvae and freshwater shrimps by walking and diving into the torrent, usually nesting under one of the numerous rocky overhangs or even behind a waterfall.
In summer the woods resound with the songs of willowwarblers and blackcaps which feed on the countless caterpillars among the leaves overhead. Herons are much the largest bird likely to be seen here, but are surprisingly light despite their five foot wingspan.This allows them to land almost like a helicopter,dropping through small gaps in the summer canopy to land with pin-point accuracy in the shallowsto stalk small fish and frogs along the banks.

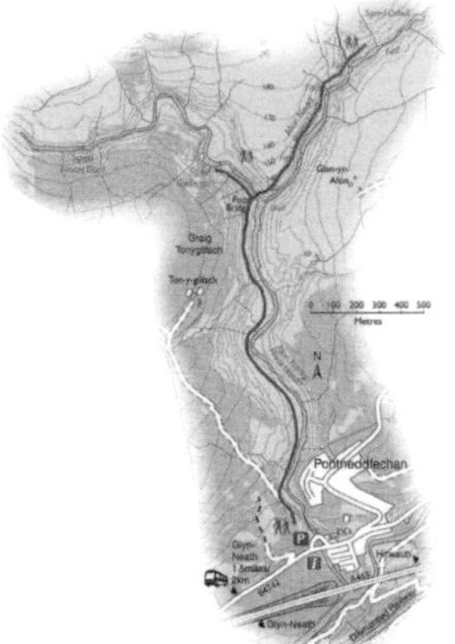

Abercastle/Aber Mawr

Half Day + Walk

The north coast of Pembrokeshire takes quite a battering from storms every year. It is part of life on the exposed coast. One storm, of 1859, is sometimes credited with having piled up the shingle banks at Aber Mawr and its neighbour Aber Bach. In fact, the banks were formed more quietly –deposited as sea levels rose at the end of the Ice Age. The storm left its mark. In all 100 ships were lost and one, the Charles Holmes, went down with all hands just off Aber Bach. At Aber Mawr look out for a small building that once put the little cove on the map. It was the terminus for the first Atlantic submarine telegraph cable, which was connected up in 1873. As the clifftop route crosses the Penmorfa peninsula look out for the impressive 2,300-year-old fort, Castell Coch. Abercastle is also known as Cwm Badau, Bay of Boats. It is so quiet now that it is hard to believe that its inlet was once a busy port. Farm produce was exported from Abercastle to Bristol and Liverpool, while limestone and coal were imported. The limestone was burned in Abercastle's limekiln, one of many around the coast. The slaked lime that the kilns produced was used on Pembrokeshire farmland. A slate bridge at the inlet was funded by the Friends of the Pembrokeshire National Park - there is an inscription carved into the top. Close by is the cromle Carreg Samson. Built as a Neolithic burial chamber, it was once buried under a mound of earth. Now, the hefty stones that formed the inner chamber do a balancing act, with the big capstone perched on supporting pillars. Local legend is that the cromlech was built by Samson, who lost a finger putting the capstone in place. The finger is said to be buried at the top of Ynys-y-Castell, an islet at the entrance to Abercastle cove.

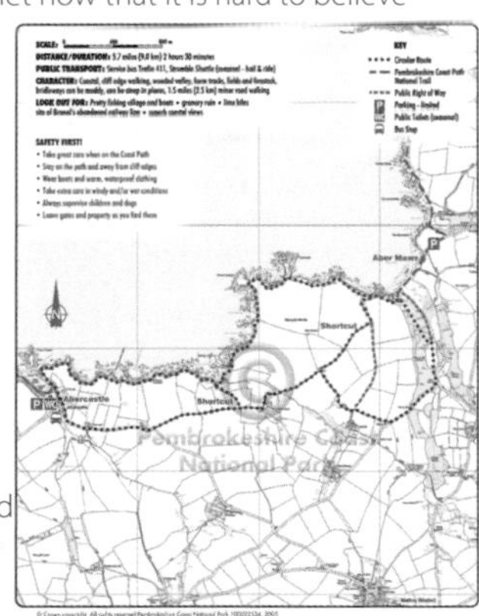

Courtesy of Pembrokeshire Coast National Park

Dylan's Walk

1:The Castle & Grist :Laugharne Castle was first established in 1116 but the towering walls date to the l5th and 16th centuries as a fortified country house. 'The Grist' is probably a shortened form of Grist Mill or Corn Mill. The salt marshes have developed in area over the last100 years or so – in the Middle Ages, boats could come right up to the castle walls.

2: The Boathouse and Dylan Thomas: A separate visit is essential to Dylan Thomas' home from 1949 to 1953, but the building dates from at least the early l9th century. It was a pub in the 1880s – The Ferry House Inn – and later a boat building and repair yard. Fine viewpoint towards Si John's Hill and over the Taf Estuary.

3: Cliffside: A much-used route to the foreshore with the remains of older cottages and small quarries. Until the 1950s, an open-boat from Ferry Point to Laugharne was operated on the tide by a single boatman. Above the wooded cliffs are the remains of an Iron Age defended enclosure, reused as a gun battery during the Civil War siege of Laugharne Castle in 1644. A very fine Victorian Boathouse below the path is a reminder of l9th century leisure.

4: A ferry crossing point close to Cwm Celyn farm, on the other side of the Taf Estuary. Upstream there were ferries from below Llandeilo Abercowin Church. These were routes used through the Middle Ages and later by travellers – kings, bishops, pilgrims, merchants and

5: Delacorse Farm: A 17th/18th century house and outbuildings, reflecting the Norman-French of the medieval lords of Laugharne – delacors, of the marsh. Mary Curtis tells of an old causeway used by limecarts from the Coygan Quarries and of Betty Fordside, who had a horse to carry travellers across the river to Black Scar at low tide. many others. Traces of causeways are revealed at low tide.

6: Carmarthen Bay: Coastal and Estuaries Trail A footpath is being created along the estuary up to St Clears.

7: St Martin's Church: The 13th century Church lies some distance from the town on the earlier site of a native Welsh church, predating the foundation of Laugharne (Abercorran). The de Brians may have changed the dedication to St Martin of Tours. Dylan Thomas is buried in the new graveyard, marked with a simple white crucifix.

8: Views to The Hugdon: Unenclosed open fields held by Laugharne Corporation and shared amongst the Burgesses. The shares or strips of land are separated from each other by unploughed grassy baulks known as 'landskers'.

9: Corporation Boundary: At the stile, look for the inscription on the rock. Excellent views back along the Taf estuary and seaward to the National Trust's Wharley Point, Cover Cliff and Black Scar Ferry.

10: Cockshilly: A choice of a higher route over Sir John's Hill or down along 'Cockshilly' to a spectacular viewpoint overlooking the former quay and tramway, extending to the Gower and Pembrokeshire.

11: Laugharne MarshLand: reclaimed from the sea since the Middle Ages,helped by the development of sand dunes. On the East Marsh some farms were sited on low hillocks. Out towards Ginst Point you can see 'The Freething' and 'The Saltings' sea walls. Late 18th century ploughing in regular ridges can still be very clearly seen today.

12: Railsgate Pill: A l9th century tramway used to run from Coygan Quarry down to a small wharf at the mouth of the Pill where limestone was loaded onto small coasting vessels. The rails are gone but the tramway causeway and remains of the small quay can be seen.

13: The Lees: Low-lying common land (40 small strips or shares) belonging to theCorporation of Laugharne, first granted by Sir Guy de Brian in 1291. and with cast-iron pillars marking the bounds.

14: Coygan Quarry: Seen at a distance, an outcrop of carboniferous limestone with an extensive cave system. Some 38,000 years ago the cave was a hyena den. Crude stone hand tools used by Neanderthal men were also found in the cave. In the 2nd century BC a large Iron Age hillfort was constructed. In the 5th–7th centuries AD the hillfort was the centre of power of a Dark Age chieftain.

15: Back Lane: According to Mary Curtis, there was much slaughter along this part of the route when the Castle was stormed by Cromwell's soldiers.

Chepstow Castle & Riverside

Detailed walk description
Riverside Walk - 30 minutes (½ mile).

This is a short stroll beginning at the Castle car park, exploring the interesting riverside area. Turn left out of the car park down Bridge Street. The old Wye Bridge at the end is a fine cast iron structure, and was until 1988 the main entrance into the town from Gloucestershire and the only crossing over the river for cars and other vehicles. It is at least the sixth bridge to be built on this site. Maintenance of the earlier stone and timber bridges was made very difficult by the extremely high tidal range here. The tide rises and falls by 40ft (12m) every day, the second highest in the world.

To continue the walk cross the road with care to join the Riverside Park. There are WCs, including a disabled WC here. Today the Riverside Park is a restful place, but until a century or so ago it was a busy port. The area was then known as Gunstock Wharf, with piles of timber on the quay and bark houses behind, for storing oak bark ready to be shipped to the tanning industry in Bristol and Ireland. Wooden sea-going merchant ships were built in three shipyards in Chepstow.

A plaque on the wall of the Wye Knot restaurant records the embarkation of the leaders of the Chartist uprising to van Dieman's Land (Tasmania), where they transported as punishment for leading a campaign to allow all men to have the right to vote. A number of old converted warehouses will be noted in this interesting area as you proceed along the path. Across the river is a natural square entrance hole in the cliff, known as the Gloucester Hole. The Union Jack was first painted on the cliff around 1935, and has been regularly repainted every since.

At the end of the path, join the road that leads away from the river. You may return to the Castle car park via St Anne's Street (turn right at the first junction), or by continuing for a short distance up Lower Church Street, crossing the road to enter the Drill Hall car park. Walk across the car park to join a tarmac alleyway to Gwy Court. The access road for Gwy Court joins Bridge Street just below the museum and the Castle car park is just opposite.

PORTHCALL WALK

To get to the start aim for Newton which is at the Eastern end of Porthcawl. Park anywhere near the village green, the Ancient Briton Pub or the 12th Century church. With your back to the Ancient Briton pub turn left to head along Church Street which passes the Church of St John the Baptist on the right and the Jolly Sailor pub on the left. Next you pass allotments on the right. As you reach level with the end of the allotments and before Bryneglwys Avenue take the tarmac footpath to the left. Where the track splits go ahead to a waymark sign by a road and metal gate. Cross the road keeping straight ahead and then another road still going ahead. There is a tall overgrown hedge to the left and the path becomes stony. After a while on the open common land you see a path off to the right but keep straight ahead – you are now walking on sand. At a junction of paths take the left path, slightly grassier. (10 mins).

The path goes gently uphill. After a while the path runs alongside a field on your left and enters a coppiced area of trees. Ignore the path off to the right and pass through two upright metal girders. 50 yards further on fine views open up to the right, whilst our path keeps to the left alongside the hedge. You pass a large house on the left and as you get level with the end of the garden (SS 84985/77549, 1.14 miles, 20 mins) the path turns sharp right and winds its way through the sand downhill. At a junction of paths turn left following the clear route continuing downhill. Just after you cross over some dark grey stones underfoot you come to an open grassy area. There are two paths off to the left, the second by a wooden post, but take the nearer path to the left, 5 yards this side of the post, winding uphill. Look ahead to note a heavily tree-covered valley which is the direction of our route. Ignore a path going off to the left and paths joining from the right – more coppiced trees on the left. You emerge from the trees and pass through a wooden kissing gate with a waymark post marked Glamorgan Heritage Coast. At the next junction take a right fork bringing you to a second wooden kissing gate. The path curves to the right, the fence on your right. Go through a third wooden kissing gate, the fence now on your left. Fork right as the fence heads off to the left, the path bringing you shortly to a stone wall. Pass through a fourth kissing gate with a large gate to the left, now turning right towards Candleston. (SS 86593/77822, 2.37 miles, 45 mins). After 20 yards take the left fork following the path which curves and then descends, becoming sandy, to a track (SS 87047/77636, 2.68 miles, 54 mins). Go right towards Candleston on the wide and often sandy track. After a while you come to a rough car parking area at which point look to the left and a short ascent brings you to Candleston Castle (SS 87136/77228). Return to the car park which you cross heading for a wide sandy area of dune. Go over a stream at the bottom of the car park and ascend through the middle of the sand, aiming for some short wooden stumps. From the top you can look across to Ogmore opposite. From the top of this sandy area take the right hand path of the two ahead and as the path descends keep to the left-hand side of the clump of trees. From the crest of any high dune you should be able to see the Coastguard centre at Ogmore on the coast. You need to aim to the right of this heading along a bit of a valley with the highest ground on your right. The general direction is South West. If you head towards the South you will come to the Ogmore River – no problem, just turn right and follow the river to the beach. Either way you should eventually come out on to the beach. (SS 85903/76261, 4.25 miles, 1hr 30 mins).

St. Fagans Circular Walk

The route of this circular walk is largely flat with some very gentle slopes. The walk is accessed from this point via a kissing gate, but users should be aware that there are three stiles situated along the route. Way-markers are posted on this route for walkers to follow. The entire circular walk is just under 2 miles in length (3km) and depending how fast you walk should take between ¾ and 1½ hours to complete.

The Battle of St Fagens

This circular walk encloses the location that most believe to be the local Civil War site of the Battle of St. Fagans, recorded as having occurred on 8th May 1648. Sources record that this battle started when disaffected Parliamentary troops declared for the King in April 1648 and then marched east into Glamorgan. News soon spread that Oliver Cromwell was despatched to Wales to see off this rebellion - a battle was now inevitable. This last major battle of the Civil War saw 8,000 Royalists bearing down on a Parliamentary force of only 3000. After around two hours of fighting (in the form of cavalry charges and handto-hand combat) the 'Royalist Rebels' were surrounded. The Royalist infantry are then said to have broken ranks in order to flee the battle scene. The Parliamentarians were victorious. Whilst each new generation probably exaggerates how the 'River Ely ran red with blood', it is fair to say that this is a significant site of the Second English Civil War history within Wales.

Landscape

The Ely Valley forms an important green 'corridor' linking the urban area to its rural surroundings. This walk passes through a mosaic of farmland, mature planted woodland and a well managed parkland character, forming part of the wider Plymouth Estate.The adjacent St. Fagans National History Museum includes St. Fagans Castle, a late sixteenth century manor house, buildings from around Wales and listed historic gardens.

It is possible to access the Ely Trail from St Fagans, on the southern side of Castle Hill. The trail is mainly an off-road, stone-dust path suitable for cyclists and walkers. It is generally flat but there are some sections which do have a gradient. On completion it will be possible to walk and cycle from St.Fagans to Cardiff Bay.

For more information about the Trail, visit the countryside website www.cardiff.gov.uk/countryside where downloadable leaflets are available.

Bodnant Gardens

Chirk Castle

Dolaucothi Gold Mines

Penrhyn Castle

Ymddiriedolaeth Genedlaethol National Trust

Only one attraction in Wales covers one fifth of the coastline, 11 of the 15 tallest peaks, 45,000 hectares of stunning landscape and includes castles, gardens, historic houses, bridges and a gold mine – the National Trust.

The Welsh countryside is enriched by fantastic attractions offering enjoyable days out and memorable experiences and so many of these inspiring places are cared for by the National Trust. You are never more than 40 minutes from a National Trust attraction, be it the imposing Penrhyn Castle in the North, majestic Chirk Castle in the East, romantic Powis Castle in mid Wales or the impressive Tredegar House in the South.

But the National Trust in Wales is not all about stately homes and fortresses, there are great days out to be enjoyed at Dolaucothi Gold mines, Aberdulais Tin Works and Waterfall and the intriguing Tudor Merchant's House. And the beautiful Bodnant Garden and Colby Woodland Garden offer so much more than simply stunning surroundings to relax and play in.

But by far the most incredible thing the National Trust offers, is unlimited access to all of this for the whole family for just over half the cost of one family visit to Alton Towers, and only £15.50 more than a family day pass to Chester Zoo.

And when you join the National Trust you can be sure that you are paying not only for access to all the 300 houses, 200 gardens, 40 castles and 76 nature reserves across Wales, England and Northern Ireland, but also helping the charity to look after our heritage and landscape forever for everyone.

Home Farm at Llanerchaeron

Brecon Beacons National Park

Pennard Cliffs, Gower, Wales.

Powis Castle and Garden

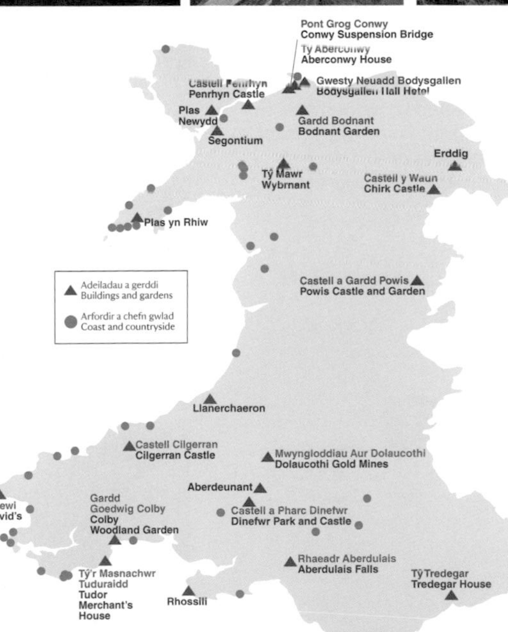

Ymddiriedolaeth
Genedlaethol
National Trust

NATIONAL TRUST

Llywodraeth Cymru
Welsh Government

A visit to a Cadw site really is a monumental day out!

We look after 127 historic sites which are visited by more than 2 million people each year. From castles that tell stories of medieval princes to sites that remind us of Wales's proud heritage as one of the first industrial nations in the world, you can explore 6,000 years of history across the country. Let us bring it to life for you.

For a full list of Cadw events near you, visit our website
cadw.wales.gov.uk

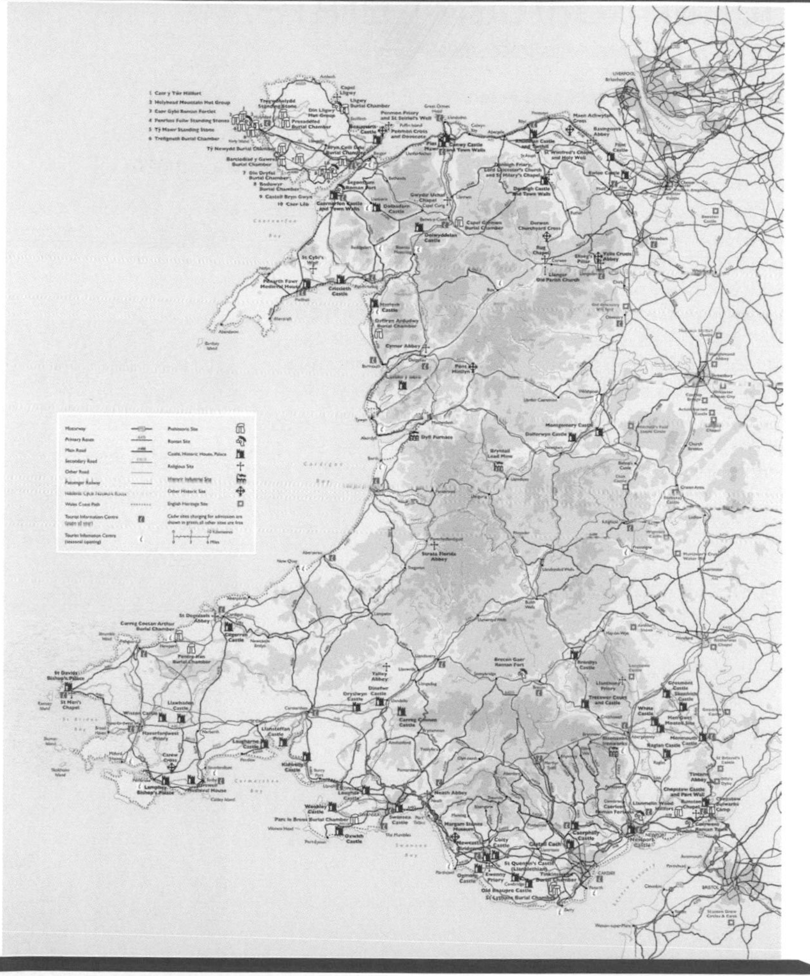
1 Caer y Tŵr Hillfort
2 Holyhead Mountain Hut Group
3 Caer Gybi Roman Fortlet
4 Penrhos Feilw Standing Stones
5 Tŷ Mawr Standing Stone
6 Trefignath Burial Chamber
Tŷ Newydd Burial Chamber
Barclodiad y Gawres Burial Chamber
7 Din Dryfol Burial Chamber
8 Bodowyr Burial Chamber
9 Castell Bryn Gwyn
10 Caer Lêb
Din Lligwy Hut Group
Capel Lligwy
Lligwy Burial Chamber
Presaddfed Burial Chamber
Beaumaris Castle
Penmon Priory and St Seiriol's Well
Penmon Cross and Dovecote
Bryn Celli Ddu Burial Chamber
Segontium Roman Fort
Caernarfon Castle and Town Walls
Dolbadarn Castle
Plas Mawr
Conwy Castle and Town Walls
Gwydir Uchaf Chapel
Capel Garmon Burial Chamber
Dolwyddelan Castle
Rhuddlan Castle
St Winefride's Chapel and Holy Well
Maen Achwyfan Cross
Basingwerk Abbey
Flint Castle
Ewloe Castle
Denbigh Friary
Denbigh Castle and Town Walls
Derwen Churchyard Cross
Rug Chapel
Llangar Old Parish Church
Eliseg's Pillar
Valle Crucis Abbey
St Cybi's Well
Penarth Fawr Medieval House
Criccieth Castle
Harlech Castle
Cymer Abbey
Pont Minllyn
Montgomery Castle
Dolforwyn Castle
Dyfi Furnace
Bryntail Lead Mine
Strata Florida Abbey
St Dogmaels Abbey
Cilgerran Castle
Carreg Coetan Arthur Burial Chamber
Pentre Ifan Burial Chamber
St Davids Bishop's Palace
St Non's Chapel
Wiston Castle
Llawhaden Castle
Haverfordwest Priory
Carew Cross
Lamphey Bishop's Palace
Tudor Merchant's House
Llansteffan Castle
Laugharne Castle
Kidwelly Castle
Talley Abbey
Dryslwyn Castle
Dinefwr Castle
Carreg Cennen Castle
Brecon Gaer Roman Fort
Bronllys Castle
Llanthony Priory
Tretower Court and Castle
Grosmont Castle
Skenfrith Castle
White Castle
Hen Gwrt Moated Site
Monmouth Castle
Raglan Castle
Blaenavon Ironworks
Tintern Abbey
Chepstow Castle and Port Wall
Runston Chapel
Caldicot Castle
Caerwent Roman Town
Llanmelin Wood Hillfort
Caerleon Roman Fortress
Newport Castle
Caerphilly Castle
Castell Coch
Neath Abbey
Loughor Castle
Weobley Castle
Parc le Breos Burial Chamber
Swansea Castle
Oxwich Castle
Margam Stones Museum
Newcastle Bridgend
Coity Castle
Ogmore Castle
Ewenny Priory
St Quentin's Castle (Llanblethian)
Tinkinswood Burial Chamber
Old Beaupre Castle
St Lythans Burial Chamber
Caernarfon Bay
Cardigan Bay
St Brides Bay
Carmarthen Bay
Swansea Bay
Severn Estuary
Motorway
Primary Route
Main Road
Secondary Road
Other Road
Passenger Railway
Wales Coast Path
Tourist Information Centre (open all year)
Tourist Information Centre (seasonal opening)
Prehistoric Site
Roman Site
Castle, Historic House, Palace
Religious Site
Historic Industrial Site
Other Historic Site
English Heritage Site
Cadw sites charging for admission are shown in green; all other sites are free
0 5 10 Kilometres
0 3 6 Miles

Bodnant Garden Centre

t: 01492 650 731 e: marketing@bodnant-plants.co.uk
www.bodnant-plants.co.uk

A Special day out at a special garden centre!

There is nowhere quite like Bodnant Garden Centre. With access to the incredible variety of plants at The National Trust's Bodnant Garden, the Bodnant Garden Centre is able to propagate over 500 varieties of plants - many not available anywhere else. From cutting to pot, Bodnant Garden Centre grows and sells special plants. Here you'll also find everything for the garden from furniture to bird feeders as well as a huge selection of seeds. In the gift shop, the emphasis is on local craftsmanship and unique, special items including pottery, antiques and home furnishings. 'Craft Street' showcases work by local artists and crafts-people including work in jewellery, textiles and wood. There is also a Welsh Food Shop, café, ample parking and children's play area, making Bodnant Garden Centre a great destination for all ages.

Bodnant Garden Centre is our first and only garden centre to be featured in our Top 100 Attractions in Wales book. The reason for this is actually quite simple, you have garden centres that are great, and garden centres that are not so great. But Bodnant Garden Centre is not just any old garden centre! It truly is the Portmeirion of all garden centres. I learned so much during my visit to Bodnant. Things about Roses, Flowers and a wide range of plants that I never knew before. The staff here are so enthusiastic about their positions, which is so refreshing to see and they go out of their way to answer any questions you may have, no matter how large or how small. Both Bodnant Garden Centre, The famous National Trust Garden and the new Welsh Food Centre adjacent make this a full day out not to be missed!

Llandudno

Bodafon Road, Llandudno, Gwynedd, LL30 3BB